Consumerist Orientalism

Consumerist Orientalism

The Convergence of Arab and American Popular Culture in the Age of Global Capitalism

M. Keith Booker and Isra Daraiseh

I.B. TAURIS
LONDON • NEW YORK • OXFORD • NEW DELHI • SYDNEY

I.B. TAURIS
Bloomsbury Publishing Plc
50 Bedford Square, London, WC1B 3DP, UK
1385 Broadway, New York, NY 10018, USA
29 Earlsfort Terrace, Dublin 2, Ireland

BLOOMSBURY, I.B. TAURIS and the I.B. Tauris logo are trademarks
of Bloomsbury Publishing Plc

First published in Great Britain 2019
This paperback edition published in 2021

Copyright © M. Keith Booker and Isra Daraiseh 2019

M. Keith Booker and Isra Daraiseh have asserted their rights under the Copyright, Designs and Patents Act, 1988, to be identified as the Authors of this work.

Cover design: Adriana Brioso
Cover image © Benjamin Booker

All rights reserved. No part of this publication may be reproduced or transmitted in any form or by any means, electronic or mechanical, including photocopying, recording, or any information storage or retrieval system, without prior permission in writing from the publishers.

Bloomsbury Publishing Plc does not have any control over, or responsibility for, any third-party websites referred to or in this book. All internet addresses given in this book were correct at the time of going to press. The author and publisher regret any inconvenience caused if addresses have changed or sites have ceased to exist, but can accept no responsibility for any such changes.

A catalogue record for this book is available from the British Library.

A catalogue record for this book is available from the Library of Congress.

ISBN: HB: 978-1-8386-0067-9
PB: 978-0-7556-4373-8
ePDF: 978-1-8386-0068-6
eBook: 978-1-8386-0069-3

Typeset by Deanta Global Publishing Services, Chennai, India

To find out more about our authors and books visit www.bloomsbury.com
and sign up for our newsletters.

We dedicate this book to each other and to our own collaboration, an example of cultural convergence that stands as proof of our main thesis.

وانقسمت الى امرأتين
فلا أنا شرقية
ولا أنا غربية

I have been split into two women,
So that I am not Eastern,
So that I am not Western.

—Mahmoud Darwish

But there is neither East nor West, Border, nor Breed, nor Birth.

When two strong souls stand face to face, tho' they come from the ends of the earth!

—Rudyard Kipling, "The Ballad of East and West"
(with a slight emendation.)

Contents

List of Figures ... vii

Introduction: Orientalism, Occidentalism, and Transnational Flow in the Age of Global Capitalism ... 1

1 From Circus Sideshows to Music Videos: Orientalism and the Rise of American Consumer Capitalism ... 33

2 "Shake Ya body like a Belly Dancer": Orientalism in American Music Videos ... 63

3 I'd Like to Sell the World a Coke: Arab Pop Music and Pop Music Video Clips ... 85

4 "They Can't Use My Music to Advertise for Coca-Cola": Arab and Arab Diasporic Rap and the Resistance to Postmodernism ... 113

5 As the World Turns from the East to the West: Tradition, Modernity, and Gender in the Arabic-dubbed Turkish Soap Opera *Noor* ... 135

6 Arabs Got TV: The "Americanization" of Arab Televisual Culture ... 161

7 Deconstructing the Myth of the Western Hero through Arab Film: *Theeb*, the Orientalist Logic of Good versus Evil, and the Birth of Jordan ... 181

Conclusion: Ideology, Utopia, and Arab Popular Culture ... 213

Notes ... 223
Works Cited ... 245
Index ... 258

Figures

2.1 Guest performer Beyoncé in all-out exotic Eastern mode in the music video for Coldplay's "Hymn for the Weekend" (2015) (screen capture)   65

2.2 Katy Perry decked out as a Cleopatra-like Egyptian queen in her 2013 music video for "Dark Horse" (screen capture)   71

2.3 Belly dancer in exotic garb from the music video for R. Kelly's "Snake" (2003) (screen capture)   75

2.4 Belly dancer from the music video for Jason Derulo's "Talk Dirty to Me" (2014), clearly designed to look as exotic as possible (screen capture)   77

2.5 Two exotic women with a phallic hookah apparatus in the music video for Massari's "Shisha" (2012) (screen capture)   82

3.1 A group of dancers in a postmodern pastiche of traditional Moroccan garb in the video clip for Saad Lamjarred's hugely popular "Lm3allem" (2015) (screen capture)   90

3.2 Title frame of the video clip for Nancy Ajram's "Hassa Beek" (2017), clearly designed to mimic the opening title of an American film noir (screen capture)   92

3.3 Screen capture from the video clip for Nancy Ajram's "W Maak" (2018), showing the performer beside a Western-style Wurlitzer juke box   93

3.4 Myriam Fares in an exotic facial covering in the video clip for "Aman" (2015) (screen capture)   94

3.5 Haifa Wehbe works out in a Western-style outfit with added Eastern-style belly dancer's coin belt in the video clip for her song "Touta" (2018) (screen capture)   95

3.6 Elissa uses her Samsung phone in the video clip for her song "Hob Kol Hayati" (2014) (screen capture)   99

3.7 Tamer Hosny and guest performer Snoop Dogg are joined by a group of female backup dancers in the video clip for Hosny's "Si Al Sayed" (2013) (screen capture)   103

3.8 Screen capture from the video clip for Hala Al Turk's "Live in the Moment" (2015), with the singer joined by a group of backup dancers who might be at home on America's Disney or Nickelodeon channels   110

4.1	Lebanese singer Farah shown at the end of the video clip for Qusai's song "Yalla" (2012), openly acknowledging the clip's affiliation with Braun shavers and Pepsi Cola	114
4.2	Syrian American rapper Omar Offendum performs in the video clip for his song "Crying Shame" (2015)	121
4.3	Tamer Nafar and Samar Qupty perform in the 2016 film *Junction 48*	126
4.4	Lowkey's video clip for "Ahmed" (2016) contains a number of powerful images	132
5.1	Muhannad (Kivanç Tatlituğ) and Noor (Songül Öden) in a quiet moment of marital communication in *Noor* (2008), the Arabic-dubbed version of the Turkish soap opera *Gümüş* (2005–7)	136
5.2	Collection of photos in the family home of Jabal (Tayem Hasan) in *Al Hayba* (2017). Note the central place accorded to Jabal's hero, Columbian drug lord Pablo Escobar (screen capture)	139
5.3	Muhannad, on the verge of tears, shows his sensitive side in *Noor* (screen capture)	154
5.4	Noor writes her memoirs in the last episode of *Noor* (screen capture)	158
6.1	Hamza Hawsawi performs "Billie Jean" on *The X Factor Arabia* (screen capture)	162
6.2	The Kuwaiti group Sheyaab performs on *Arabs Got Talent*	165
6.3	Haifa Wehbe sings to host Adel Karam on the Lebanese talk show *Hayda Haki*	174
7.1	T. E. Lawrence poses heroically atop a captured Ottoman train in *Lawrence of Arabia* (1962), while a crowd of his Arab followers cheer him from below	192
7.2	Theeb's brother Hussein with camels at one of the wells that are crucial to the survival of the Bedouins in *Theeb* (2014) (screen capture)	194
7.3	Theeb sits on the cracked earth of his arid homeland in *Theeb* (2014) (screen capture)	196
7.4	Theeb heads for home at the end of *Theeb* (2014). Note the Ottoman train in the distance (screen capture)	198
7.5	The title character pokes his head into a Bedouin tent in *Theeb* (2014) (screen capture)	205
7.6	Henry Fonda is ready for his close-up in the Spaghetti Western *Once Upon a Time in the West* (1968). Even very big American stars sometimes appeared in these Italian films	205

Introduction: Orientalism, Occidentalism, and Transnational Flow in the Age of Global Capitalism

One character in Kim Stanley Robinson's American science fiction novel *New York 2140* (Amelia Black, the host of a "cloud" program that is the 2140 equivalent of today's "web series") complains about those who believe in maintaining "pure" versions of local environments or cultures:

> We've been mixing things up for thousands of years now, poisoning some creatures and feeding others, and moving everything around. Ever since humans left Africa we've been doing that. So when people start to get upset about this, when they begin to insist on the purity of some place or some time, it drives me crazy, I can't stand it. It's a mongrel world. (259)

The "cloud" itself is, like today's "web," a key example of this mongrelization, aspects of which more scholarly observers have described with terms such as "globalization" or "transnational cultural flow." The eminent Palestinian American scholar Edward Said has himself noted that "partly because of empire, all cultures are involved in one another; none is single and pure, all are hybrid, heterogenous, extraordinarily differentiated, and unmonolithic" (*Culture* xxv).

We agree with both Amelia Black and Said, except that we would argue that today's transnational flow of culture, while it has "empire" as an important part of its historical background, is enabled even more by the *fall* of the great European colonial empires, a demise that opened the way for today's global capitalist system. Transnational flow has, among other things, done a great deal to break down localized distinctions between cultures, rendering ideas such as the Orientalist notion of a polar opposition between Eastern and Western cultures spectacularly obsolete, but it has been able to do so partly because the empires that once upheld such distinctions have been replaced by a global capitalism that depends on free flow and interchangeability. Under such a system, the mongrelization of the world's cultures is inevitable.

This mongrelization, however, does not imply homogeneity, but in fact can produce interesting (if confusing and unsettling) new forms of diversity.

Human cultures have often been destroyed by contact with other cultures in our planet's bloody history, but cultures have also frequently been enriched and diversified through contact with outside forces. The culture of the Middle East might seem to be under threat due to the influence and power of the West in the region (many there certainly see it that way), but in fact the culture of the Arab world has never been more diverse—to the point that the very term "Arab world" is now useful primarily as a rhetorical convenience, rather than as a label for some actually existing phenomenon. Algeria is different from Saudi Arabia in many, many ways, for example, and even neighboring countries with intertwined histories (say, Egypt and Libya, or Jordan and Lebanon) have developed distinctly different cultural identities. Perhaps more importantly, even those identities themselves are complex and multiple. There is no Jordanian point of view or culture, for example, only points of view and cultures. Ramtha and Amman differ as much as Arkansas and New York, and the attitudes and opinions of individuals (especially in metropolitan centers) can vary significantly even in a given locale.

We are writing in the year 2018. Radical Islamist imams in the Middle East are at this moment furiously conjuring up *fatwas* against the evils of America and American culture. In retaliation for the threat to their beliefs that they find in Western culture and American foreign policy, extremist Islamist groups—their minds apparently immersed in the eighth century despite their facility with high-tech weaponry and communications—are no doubt currently planning more terrorist attacks against targets in the West. These Arabs live in a harsh and morally rigid world starkly opposed to the seductive gleam of Western consumer culture. On the other hand, their world is also starkly opposed to the world in which the majority of people in most Arab countries live their daily lives. Severe-looking Muslim men in flowing beards and robes walking down the street in an American town might make many nervous, but many Arabs would be made uncomfortable by this sight in their own towns as well. For every staunchly anti-American Arab who thinks American culture is a tool of Satan, many more Arabs are clustered around their television sets in modern living rooms that look like they might be in Peoria, watching Arabic-dubbed versions of the latest American action movies via satellite television, rooting for the same heroes that American audiences root for. And three- and four-year-old girls all over the Arab world are gleefully dancing and singing tunes from *Frozen* and dreaming of becoming Disney princesses; children of their age are often exposed to so much American popular culture that they speak English as well as or better than Arabic.

Most Americans, for their part, are very much aware of the extremists and the terrorists, but not so much aware of Arab television-viewing habits or Arab Disney princesses. They know about ISIS and its attacks in Europe, but many don't know that most ISIS violence occurs in the Middle East and is directed at other Muslims. They know that the Middle East has oil and deserts and camels and that there are Arab Islamist fanatics who are willing to blow themselves to bits in suicide bombings just to disrupt the peaceful pursuit of the Western democratic way of life. They know that Americans must be vigilant in order to protect themselves from these attacks. They are even vaguely aware that the American military machine visits its high-tech fury upon the Middle East on a regular basis in a supposed attempt to help provide this protection, though they might not like to think about the details of what this really entails. As British-Iraqi rapper Lowkey puts it in his 2011 song "Terrorist?," these attacks produce "screams" that never reach the "earholes" of the American public. Finally, most Americans know next to nothing about the history of the Middle East or about how we really got to this point.

Americans do, however, come more and more into contact with Middle Eastern culture every day. The increasing penetration of Middle Eastern foods into American markets (and into the popular American consciousness) is a good case in point—and an important one, given the key role often played by food in establishing and maintaining cultural identities. Americans have been consuming various forms of Middle Eastern food as exotic specialties at least since the nineteenth century, of course, but the twenty-first century has seen a shift in which such foods are becoming less exotic and more routine.[1] What self-respecting American supermarket, for example, does not now stock a variety of brands and flavors of hummus? Granted, the leading line of hummus sold in America might be the Israeli brand Sabra, but other Arab foods are also becoming more and more popular in both restaurants and supermarkets nationwide. In the current age of globalization, this should come as no surprise. Indeed, American supermarkets routinely stock foods from all over the world. Virtually all of them sell French cheeses and Italian pasta sauces, for example, while various forms of Mexican and Asian foods are increasingly popular as well.

Even during the Cold War years, when their stock was significantly less international, American supermarkets became a key element of Western propaganda, their clean, well-lit spaces and well-stocked shelves, neatly stacked with an amazing variety of foods, standing in sharp contrast to the grungy, poorly stocked grocery stores of Eastern Europe. Such contrasts still exist around the world, and the quest for food and clean water is a daily struggle for many millions of people on our planet. But supermarkets in general provide one of the best examples of globalization, with stores all over the world stocking products from all over the world. For that matter, some of the most popular of America's famed supermarkets are now foreign-owned, as in the case of the German-owned Aldi chain, which also happens to own as a subsidiary one of America's favorite (and most American-sounding) supermarket chains, Trader Joe's.

Of course, in places like the Middle East, there are still quaint shops specializing in local delicacies, providing still another sort of contrast—though these shops sometimes serve as many Western tourists as they do Eastern locals.

Meanwhile, it is also the case that urban centers in the Middle East typically feature small specialty shops that stock mainly (and often *only*) Western products. In addition, most cities of the Middle East feature large, ultra-modern supermarkets that can easily rival the best America has to offer in both quality and variety of food on offer, though many of these supermarkets are themselves Western-owned. For example, in Amman, Jordan, one can go to a huge, ultra-modern superstore operated by the French conglomerate Carrefour that includes a large, well-equipped supermarket section. (Carrefour also operates several smaller stores around the city, in addition to this superstore.) The Amman superstore certainly carries more Middle Eastern foodstuffs than the typical American supermarket (though there are American stores, such as Houston's Phoenicia Specialty Foods, that actually have more of a Middle Eastern flavor to their stock than does an Amman Carrefour). But Carrefour and other Middle Eastern supermarkets also stock a variety of international foods (including American ones, such as soft drinks) manufactured specifically for the Middle Eastern market, generally featuring labels printed in both English and Arabic—as are the store signs in Carrefour. And many international foods stocked in Carrefour—such as the aforementioned French cheeses and Italian pasta sauces—feature labels printed *only* in English, the international language of food (like so many other things). These products thus appear pretty much the same on the shelves of an Amman Carrefour (or a Lulu Hypermarket in the Gulf) as they would on those of an Arkansas Walmart.

Orientalism and capitalism

Given such phenomena, we would surely seem to be nearing the end times for the sort of binary thinking described in Said's *Orientalism* (1978), thinking that would imagine the "East" as a mysterious and exotic (if degraded and inferior)

Other to the "West." Yet Orientalist stereotyping persists, and Said's book remains a useful, if now somewhat dated, text for understanding the history of interactions between the Eastern and the Western worlds—even if such separate worlds no longer really exist. *Orientalism* is also one of the founding texts of the contemporary discipline of postcolonial studies and one of the most important academic books of all time, even if some scholars have argued that it has done more harm than good.[2]

Orientalism hovers in the background of the current study, as we seek to use Said's work as a springboard for a study of contemporary Arab popular culture in dialogue with contemporary Western (and especially American) culture. Both widely criticized and widely admired, Said's book has certainly drawn attention to its topic in ways that cannot help but be useful, whatever the arguments about the specifics of Said's methods or conclusions.[3] Using examples drawn primarily from eighteenth-to-twentieth-century French and English texts (both fiction and nonfiction, both scholarly and sensational) Said describes the long process by which the "Orient" (basically anything roughly east or south of Europe, though his interest is specifically in the Arab Middle East) has been described by Western writers through a systematic series of stereotypes designed to depict the Orient as the inferior Other of Europe in ways that have helped Europe (and later the United States) to exert political, cultural, and/or economic power over this Other.

For Said, this Othering process proceeds according to a binary logic in which Europe and the Orient are conceived as polar opposites, with negative depictions of the East having less to do with the reality of the Orient than with the attempt to produce positive representations of the West. This kind of thinking, of course, is closely aligned with the ideology of colonialism. As Frantz Fanon famously states in *The Wretched of the Earth*, "The colonial world is a Manichean world" (41). Said (who, oddly, does not mention Fanon's work directly in *Orientalism*[4]) notes that, in this kind of thinking, "On the one hand, there are Westerners, and on the other there are Arab-Orientals; the former are (in no particular order) rational, peaceful, liberal, capable of holding real values, without natural suspicion; the latter are none of these things" (49). Or, as he puts it a few pages earlier, "the Orient is irrational, depraved (fallen), childlike, 'different': thus the European is rational, virtuous, mature, 'normal'" (40).

Drawing upon the work of Michel Foucault, Said concludes that Orientalism is best understood as a discourse that sets the conditions under which one is able to think or talk about the Orient:

> Orientalism can be discussed and analyzed as the corporate institution for dealing with the Orient—dealing with it by making statements about it,

authorizing views of it, describing it, by teaching it, settling it, ruling over it: in short, Orientalism as a Western style for dominating, restructuring, and having authority over the Orient. (3)

Further, for Said, this discourse (which pertains both to scholarly study of the Orient and to artistic representation of the Orient) is inseparable from the history of real-world material relations between the East and the West, relations that have for centuries been informed by the domination and exploitation of the former by the latter: "The relationship between Occident and Orient is a relationship of power, of domination, of varying degrees of a complex hegemony" (5). Indeed, it is the fact of these real-world power relations that gives Orientalism its strength and longevity, while simultaneously making it more sinister and harmful. However, Orientalism is a fundamental component of the modern Western mindset, and not simply something that is tacked on after the fact. In particular, Said argues that "to say simply that Orientalism was a rationalization of colonial rule is to ignore the extent to which colonial rule was justified in advance by Orientalism, rather than after the fact" (39).

Going on, Said further elaborates on his Foucauldian vision of Orientalism as a discourse by noting that "Orientalism is better grasped as a set of constraints upon and limitations of thought than it is simply as a positive doctrine" (42). But Said is also heavily influenced by the work of the Italian Marxist Antonio Gramsci, whose pioneering work in describing how a bourgeois minority can use ideological manipulation to maintain the largely voluntary support and obedience of a working-class majority was a crucial breakthrough in our understanding of how modern societies function. It is thus no accident that Said's description of Orientalism as a discourse often sounds so similar to modern Marxist descriptions of ideology. Indeed, the various readings of Western texts that Said produces in order to demonstrate the workings of Orientalism as a discourse in these texts can also be viewed as an essentially Marxian exercise in ideology critique.

We would argue, however, that Orientalism should not be regarded as an ideology in its own right, however ideological it might be. It is, like the colonialism with which it is intertwined, a particular manifestation of the bourgeois ideology of capitalism, an ideology which—with its individualist emphasis on a dynamic of self versus other and its glorification of competition—lends itself particularly well to the kind of binary thinking that underlies Orientalism (and colonialism). Bourgeois ideology, however, is a complex phenomenon that operates very differently in different contexts. In Western Europe in the eighteenth century, for example, it was a radical ideology that challenged the power of the *ancien régime*, leading to the French Revolution and to what historian Eric Hobsbawm has dubbed "the age of revolution." By the nineteenth century, however, capitalism was firmly established in Western Europe and the bourgeoisie became staunchly conservative, more interested in preserving what they had already gained than in trying anything new. In nineteenth-century Russia, on the other hand, bourgeois ideology remained a radical, progressive force amid a social and political system that was still essentially medieval.

The specifics are very different, of course, but today's Middle East is in somewhat the same situation as nineteenth-century Russia with regard to the status of bourgeois ideology. While the basic content of that ideology is the same whether one is in Bentonville or Baghdad, the meaning (and some details) of this content can vary widely depending on the context in which it operates. The same ideology that serves to reinforce and maintain the status quo in the West represents a radical challenge to the powers-that-be in the Middle East, creating a tug of war of forces that creates an extremely complex and agonistic ideological climate. Thus, as opposed to the Western world of contemporary capitalism, in which the process of capitalist modernization is essentially complete, leaving capitalism itself in a thoroughly dominant position without any real rivals, the Arab world is very much contested terrain, with radically different ideologies—and radically different forms of social organization—striving for supremacy. The most important of these alternative ideologies is Islam, of course, but even Islam itself is contested terrain, with radical fundamentalists struggling with more modern and progressive Muslims for the power to define what Islam really is—not to mention other rifts within Islam, such as the Shia-Sunni conflict.[5] Even in the seemingly "pure" Wahhabist stronghold of Saudi Arabia, visions of Islam can vary greatly. As the narrator of Fahd al-Atiq's 2004 Saudi novel *Ka'in mu'ajjal* (*Life on Hold*) puts it, describing the sweeping changes he has seen in Riyadh in his lifetime, "Society had split into two camps, one camp adopting the slogan that God is strict in punishment, the other insisting that God is forgiving and merciful" (19).

Similarly, it is obvious that the opposition between the West and the Middle East today is not a simple Manichean one between modernity and tradition. In a sense, it is an opposition between a Western society in which capitalist modernization is complete and an Eastern society in which modernization is very much incomplete, leaving room for alternative social visions, especially Islamic ones, but also showing a strong presence of capitalist modernity. But, in reality, "opposition" itself is no longer the appropriate term for the relationship between the East and the West, especially in the realm of culture, where increasing globalization is far more complicated than the simple exportation of American culture to the rest of the world, which then absorbs the Westernizing messages of that culture—a model that Brian Edwards calls the "logic of broadcasting" (22). Instead, Edwards rightly insists that "circulation" is a better model for the way culture flows about the world, with different cultures interacting with one another in multiple (and multidirectional) ways.

Said's bête noire Bernard Lewis has spoken of a civilizational "clash" between Islam and modernity in the Middle East. Ben Barber has spoken of a global confrontation between Islam on the one hand and the Americanization, or McDonaldization,[6] of the world on the other. But Jan Nederveen Pieterse more accurately describes the entanglement between Eastern and Western interests when he argues that "the interlacing of western capitalism and consumerism and Islamic values and institutions, is much closer to the mark" (139). Timothy Mitchell, for example, notes the extensive collusion among American oil interests, the Saudi government, and radical Wahhabism in Saudi Arabia, referring to the outcome as "McJihad."[7] It is this global mishmash of cultures that constitutes the mongrelized contemporary world, in which one might imagine a French novel inspiring an American television series, which is then adapted into a Bollywood film, which then supplies an idea for an Arab video clip, and so on. Importantly, though, each of these might add its own local touches to the product, in the process often referred to as "glocalization," a term that originally arose in the 1980s to the adaptation of global business practices to local conditions (especially in Japan) but that has recently been increasingly used in a cultural context. Of course, in the era of global capitalism and postmodernism, business and culture are increasingly inseparable—as, for that matter, are the global and the local.[8]

Our thinking about the nature of contemporary capitalism is fundamentally informed by the work of Fredric Jameson, who follows Marxist thinkers such as Ernest Mandel in believing that, in the wake of the collapse of the great European colonial empires after the Second World War, capitalism has entered a new "late" era of globalization and transnationalism, informed by a

> new international division of labor, a vertiginous new dynamic in international banking and the stock exchanges (including the enormous Second and Third World debt), new forms of media interrelationship (very much including transportation systems such as containerization), computers and automation, the flight of production to advanced Third World areas, along with all the more familiar social consequences, including the crisis of traditional labor, the emergence of yuppies, and gentrification on a now-global scale. (*Postmodernism* xix)

Also crucial to our thinking is Jameson's seminal theorization of postmodernism as the "cultural logic" of this late capitalism, that is, as the cultural dominant that appears when capitalist modernization is complete, leading to the incorporation of culture as simply another commodity within the capitalist economic system. All parts of the world now participate in this process, but that does not mean that some parts are not more thoroughly saturated by it, more thoroughly modernized, than others. In the West, especially in the United States, postmodernism thus reigns supreme as a cultural dominant, while in the Middle East postmodernism still contends for supremacy with other powerful cultural forces. In fact, while Jameson himself emphasizes that postmodernism, like late capitalism itself, is a global phenomenon, he has consistently insisted that the phenomenon is further advanced in the West than in what used to be called the "third world," where localized pockets of cultural resistance remain. This does not mean, however, that postmodernism exerts no gravitational pull there. It simply means that other forces (like Islam) still have power there as well and that these forces are not necessarily aligned with capitalism—or might even be aligned against it.

It is clear that this global situation is far different from the Manichean one with which Said associates Orientalism. The world has simply changed a great deal since the appearance of the texts on which Said concentrates—and even since the appearance of *Orientalism* itself in 1978. Because bourgeois ideology changes over time (as the capitalism it supports evolves through various phases), viewing Orientalism as the product of bourgeois ideology leads us to expect that Orientalism should change over time as well—in addition to operating differently in different contexts in general. In our view, a major weakness in Said's conception of Orientalism is his depiction of it as a monolithic and virtually transhistorical force, a view he takes because he believes Orientalism to be somehow more fundamental than capitalism, and thus somehow impervious to the historical changes wrought by capitalist modernization.

Our view of history is very different in that we see capitalist modernization as the principal driving force behind the evolution of world history in the past several centuries. While it is true that certain attitudes and ideas that might be described as "Orientalist" clearly predate capitalism, this fact does not make Orientalism a more fundamental driving force for history in the modern era. To us, it simply implies that capitalism has appropriated Orientalism for its own purposes over the centuries, just as it has appropriated so many other things, Christianity included. In the same way, we would argue that Orientalism has survived colonialism not because it is a more fundamental historical phenomenon than colonialism, but because Orientalism is more fundamentally aligned with capitalism than with colonialism. Similarly, it is clear that the rise of modern capitalism in Europe was possible only after the colonization of the Americas had brought sufficient wealth (i.e., sufficient *capital*) to Europe to make the capitalist system viable there. But this does not mean that colonialism is more fundamental than capitalism or that colonialism is the force the drives capitalism. It simply means that colonialism was a valuable resource for capitalist modernization from the very beginnings of the modern era.

For us, Orientalism is deeply intertwined with the historical phenomenon of colonialism, but both Orientalism and colonialism, during the modern period, are *results* of capitalist modernization, not causes. And, of course, capitalist modernization is a dynamic historical phenomenon that takes on different characteristics (and has different results) over time. By extending his examples of Orientalism to twentieth-century American texts, Said demonstrates the ongoing relevance of his analysis of Orientalism to the vexed present-day relationship between the United States and the Middle East, something he would continue to demonstrate through the rest of his career, until his death in 2003. Unfortunately, we believe he took insufficient account of the ways in which twentieth-century Orientalism, especially in America, differs from the classic eighteenth- and nineteenth-century European Orientalism that he concentrates on in his analysis.

One reason for this failure might be the fact that Said largely limits his twentieth-century examples to the work of academic Orientalists, diminishing his coverage of culture and instead concentrating on the work of scholars such as H. A. R. Gibb and Bernard Lewis—reserving particular choler for the latter. There can be no doubt that such explorations of more contemporary Orientalist scholarship continue to be necessary—perhaps more urgently than ever before—as of this writing in 2018, when the complexities of increasing globalization make understanding and communication among different cultures more important than ever before, but when *mis*understanding between the United States and the Middle East seems to have reached an all-time high. However, we feel that these explorations need to include culture, and particularly *popular* culture in order to understand the true relationships between American and Arab cultures in the changed circumstances of today's world system.

In particular, popular culture tends to be more in tune with the currents of capitalism than does scholarship or high art, partly because it is itself so thoroughly commodified. Moreover, popular culture in its contemporary form is very much a product of capitalist modernization. Cultural phenomena such as the films, television programs, and video clips discussed in this study only came into existence as a result of capitalist modernization and took the form they did only as a result of the way in which capitalism transformed itself from the classic production-oriented nineteenth-century form that produced the great European colonial empires to the late consumer-oriented form that has produced the phenomenon of globalization in the late twentieth and early twenty-first centuries.

Capitalism underwent sweeping changes in the last years of the nineteenth century and the first years of the twentieth, changes whose ramifications ultimately brought about the late capitalism of today. If one believes, as we do, that Orientalism is a product of capitalist modernization, then it only makes sense that Orientalism, too, would take on different forms during this time period. Moreover, given the increasingly pluralist nature of capitalism and the ideology that supports it since the beginning of the twentieth century, it only makes sense that Orientalism would be plural as well. In Chapter 1 of this study we examine the ways in which the rise of a consumerist form of capitalism in the United States led to the development of a distinctively new form of Orientalist discourse that was related less to colonial power relations between the West and the East and more to the tendency of consumer capitalism to treat any and all images from any and all cultures as fodder for its marketing machine. This new consumerist Orientalism has been an important strain of American Orientalism ever since, though elements of European-style colonial Orientalism have continued to exist in America as well, seeing periodic resurgences—as in anti-Ottoman sentiment during the First World War or anti-Arab sentiment in the wake of the 9/11 bombings. There are also other forms of Orientalism in American culture, as in the special emphasis placed on the Holy Land in much of the thought of the religious Right.

Orientalism in general is a form of Othering that can usefully be described via Julia Kristeva's theorization of the concept of abjection, a process through which certain objects or ideas are identified as wholly foreign to us, then regarded on the one hand with horror and revulsion and on the other hand with an odd sort of fascination, both aspects of this twinned response going well beyond what is rationally justified. Kristeva describes the process largely in psychological terms, though large-scale phenomena such as Orientalism are clearly best described in ideological ones. Still, the analogy remains. One can then say that the classic colonialist Orientalism described by Said includes both horror and fascination, but tends more toward horror, while the consumerist Orientalism we describe in this book tends more toward the pole of fascination, while also still including elements of horror.

As consumerist (and American) capitalism has become more and more ascendant, the new style of consumerist Orientalism has gained traction worldwide, helping to set the stage for the transnational cultural flows that are a central concern of this study. We particularly seek to outline some of the many ways in which the popular culture of the Arab Middle East (for better or worse) is coming more and more to resemble the culture of the United States, or, more accurately, the culture produced and distributed globally by a late capitalism that, however international, remains centered in the United States.

We believe our shift in focus (relative to Said) from high culture and classical scholarship to contemporary popular culture, especially from the Middle East, is desirable, even necessary, to fully understand the contemporary cultural relationship between the United States and the Middle East. For one thing, today's popular culture, driven by advances in media and communications, is inherently more mobile than the eighteenth- and nineteenth-century texts explored by Said, facilitating much more rapid and extensive cultural exchange between the East and the West. In addition, popular culture exerts a more powerful influence on more people than do the texts of high culture or academia. Indeed, the explosion in Middle Eastern pop cultural production (influenced heavily by American popular culture) in recent years means that the cultures of the East and the West are now engaged in a much more extensive dialogue than they were when *Orientalism* was written and published—and certainly more than they were when the texts with which *Orientalism* mostly deals were originally written. Of course, the growing similarities between contemporary Arab popular culture and American popular culture should themselves be enough to demonstrate that the kind of strict binary logic through which Orientalist thinking views the West and the East as polar opposites has no basis in contemporary reality. However, most Americans are not even aware of the growing convergence of American and Middle Eastern culture, while many in the Arab world view this phenomenon primarily as an occasion for horror and dismay.

Meanwhile, the kind of binary thinking that underlies Orientalism continues to hold sway on both sides of this supposed binary, with each viewing the other as a dangerous and mysterious Other that represents a fundamental threat to their most basic values and even their very way of life. In the West, the classic time-honored Orientalist images of the Arab world—such as fiercely savage men riding about the desert on camels or exotically seductive women undulating in belly-dance costumes that might have been borrowed from

Barbara Eden—continue to maintain a surprising grip on the American mind. Indeed, if such images are losing any purchase at all, it is because they are being replaced by even more harmful images of obscenely rich (and sexually depraved) oil sheikhs, crazed suicide bombers, beaten-down and submissive veiled women, and hooded executioners lopping off the heads of children because they were caught listening to Western music. Meanwhile, on the other side of the East-West divide, in a surge of what one might call "Occidentalism," the tendency to view Western culture in stereotypical terms that lead to the notion of America as the "Great Satan" seems to be gaining, not losing purchase in the contemporary Arab world.

Orientalism and Occidentalism

It is not difficult to see why Iranians, Iraqis, and others in the Middle East, given their special experience with American interventionism, might be suspicious of the agenda of the United States in the region. For example, it is clear why so many Arabs in the Middle East might view the United States with fear and loathing, given events such as the 2003 invasion of Iraq and the continued US support for an Israeli regime that seems to have gone over into all-out anti-Arab fanaticism. Indeed, it would be difficult to overestimate the extent to which anti-American sentiment in the Arab world is tied up with the seemingly blind US support for an extremist Israel, widely regarded in the Arab world as America's pampered child. For their own part, from the 9/11 bombings to the continuing atrocities being committed by ISIS and other fundamentalist groups in the Middle East itself, Arabs have provided plenty of fuel for Orientalist antagonism toward their world in the United States. Indeed, rising religious fundamentalism on both sides of the Atlantic would seem to provide key fuel for both Orientalism and Occidentalism in the twenty-first century, with both Christian and Muslim fundamentalists being so convinced of the righteousness of their views (and the downright evil of any who oppose those views) that intercultural dialogue becomes well-nigh impossible.

Christian fundamentalists in the West and Muslim fundamentalists in the East (as well as Jewish fundamentalists in Israel) have a great deal in common in terms of their basic inability to understand and appreciate perspectives other than their own. They also have other things in common, such as a patriarchal tendency to view women as less than fully human and as a possible threat to moral rectitude whose sexuality must be contained and controlled at all costs. Indeed, the noted

Egyptian writer and social activist Nawal El Saadawi has argued that such similarities among these different fundamentalisms are far from coincidental, and that this patriarchal tendency (along with economic systems that support class inequality) overrides what seem to be glaring differences among these points of view. "Everything," she said in a 2006 interview, "is linked—George Bush and Bin Laden are twins. All the fundamentalist movements—Jewish, Christian, Muslim—they all have the same face. It is a religious revival to protect patriarchy, linked to class and gender oppression" (Bhaduri).

In short, even the extremist positions that would seem to oppose the East to the West in the starkest of terms are underwritten by certain fundamental similarities in our globalized age. A common reliance on systems of oppression and inequality in terms of class and gender and a common tendency toward suspicion of racial Others might not, of course, provide the most positive and fruitful basis for intercultural communication between the East and the West. In this study, we remain cognizant of these ominous similarities, but seek to focus on developments in the contemporary cultures of America and the Middle East that might further cross-cultural communication in more positive ways, overcoming tendencies toward Orientalist thought in the West and Occidentalist thought in the East.

These developments, we believe, are related to transnational forces that potentially have a strong utopian potential, just as globalization itself has considerable utopian potential. Even Jameson, who sees globalization primarily as the process by which capitalism exerts its global supremacy, squelching utopian energies along the way, grants that globalization can "pass effortlessly from a dystopian vision of world control to the celebration of world multiculturalism with the mere changing of a valence" (*Archaeologies* 215). Robert Tally, meanwhile, points to specific examples—such as the Arab Spring and the Occupy Wall Street movement—that suggest that this change in valence might well already be underway. As Patrick Hayden puts it, "utopia and globalization are intrinsically linked," both being driven by "the desire to transgress borders and to encounter other lands and peoples, to connect together otherwise disparate places and identities across the globe" (51).[9] Much of our work in this volume is in the spirit of such observations.

Of course, negative forces circulate freely in today's world as well, and even such seemingly rigid ideologies as Orientalism are in many ways quite fluid. Stereotyping is notoriously portable, given that stereotypes reside primarily in the mind of the beholder rather than in physical reality. Much of the work of Foucault, who is so important to Said in *Orientalism*, illustrates this very point. Indeed, Said draws extensively upon the work of Foucault not only in elaborating the idea of Orientalism as a discourse, but in his focus on the way in which European society has long developed positive images of itself through contrast with despised Others. For Foucault, these Others might be lepers, or madmen, or criminals, or homosexuals. One might add women and the poor to this list as well, though Foucault does not explicitly examine these categories. Very much the same mechanisms of stereotyping (and even many of the same stereotypes) operate in all of these cases, in which affluent, white, law-abiding, heterosexual, male Westerners hold themselves up as paragons of capability and virtue in contrast to the laziness, depravity, and untrustworthiness of the poor, the nonwhite, the criminal, the homosexual, the female, or the Oriental.

Stereotypes, generated by the assumptions of a discourse and thus unmoored from material reality, are free to float about in this way, operating very much in the same manner as commodities, which are endlessly interchangeable. Indeed, at least as it operates under the auspices of capitalism, such stereotyping is essentially a form of commodification, removing Arabs (or gays, or manual workers, or whomever) from the real world of use value and plunging them instead into the abstractly artificial world of exchange value. The representations involved in these stereotypes derive value not from how well they describe reality but from how well they allow one to achieve what one wants to achieve with them. Said, of course, is aware that the kind of stereotyping that he associates with Orientalism is part of a broader tendency in Western social history, a fact that he makes especially clear in the "Afterword" that he wrote, not long before his death, for the twenty-fifth anniversary edition of *Orientalism*:

> Each age and society re-creates its "Others." From a static thing then, identity of self or of "other" is a much worked-over historical, social, intellectual, and political process that takes place as a contest involving individuals and institutions in all societies. (332)

Said's work has prompted decades of intense academic investigation of the phenomena he describes in *Orientalism*, so that the complex of rhetorical strategies by which the West has historically described, contained, and to an extent even created the East is now fairly well understood in academia. On the other hand, ongoing suspicion of Arabs and Muslims (the two are barely distinguished among many Americans) in the popular press and in the general American population suggests that this knowledge has not quite sunk in on a wider level. But the same can be said for the panoply of stereotypes, suspicions, and even downright superstitions that inform popular attitudes toward the

West—and especially the United States—in the Arab world. These attitudes in themselves constitute the discourse that one might call Occidentalism, though this discourse is of course less fully supported by scholarly study and less involved in the exertion of dominative power in the East than Orientalism is in the West.

The relationship between Orientalism and Occidentalism is itself, however, not a binary one. The two discourses are extensively intertwined. Among other things, as Ian Buruma and Avishai Margalit have convincingly argued, the discourse of Occidentalism actually originated in the West, in critical reactions to the phenomenon of modernity, according to which the lure of wealth leads to greed and depravity, while devotion to change leads to a dehumanizing impermanence, instability, and loss of values. For example, the novels of Honoré de Balzac in the early nineteenth century (still perhaps showing a hint of the medieval Catholic horror of money and commerce) depict a postrevolutionary France in which Gordon Gekko might have found himself very much at home amid a mad scramble for cash that leads to a furious struggle of each against all. Meanwhile, Balzac's novels, while positioning themselves resolutely in opposition to modernity as whole, are shot through with a bourgeois ideology that helped them to become one of the paradigms of realist fiction, the ultimate bourgeois literary form. Bourgeois ideology is so complex, multiple, and nefarious that it is virtually impossible to position oneself in direct polar opposition to it or to engage with it without being seduced by it to some extent.

Karl Marx understood this property of bourgeois ideology (and of capitalism as a whole) quite well. He and Friedrich Engels, then, positioned themselves not in polar opposition to capitalist modernity, but in dialectical relation to it, launching a critique of that phenomenon from within modernity itself. Thus, in the *Communist Manifesto*, they express not only considerable admiration for the ability of capitalism to transform traditional societies into modern ones, but also considerable dismay at the brutal way in which this transformation sweeps away everything in its path, leading to an arrant economism that reduces human relationships (and human beings) to mere commodities. Meanwhile, the capitalist devotion to seeking greater profits leads to a fierce emphasis on change and innovation that leaves individuals disoriented and dehumanized. In one of their more famous passages, they note that

> constant revolutionizing of production, uninterrupted disturbance of all social conditions, everlasting uncertainty and agitation distinguish the bourgeois epoch from all earlier ones. All fixed, fast-frozen relations, with their train of ancient and venerable prejudice and opinions are swept away, all new-formed ones become antiquated before they can ossify. All that is solid melts into air, all

that is holy is profaned, and man is at last compelled to face with sober senses, his real conditions of life, in his relations with his kind. (Marx and Engels 6)

Such concerns about the instability and lack of substance of life under capitalism form a crucial part of the background of contemporary Occidentalism. However, contemporary Islamic fundamentalism has introduced a new stridency in the furious moral indignation of its thoroughgoing rejection of modernity and everything it represents. Thus, Buruma and Margalit note that

> Islamism, as an ideology, was only partly influenced by Western ideas. Its depiction of Western civilization as a form of idolatrous barbarism is an original contribution to the rich history of Occidentalism. This goes much further than the old prejudice that the West is addicted to money and greed. Idolatry is the most heinous religious sin and must therefore be countered with all the force and sanctions at the true believers' disposal. (102)

Marx and Engels, of course, would predict that Islamism is here fighting a losing battle. For them, capitalist modernity is an irresistible force that can only be defeated when it finally collapses beneath its own weight, brought down by the proletarian class that it itself created. They base this analysis, of course, on primarily economic terms, well before the birth of today's global capitalist popular culture, a force that makes capitalism considerably more formidable than it had been in the nineteenth-century context in which Marx and Engels worked.

The American Muslim journalist and writer G. Willow Wilson (whose 2012 World Fantasy Award–winning novel *Alif the Unseen* is a key example of the flow of Middle Eastern culture into American culture) has argued that Arab antipathy toward the United States comes in two distinctly different flavors, which one might describe as two different strains of Occidentalism. More moderate Middle Easterners, she argues, are resentfully aware of the military and economic power of the United States and of the way in which this kind of American muscle has often been flexed to the detriment of the Middle East. This sort of antipathy, she concludes, has very little to do with religion, but has everything to do with a perceived imbalance of power (*Butterfly* 135). On the other hand, Islamic fundamentalists base their hostility toward the United States very much on religious principles, informed by a fierce sense of the sinfulness not of American foreign policy, but of American popular culture. For these fundamentalists, she argues, American culture is like a cancer spreading through the Middle East, bringing materialism and loss of traditional Islamic values in its wake. The fundamentalists she observed while living in Egypt "hated the materialism that was spreading through Egypt and the Gulf like a parasite, turning whole cities—Dubai, Jeddah—into virtual shopping malls, and blamed this materialism on Western influence" (136).

We would argue that these two forms of Occidentalism are far more intertwined than Wilson indicates, with many in the Middle East making little distinction between American political power and American cultural power. Meanwhile, Wilson (perhaps falling into more problematic binary logic) argues that materialism is very much at home in the West and so does relatively little damage there. "But the Middle East," she argues, "is peopled by cultures that struggled for centuries to rid themselves of anything iconic or graphic or unnecessary; there, materialism acts as a kind of cultural smallpox, leaving mindless ostentation and artistic sterility in its wake" (136). The messages conveyed by American-style popular culture are thus, at least to Islamic fundamentalists, like a disease.[10] Moreover, they are a disease that is very hard to treat except by extreme measures. These fundamentalists "knew they could not make the ritualized, morally appraising culture of traditional Arab Islam—in which one must be worthy of truth, love, and God to attain them—more attractive than the lifestyle endorsed in the West. So they demonized attraction itself" (137).

Wilson's two versions of Arab Occidentalism—which might be described as political (or anticolonial) Occidentalism and cultural (or anti-consumerist) Occidentalism—correspond in many ways to the two principal forms of Orientalism that we discuss in this study. In any case, Wilson sees Islam (at least of the fundamentalist variety) as inherently at odds with the culture of the West, though this does not mean that more progressive forms of Islam cannot reach an accommodation with that culture—as has Wilson herself in, for example, her work in the American comic book industry, as well as in *Alif the Unseen*. In any case, her comments help to shed light on one of the central points we make in this volume—that Arab popular culture is heavily informed by Western (especially American) influences, though it has often taken ownership of those influences and made them into something new—which means that it mostly falls within the realm of the postmodern.

The many anti-consumerist Occidentalist Muslims who see Islam as the polar opposite of American culture do not produce pop cultural alternatives to that culture directly, but instead opt out of the Arab Culture Industry as inherently contaminated by the West.[11] This form of Islam rejects that industry out of hand, as when ISIS urges its followers to destroy satellite dishes throughout the Arab world to cut off access of the Culture Industry to the hearts and minds of its Arab consumers.[12] ISIS, of course, represents an extreme case, but conservative Arabs have been highly critical of the Westernization of Arab popular culture in recent years, especially in areas such as music video clips, which have been widely seen in the Arab world as scandalous, especially in their representation of women and sexuality, though also in their seeming endorsement of materialism. This sort of reaction might seem to verify certain Orientalist stereotypes about Arab culture, but it in fact has numerous Western equivalents, as when (especially white) American parents saw the newly emergent black-inflected rock music of the 1950s as the "devil's music." Similarly, Elouardaoui has specifically argued that the reaction against Arab video clips resembles the reaction of older, more conservative elements of British culture against the musical culture of British youth, as discussed by Stuart Hall and Paddy Whannel. In any case, as Mellor notes, media-based popular culture remains contested terrain in the Arab world, with many seeing it as having great promise for building a viable pan-Arab cultural identity and others seeing it as destroying Arab identities and replacing them with Western ones (27).

While much has been made (especially in the West) of the rapid growth of Islamic fundamentalism in recent years, much less has been said about the even faster growth of the Western-style Culture Industry in the Middle East in the past couple of decades. The proliferation of delivery systems such as satellite television and the internet has facilitated greater access not only to works imported from the West but to the rapidly growing number of films, television programs, and music video clips that now form such an important part of popular culture in the Arab world. And Arab audiences have eagerly consumed this new culture, a phenomenon that might well demonstrate the seductive power of American popular culture, proving one of the fundamentalists' points. However, the fact that this same seduction works so well on both Arabs and Americans can surely also be taken as an indication that Arabs and Americans are not as different as the fundamentalists on both sides would have us believe.

Contemporary transnational flow

We demonstrate in this volume that American popular culture now exerts a powerful influence in the Arab world, where it is both consumed directly and used as a model for the creation of Arab popular culture. We argue, though, that the impact of American popular culture on the Arab world—however much it might appall some Arabs, driving them to conspiracy theories that the United States is plotting to rob them of their cultural heritage—is far more complex than a simple case of cultural imperialism in which one culture overwhelms and colonizes another. The impact of the Arab world on America is complex as well. Melani McAlister has thus argued that, while the United States still partly constructs its national identity by playing that identity off against the Middle East, this process has, since the Second World War, been "distinctly post-Orientalist." For McAlister, "The meanings of the Middle East in the United States have been far more mobile, flexible, and rich than the Orientalist binary would allow" (304).

Meanwhile, we would go so far as to argue that the increasing impact of American popular culture in the Middle East works *against* the proliferation of genuinely Orientalist ideas of the kind Said identified in his masterwork. And we argue this for two reasons. On the one hand, both American and Arab popular culture have been ideologically colonized by the power of global capitalism, for which the United States might serve as the corporate headquarters, but which is hardly a purely American phenomenon, under purely American control. It is not an American conspiracy that drives world history in the early twenty-first century but a capitalist (post)modernity that is far bigger than any nation and that in many ways renders nations in the traditional sense secondary players on the world stage. On the other hand, there is also a utopian dimension to this seeming Americanization of Arab popular culture. For one thing, however contrary to the values of multiculturalism it might seem, there is surely something positive about cultural convergence in the sense that it furthers communication between different, previously disparate cultures. Perhaps more importantly, though, the coming together of different cultures has the potential to produce new hybrid cultures that are richer than either of the previous ones. Thus, Brian T. Edwards argues that American dominance in the Middle East is waning, even as Middle Eastern culture seems to be building itself more and more on American models—partly for political reasons, and because Middle Eastern artists often add their own creative elements to the extent that their work is divorced from any specifically American resonances. As a result, American cultural artifacts such as "cyberpunk fiction, superhero comics, social networking software, and text-messaging language" are "imbued with rich new sets of meanings" (35).

In fact, any number of observers have discussed such phenomena. Pieterse thus speaks of the "braiding" and "osmosis" of Eastern and Western cultures in the age of globalization, while Bill Ashcroft has discussed the "transformation" of postcolonial societies, arguing that culture in general is a fluid phenomenon, always in flux, and that one should not underestimate the "resilience, adaptability and inventiveness" of postcolonial societies (6). In our view, contemporary Arab popular culture does not simply represent the substitution of American culture for preexisting Arab culture but is in fact the product of a complex and dynamic process of creative cultural exchange and adaptation perhaps best captured in the concept that Fernando Ortiz refers to as "transculturation." For Ortiz, transculturation

> does not consist merely in acquiring another culture . . . but the process also necessarily involves the loss or uprooting of a previous culture, which could be defined as a deculturation. In addition it carries the idea of the consequent creation of new cultural phenomena, which could be called neoculturation. (103)

Ortiz thus acknowledges that there is always an element of loss of a former culture when a new culture is acquired, and it is certainly the case that some aspects of traditional Arab culture are likely to be diminished, if not entirely lost, as a result of the increasing prominence of Western-style popular culture in the Middle East. This loss, however, comes about not due to the forced imposition of American or other Western culture on the Arab world, though of course the American political rhetoric of liberating the Arab world from Oriental tyranny (as in the lead-up to the 2003 Iraq invasion) can easily lend itself to seeing modernization in the Arab world as an imposed Americanization.[13] But the loss of traditional cultures, Arab or otherwise, is simply a natural consequence of living in the "all-that-is-solid-melts-into air" world of capitalist modernity. The opposition involved is not between the East and the West, but between modernity and tradition—an opposition that is itself not a simple one, given that tradition as a concept is at least partly a product of modernity: tradition, after all, is partly the invention of those who would seek to provide reassurances that modernity has not, in fact, caused everything solid to melt into air and partly the invention of those who would offer the comforts of tradition as an alternative to the dizzying destabilization of modernity.

The United States, of course, is at the epicenter of modernity (or, now, postmodernity), so that the contemporary postmodern culture of late capitalism might seem to emanate from there. However, just as this late capitalist culture threatens to sweep away an older Arab culture, we should remember that it has already swept away older American cultures—and that, before the United States even existed, an emergent modernity had already swept away the traditional societies and cultures of medieval Catholic Europe. It is not for nothing that, as Jameson repeatedly notes in his study of postmodernism, nostalgia is a particularly crucial element of the postmodern experience. As the surprising success of the 2016 Donald Trump presidential campaign should make clear, Americans are also suffering from a strong sense of loss these days, as are people all over the world. Nor is it surprising that so much of the energy of American nostalgia is directed at the 1950s, the last decade in which late capitalism had not become hegemonic in the United States and when the pace of change was just beginning to kick into hyperdrive. All that was solid already melted into air in the 1950s (or even the 1850s), but, in the contemporary postmodern era, all that is solid melts into air at a more and more rapid rate—to the point that nothing ever really has time to become solid in the first place.

Writing at a time when late capitalism was still in its infancy (or at least early childhood), the eminent anthropologist Margaret Mead already marveled not only at the increasing rate of change in the modern world, but also at the way that change was leading to a convergence of global cultures. For her, modern culture changes so rapidly that only the very young are living in their own culture; by the time they reach adulthood, they will already be living in a culture that is foreign to the one they grew up in:

> Today, everyone born and bred before World War II is an immigrant in time—as his colonizing forebears were in space—struggling to grapple with the unfamiliar conditions of life in a new era. Like all immigrants and pioneers, these immigrants in time are the bearers of older cultures. The difference today is that they are represented in all the cultures of the world. (70–71)

This last point is a crucial one for the phenomena we discuss in this volume. "It is as if," Mead notes, "all around the world, people were converging on identical immigration posts, each with its identifying sign: 'You are now about to enter the post–World War II world'" (70). For Mead, then, all of the people of the world, "whether they are sophisticated French intellectuals or members of a remote New Guinea tribe, landbound peasants in Haiti or nuclear physicists, have certain characteristics in common" (71).

Since the time that Mead was developing this argument in the 1960s and 1970s, of course, the pace of change has gotten even faster and the scope of change has become even more global, with certain technological advances playing key roles in that process. Robert Crary convincingly argues that human identities have come, in the twenty-first century, to be defined more and more in relation to our consumption of specific technological objects and devices that themselves are continually replaced by newer models and thus rendered obsolete.[14] This rapid pace of innovation means that our identities must themselves be revised and updated at a faster and faster pace, while those identities are rendered more tenuous in the first place by the knowledge that the devices we so cherish are temporary and provisional:

> Now the brevity of the interlude before a high-tech product literally becomes garbage requires two contradictory attitudes to coexist: on the one hand, the initial need and/or desire for the product, but, on the other, an affirmative identification with the process of inexorable cancellation and replacement. (45)

In short, eventually, the consumerist desire that drives subjects under late capitalism becomes a desire not for the commodity itself but for the newness of the commodity and for the sense of being up-to-date on all the innovations being produced by the consumerist system.

As late capitalism penetrates the Arab world more and more extensively, with Arabs more and more using the same devices as Americans for very much the same purposes, it is only to be expected that this texture of continual change—so drastically antithetical to any sort of reliance on monotheistic tradition—should become a central part of day-to-day experience for Arabs as well. Granted, Islam stands as a mighty force in opposition to this sort of frenzied innovation (just as the Catholic Church long tried to block the spread of capitalism in the West), but it should also be said that Orientalism plays a role in promoting the transition to Western-style rapid change. Crary argues that individuals (and he primarily means *Western* individuals) submit to this situation of continual rapid innovation because of "the portent of social and economic failure—the fear of falling behind" (46). Facing an Orientalist legacy in which they have continually been depicted as primitive and backward and in which their society has been depicted as trapped in an unchanging sameness, Arabs might understandably tend to feel a special pressure to keep up with all the latest innovations as a partial refutation of that legacy. It is not for nothing, for example, that the "New Quarter" of the city of Dubai—looking for all the world like a CGI cityscape from a science fiction film[15]—looks far more futuristic than any Western city, more like a Baudrillardian simulacrum than like a "real" city. Many millions of oil dollars have been spent there in the quest to present an ultra-modern image to the world.

Of course, many aspects of the Arab world remain far less modern than the same aspects of the Western world, and the Arab world as a whole has certainly not experienced the complete modernization that Jameson associates with postmodernism in the West. As Pieterse puts it, "The Middle East is deeply and yet unevenly modern" (139). But the very fact that some aspects of the Arab world (such as the Dubai skyline—and certain characteristics of Abu Dhabi, Kuwait City, Doha, Jeddah, Riyadh, or even Mecca) are actually *more* modern than their American counterparts should make it clear that modernity does not *necessarily* emanate from the West, even though it has typically done so, simply because modernity *began* in the West. Modernity, in fact, emanates from capitalism, so it should come as no surprise that the cities listed above all exist in areas of the Arab world where capital is abundant. Nor should it come as any surprise that the popular culture being produced in the Arab world should tend more and more toward the postmodern: such is the direction of history.

One might argue that it makes little difference whether traditional Arab culture is being swept away by American culture or by late capitalism, but in fact it makes a great deal of difference. The homogenizing tendencies of late capitalism might have certain ominous implications for the richness and authenticity of individual subjective experience, and it is certainly the case that the ideology of late capitalism lurks behind all of the cultural phenomena we will discuss in this volume. But at least the leveling effect of late capitalism dismantles the Manichean structure of colonialism and leaves the Arab world in a position that is no longer inherently subaltern. Granted, the postmodern culture of late capitalism might still be dominated by the West, as is the economic system itself, but the cultures of America and of the Arab world are now free to intermix and to cross-fertilize each other in ways that would never have been possible were it simply a case of American culture wiping out traditional Arab culture and replacing it with a cheap knockoff of American culture. It should also be noted that many elements of Arab culture have been using Western culture as an inspiration for their own modernization at least since the *Nahda* period of the nineteenth century, and that this process (like most processes) has only accelerated in recent years, rather than emerging out of nowhere.

East is East and West is West—but the Twain have long met in culture

Beginning with the Moorish invasion of Spain in the early eighth century and continuing through the European invasion of the Middle East in the Crusades and the Ottoman conquest of much of southeastern Europe in an outburst of imperial expansion, the relationship between Europe and the Middle East has long been one of opposition and antipathy. However, even these events brought about significant cultural exchanges that undermine the notion of Europe and the Orient as polar opposites. As Said notes, modern-day Orientalism has its roots specifically in more recent events, including tensions between the Ottoman Empire and the French and British colonial empires as they competed for influence, especially in the Middle East. Said, for example, puts great emphasis on the crucial importance of Napoleon's invasion of Egypt in 1798, an event that formed a key component of the general's subsequent rise to power in France and of his assumption of a crucial historical role as the destroyer of the Holy Roman Empire and as a bringer of modernity to areas of Europe that were still steeped in medievalism at the beginning of the nineteenth century.

The final destruction of the medieval-style Russian and Austro-Hungarian Empires would not be completed until the First World War, of course, via a conflict that would finish off the Ottoman Empire as well. But Napoleon's Egyptian adventure and subsequent campaigns of conquest in Eastern Europe initiated a chain of events that were a crucial part of the background to the First World War and to the making of the modern Middle East, as well as of modern Orientalism and Occidentalism. Among other things, the destruction of the Ottoman Empire in the First World War led directly to the radical program of modernization instituted in post-imperial Turkey by Kemal Atatürk, whose project can be read as a sort of Orientalism-from-within. Atatürk privileged the modern over the traditional, the secular over the religious, and indeed evinced an Orientalist rejection of the more anti-modern aspects of Islamic thought as steeped in ignorance and superstition. Moreover, much of Atatürk's war on Islamic tradition was a cultural one. Buruma and Margalit note that Atatürk promoted "Western-style entertainment" as a means of encouraging the population of Turkey to think in more modern and secular ways. Atatürk, they conclude, "believed that a Western style was essential to becoming a modern nation" (113).

Atatürk's traditionalist (Occidentalist) opponents were of course horrified by this incursion of Western-style popular culture into postwar Turkey, and indeed much of the confrontation between Westernized popular culture and Islamic traditionalism in today's Middle East was already exercised in the post–First World War Turkey, with the notable exception that the Westernization of culture in Turkey came with strong, overt government support of a kind that is largely lacking in the contemporary Arab world—but also with the exception that Western popular culture itself is now far more sophisticated and has far more global power than it had in the 1920s, thanks partly to the availability of better technologies (such as satellite television and the internet) for delivery of that culture to more people around the world.

In any case, if the modernization of the post–First World War Turkey provides a precedent for the contemporary convergence of Arab and American popular culture, it is also the case that Western-inspired modification of Middle Eastern culture has roots that go back considerably earlier. The Islamic (and pre-Islamic) Middle East has a long and rich tradition of literature in Arabic that stands very much apart from the Western literary tradition. For example, that tradition (with notable exceptions such as *One Thousand and One Nights*) was largely dominated by distinctly Arabic forms of poetry (and by the Quran) at least until the nineteenth century. In that century, however, Arab *Nahda* thinkers struggled to modernize Arab culture along the lines of Western models, thereby re-energizing Islamic culture in ways that would help it to recover the best elements from its own past.[16] However, even as fictional narratives became more prominent during the *Nahda* period, those narratives (produced mostly in Egypt, Syria, and Lebanon) continued to be dominated by classical Arabic forms, so that it was not until well into the twentieth century, with pioneers such as the Egyptian Taha Hussein (1889–1973) leading the way, that a modern novelistic tradition in Arabic began to emerge.[17]

Often called the "Dean of Arabic Letters," Hussein was a cosmopolitan figure with doctorates from both Cairo University and the Sorbonne, and his work—as in the novel *Adib* (1935, rendered into English in 1994 as *A Man of Letters*)—often deals with cross-cultural encounters between the East and the West. Perhaps the best-known Arabic literary work to focus on such encounters is *Mawsim al-hijrah ilá al-shamāl* (1966, available in English as *Season of Migration to the North*), by Sudan's Tayeb Salih. A sophisticated novel that employs virtually all of the technical resources of Western modernism (and that has been seen as a sort of rejoinder to Joseph Conrad's *Heart of Darkness*), *Season of Migration to the North* seemed to announce that the *Nahda* dream of the modernization of Arab literature had been fully realized.

Of course, the Arabic-language novelist who is best known in the Western world is undoubtedly Egypt's Naguib Mahfouz (1911–2006), the first (and so far the only) Arab writer to win the Nobel Prize in Literature. Even a decade before *Season of Migration*, Mahfouz, with the Cairo Trilogy (1956–57), was publishing novels that were not only overtly modern in form but explicitly *about* the process of modernization in an Egypt transformed by a number of forces, including contact with the West.

The trilogy focuses on the experiences of three generations of a family in Cairo, at the same time placing the private experiences of the characters in close proximity to historical events (and changes) underway in Egypt during the time period covered by the trilogy, which ranges from the First World War and the subsequent Egyptian Revolution against British rule to 1944, with further political unrest as the Second World War is coming to a close. In this sense, the closest thing in British literature to the Cairo Trilogy is probably John Galsworthy's *The Forsyte Saga* (1906–21, published as a single volume in 1922), which focuses on a single upper-class British family as British society underwent a dramatic process of historical change from the late nineteenth century to the beginning of the 1920s. However, while British history simply provides a backdrop for the personal stories of the Forsytes, the priorities are reversed in Mahfouz, whose real story is the story of Cairo and Egypt, with the stories of individual characters merely providing a focal point for that larger historical narrative.

This shift in emphasis makes Mahfouz's sequence seem altogether weightier and more adept than Galsworthy's. Perhaps what is most impressive about the Cairo Trilogy is the way its narrative of transformative changes in Egyptian society during the time period spanning the two world wars is so carefully reinforced by its formal structure. Just as Egypt modernizes in the course of the narrative, so too does Mahfouz's narrative technique modernize. For one thing, the rather leisurely pace of the narrative does pick up as the trilogy proceeds. Each volume, for example, is shorter than the one before, but covers a longer period in Egyptian history. Moreover, Mahfouz's technique also moves from a reliance on an essentially Balzacian omniscient narrative voice in the beginning, through more and more use of a Flaubertian indirect free style, into an increasing prominence of modernist-style interior monologues. The trilogy thus stands at the pivot point of Mahfouz's career, enacting his own transition from his earlier historical romances to a period of high realism, but also already showing the beginnings of his transition to literary modernism.

The trilogy is a towering achievement, though in a sense not a surprising one. Change, the resistance to change, and the need for change are topics that lie at the very heart of modern Arabic literature, which has been reaching out since the *Nahda* period in an effort to participate in the transnational flow of literature and the arts and which has in turn offered its own substantial contributions to that flow, with the Cairo Trilogy serving as perhaps the most impressive single example.[18] But there are many impressive examples of this process, such as Abdelrahman Munif's *Cities of Salt* quintet (*Mudun al-milh* in the original Arabic), which not only displays many of the literary characteristics of Western postmodernism but is explicitly built around events related to the development of the Arab oil industry, the central historical event that has dominated political and economic relations between the Arab world and the West since the 1930s and that lies at the heart of the political form of American Orientalism.

Contemporary Arab literature shows even stronger signs of precisely the kind of transnational flows and resultant cultural convergences that are found in film, music, and television. For example, Lebanon's Elias Khoury has for some time been producing fiction that many critics have regarded as postmodern,[19] while important writers of Arab literature are beginning more and more to write primarily in English—as in the case of Sudan's Leila Aboulela or Libya's Hisham Matar, both of whom live in London, or Egypt's Ahdaf Soueif, who lives in Cairo. This phenomenon goes beyond Arabs to other Middle Eastern writers, as when the distinguished Turkish novelist Elif Şafak also now writes largely in English. And it should be noted that even the recent retelling of *One Thousand and One Nights* (2014) by Lebanon's Hanan al-Shayk, well established as a writer in Arabic, was written in English, thus making it more accessible to a Western audience. Finally, some of the trendiest recent novels in Arabic clearly follow along the lines of Western models, including such examples as the hip *Banat al-Riyadh* (2005, available in English as *Girls of Riyadh*); Ahmed Khaled Towfik's Egyptian dystopian novel *Utopia* (2009); Ahmed Alaidy's Egyptian cyberpunk novel *An Takoun Abbas El Abd* (2003, available in English as *Being Abbas el Abd*)[20]; and *Frankenstein in Baghdad* (2013) by Iraq's Ahmed Saadawi, which builds upon Mary Shelley's classic story to express the horrors of contemporary Baghdad.

About this volume

The current study grows first and foremost out of a recognition of the growing prominence of Western-style popular culture in the Arab world, as witnessed by everything from the increasing frequency with which American and other Western movies and television programs are rebroadcast in the Middle East (generally with Arabic subtitles), to the replication of American-style television programs and genres in an Arab context (and in Arabic), to the production in the Arab world of wildly popular music video clips that are clearly based on Western models. Our work also grows out of a recognition that this phenomenon is a complex one. While the majority of younger Arabs in much of the Arab world have enthusiastically greeted American and American-style movies, music, and television when given the chance, many Arabs (especially those who are older and/or religiously conservative) have greeted the intrusion of American culture into their lives as a threat to the cultural and moral foundations of their Islamic world. Meanwhile, the whole phenomenon of contemporary Arab popular culture is part of the larger process of capitalist globalization, the implications of which we remain cognizant throughout this study.

After we look in Chapter 1 at the birth of popular forms of Orientalism in conjunction with the rise of consumer capitalism in the United States throughout much of the twentieth century, we turn our attention in Chapter 2 to the music industry, one of the most extensively globalized aspects of contemporary popular culture. Here, we look at the flow of images from the East to the West, concentrating on the Orientalist way in which stock images of Arab culture (such as camels and belly dancers) have been appropriated for use in American music videos and other aspects of American popular culture. These videos and other works, crucial parts of American popular culture during the past few decades, demonstrate how thoroughly ingrained Orientalist images are in the popular American consciousness. Some are overt in their appropriation of images from the Arab world to create humor or an air of exoticism; others are more subtle. But there is generally little concern about whether the images of the Arab world presented in the videos are accurate. Moreover, the use of the images is consistent enough that they clearly participate in an Orientalist discourse, even though we believe the Orientalism of these videos to be more of the consumerist variety than of the colonialist variety described by Said. We believe that an examination of these videos is particularly useful because American music videos as a whole (including many of those discussed in this chapter) have been so popular in the Arab world and because such videos (generally called "video clips" in the Arab world) are among the American cultural forms that have been most successfully replicated in the Middle East. As a result, the phenomenon of music videos/video clips provides one of the clearest examples of transitional cultural flow from the West to the East, while at the same time helping to show how the consumerist form of Orientalism facilitates such flow (as opposed to colonialist Orientalism, which should impede it).

In Chapter 3, we focus on the Arab music industry and on Arab video clips, which also, as it turns out, frequently employ Orientalist imagery, sometimes in ways that seem to have circulated back to the East from the West. In this chapter we will survey many aspects of Arab pop music, concentrating on the ways in which it maintains an ongoing dialogue with American and other Western pop music. We will also particularly focus on the thoroughgoing commercialization of the Arab pop music industry, a phenomenon that places this industry firmly within the circuits of global capitalism, while placing the products of that industry clearly in the realm of the postmodern.

Chapter 4 then completes our coverage of the Arab music industry with a consideration of Arab rap music, which can sometimes also be highly commercialized, but which also frequently maintains an oppositional stance with regard to the operations of global capitalism. The latter is particularly the case in the work of artists of the Arab diaspora, such as Lowkey and Shadia Mansour in Great Britain, or Omar Offendum in the United States and Narcy in Canada. Among other things, the fact that these "Arab" artists operate mainly in the West (while performing in both English and Arabic) suggests the way in which it is not only music that circulates throughout the world, but sometimes the musicians themselves.

In Chapter 5 we turn our attention to the Arab television industry, which has seen explosive growth since the introduction of satellite cable systems in the Middle East at the beginning of the 1990s. This phenomenon has widespread implications, including the exposure of Arab audiences to images and ideas from Western culture at an unprecedented level. In this chapter, however, we concentrate on the soap opera *Gümüş*, originally broadcast in Turkey from 2005 to 2007 and then rebroadcast (as *Noor*) throughout the Arab world in a hugely successful Arabic-dubbed version in 2008. This series itself touches on a number of crucial issues related to the transnational flow of culture, particularly in the way it addresses the confrontation between tradition and modernity in contemporary Turkey. But what is also interesting is the strong response (both positive and negative) that *Noor* triggered in the Arab world. In particular, its vision of a strong, confident liberated wife whose kind, considerate, enlightened husband treats her as an equal struck a chord in the Arab world that revealed a great deal about contemporary tensions over gender roles in that world—tensions that reveal a far more complex situation than that encompassed by Orientalist stereotypes.

In Chapter 6 we provide a broader survey of the kinds of television programming that are being produced in the Arab world. The similarity of this programming to much American programming provides some of the clearest examples of the convergence of Arab and American popular culture in recent years, while also providing examples of the some of the ways in which these cultures remain distinctly different. Focusing on such TV genres as singing competition shows, talk shows, and game shows, we explore the implications of these similarities in terms of whether they simply represent an instance of cultural imperialism in which Arab culture has been hijacked by American culture or whether they represent a utopian example of two cultures coming together in a productive way.

The Oscar-nominated Jordanian film *Theeb* (2014), set during the Great Arab Revolt of the First World War, is the focus of Chapter 7. The discussion of this film helps to indicate the participation of the Arab film industry in the global film industry essentially from its very beginning. Meanwhile, the particular subject matter of *Theeb* deals with the birth of the modern Jordanian nation (largely as a result of Western interventions in the region) and touches on a number of important topics related to colonialism and nationalism—and to the ways in which Arab "nationalism" can be seen as a part of the process of globalization. But the film also addresses a number of crucial issues related to cultural flow between the East and the West, especially in the way it derives its style so directly from Western cinema, especially the genre of the American Western— but also of the Italian Spaghetti Western. However, among other things, the film systematically deconstructs the binary logic of heroism that underlies the American Western—and that also, in a different way, underlies *Theeb*'s most important Western predecessor (which deals with the same historical material), *Lawrence of Arabia* (1962). *Theeb* thus undermines the self versus other thinking that has been crucial to Orientalism in all its forms, potentially helping to point the way toward new ways of thinking that surmount Orientalism altogether.

1

From Circus Sideshows to Music Videos: Orientalism and the Rise of American Consumer Capitalism

Noting the many new strategies that were developed to market products as American capitalism shifted into a new phase at the beginning of the twentieth century, William Leach, in a study of the rise of consumer capitalism in the United States, concludes that "perhaps the most popular of all merchandising themes in the years before World War I was the oriental theme, fashion from the bottom up, as it were, not, as with much of Paris couture, from the top down" (*Land* 104). Fashion based on Oriental (especially Middle Eastern) themes had, according to Leach, a hint of something "luxurious," but also "impermissible," certainly exotic and perhaps a bit risqué. From the 1890s forward, circuses, world's fairs, movies, live theater, fiction, and even public parks began to display Oriental themes in their design. Importantly, these themes were attractive to Americans because they suggested an air of something vital and energetic and mysterious that the increasingly routinized and commodified lifeworld of individuals under capitalism sorely lacked.

To an extent, this phenomenon is an extension of one described by Said in a nineteenth-century European context. He notes, for example, that "the regeneration of Europe by Asia was a very influential Romantic idea" (*Orientalism* 115). We would argue, however, that this new American use of the Middle East as a source for exotic fantasies to provide relief from capitalist routine is fundamentally different from the European vision of the East as a source of vital (and sexual) energies. After all, this European Orientalist desire had an outlet in the literal conquest and domination of the East. Modern American Orientalist desire was, on the other hand, from the beginning oriented toward the consumption of specific goods and services. This consumerist Orientalism would, of course, spill over into Europe in the century to come, just as European-style colonialist Orientalism would continue to be a force in America.

But Europe was the birthplace and principal home of colonialist Orientalism, just as America played the same roles for consumerist Orientalism.

As a key example of how the Middle East was seen in early-twentieth-century America, Leach cites the 1904 novel *The Garden of Allah*[1] by Englishman Robert Hichens, an author who had traveled extensively in the Islamic world before writing several novels set in that world. According to Leach, Hichens's novel, written in overwrought, sentimental, purple prose, "expresses European disenchantment with rational civilization, with conventional order and behavior" (*Land* 108). Its heroine, Domini, an Englishwoman, travels to North Africa in search of elemental passions and exotic libidinous thrills unavailable in staid, bourgeois Europe. And the wild, Arabic atmosphere nearly delivers—until Hichens has second thoughts and hastily retreats into bourgeois propriety at the book's end.

Hichens's book was a big seller in the United States (though not, oddly enough, in England) and was adapted to the Broadway stage in 1907, then later to film three different times, including the 1936 Technicolor adaptation directed by Richard Boleslawski and starring Marlene Dietrich as Domini—which predictably strips the novel of most of its sensuality and turns the story into one about Catholic piety, of all things. The novel even became the inspiration for new Arabic-themed clothing lines and fashion shows in major department stores. Indeed, when the stage version was revived in 1912, it was such a success that it triggered an entire line of tie-in merchandise. Clearly, American business quickly sensed the profit potential in Orientalism and moved to cash in on Orientalist desire, commodifying Orientalism like everything else. As Holly Edwards puts it, "The migration of Garden of Allah imagery from story to product epitomizes the process whereby the Orient was constructed and then disseminated in forms that conformed with American dreams and patterns of consumption" (44). And yet, the Orient maintained its own stubborn material reality, and real-world Arabs continued to inhabit the Middle East however many stage Arabs were used to market products in America.

Colonialism, routinization, and the historical background of consumerist Orientalism

The fascination with Oriental motifs that erupted in American culture around the beginning of the twentieth century did not emerge from nowhere, though it did gain momentum and new modes of expression from the important changes that were going on in America at the time. For example, American Orientalism clearly has roots in the eighteenth- and nineteenth-century European Orientalism on which Said focuses, and it borrows its initial iconography directly from European representations of the East. John Carlos Rowe, for example, traces the long history of American Orientalism through an analysis of literary sources that reach back to the eighteenth century ("Arabia Fantasia"). Using Royall Tyler's *The Algerine Captive* (1797) as a starting point, Rowe notes that Barbary captivity narratives became immensely popular in the new United States as long ago as the beginning of the nineteenth century, while an Orientalist fascination with the Middle East persisted in American literature throughout the nineteenth century and in phenomena such as "Egyptomania," or the popular fascination with exploring the tombs and monuments left by the ancient Egyptians.[2]

In a similar way, Malini Johar Schueller notes the extent to which nineteenth-century American authors from Washington Irving to Emerson and Whitman often demonstrated a fascination with an imaginative conception of the Orient that stretched from the Barbary Coast to India. For Schueller, these authors helped to shape an imperial vision of American statehood (and a notion of the United States as the culmination of the evolution of global culture) that has informed American foreign policy since the early twentieth century. However, American Orientalism underwent important changes in the early twentieth century in conjunction with sweeping and fundamental changes in capitalism itself, setting in motion a new form of consumer-oriented capitalism that eventually became the late capitalism of today.

Granted, there is always a geopolitical dimension to the representation of foreign cultures. And it is probably no accident that a stepped-up fascination with Oriental motifs in American culture occurred at about the same time new rumblings of imperialist tendencies arose in American politics with the Spanish-American War of 1898. Similarly, it is no coincidence that these imperialist tendencies gained energy just as the conquest of the American frontier—which had provided so much imaginative energy to the formulation of an American national identity throughout the nineteenth century—was coming to a close.

This notion that the closing of the frontier might have a profound impact on American national attitudes and policy emanates, of course, from the so-called Frontier Hypothesis advanced by historian Frederick Jackson Turner in his essay "The Significance of the Frontier in American History," first presented at a conference of the American Historical Association held in conjunction with the World's Columbian Exposition, which took place in Chicago in 1893. Among other things, this exposition announced a new interest in global cultures on the part of a formerly isolationist America, even as it "trumpeted American cultural superiority" (Holly Edwards 37). It can also be taken as a key starting point for the fascination with the Middle East noted by Leach in his discussion of the rise of consumer capitalism in the United States. After all, one of the key exhibits at the exposition was an Orientalist spectacle identified as a "Street in Cairo," where visitors could view various Middle Eastern wonders, including the obligatory belly dancer, in this case a performer billed as "Little Egypt," who headlined a show entitled "The Algerian Dancers of Morocco." The dancer herself (Fahreda Mazar Spyropoulos) was actually Syrian, but this conflation of Egypt, Algeria, Morocco, and Syria is not surprising. One of the central characteristics of Orientalist stereotyping is the tendency to lump all of the East into one undifferentiated category, and Americans at the time were, by and large, far from knowledgeable enough to make distinctions.[3]

Holly Edwards has suggested that the popularity of these dancers—whom American audiences seemed to find quite titillating despite the fact that they were modestly dressed—centered on certain American practices at the time. In particular, she notes that American women's attire at the time featured a heavy dose of corsetry and other devices that "conspired to camouflage, restrict, and generally deny the free flow of energy at the core of the female body" (39). In contrast, the free and fluid movements of the midsections of these "Algerian" dancers must have seemed shocking and suggestive of forbidden sexual pleasures.

Orientalist fantasies are, in general, underwritten by elaborate visions of pageantry and spectacle and magic, so Orientalist images were ideal for an American culture that was rapidly embracing modernity, excited by the notion that the United States might very well emerge from the flurry of modernization that marked the first decades of the twentieth century as the most modern nation of all. But modernity—especially capitalist modernity—comes at a high cost. For one thing, the "time is money" ethic of modern capitalism meant that every moment suddenly had to be scheduled and administered for maximum efficiency, a phenomenon T. S. Eliot's "Prufrock" captures well when he complains that "I have measured out my life with coffee spoons." More fundamentally, as Max Weber has so influentially described, the basic worldview of capitalism reduces everything in the world to an instrument of capitalist productivity, stripping human experience of anything and everything that can't be rationalized, routinized, packaged, and marketed. In *The Protestant Ethic and the Spirit of Capitalism*—originally composed in 1904 and 1905, just as the Orientalist craze in America was hitting its stride—Weber describes how capitalism—with Protestantism as its accessory and ideological handmaiden— produces a world bereft of magic, in which everything makes sense, everything has a price, and nothing has real value. The particularly strong confluence of Protestant repression and capitalist modernization that marked the American ideological climate combined with the closing of the frontier in the late nineteenth century to produce a perfect storm of routinization and rationalization that left Americans desperate for a life of more color and adventure than the one they saw around them.

As Leach notes, the first years of the twentieth century saw an outburst of pageants, parades, and other spectacles all over America. From the very beginning, though, the content of these spectacles was rather confused, often turning a fundamentally anti-capitalist impulse into a new marketing opportunity. Pageants and parades often featured shiny and impressive examples of a potential better world, and what could be more marketable than that? As an extreme example, Leach cites the 1913 silkworkers' strike in Paterson, New Jersey, for which organizers attempted to gain the support of workers in nearby New York by literally re-enacting the strike in fictionalized form as a pageant held in and around Manhattan's Madison Square Garden. The ensuing spectacle, however, did little to win support for the strike and in fact diverted so much energy *from* the strike that it ultimately might have contributed to its collapse (Leach, *Land of Desire* 188). More importantly, the very idea of converting the strike into a pageant was shot through with the premises of capitalist marketing, representing an unconscious and inadvertent capitulation to the very capitalist ideas that the strike was meant to oppose. For Leach, then, this pageant "exposed the extent to which the new commercial culture was beginning to penetrate the ideological center of American life, and to what degree it had established—even in the heart of labor radicalism—the character of what people longed for and fought for" (189).

The fascination with Oriental motifs that permeated the culture of pageant and spectacle in American society in the early years of the twentieth century might have been less obviously anti-capitalist than the Paterson strike pageant, but it almost certainly grows out of a desire, conscious or not, to escape the mind-numbing routine of day-to-day life under modern capitalism. Just as surely, though, the romantic and exotic images that informed the Orientalist craze of the early twentieth century were themselves quickly commodified, appropriated as part of the capitalist system from which they were meant to provide escape. This commodification can perhaps be most easily seen in the use of such images in the emerging popular culture of the early years of the twentieth century. Orientalist images quickly became the stuff of show business—with the emphasis equally on *show* and on *business*.

The Orient as show business spectacle in early-twentieth-century America

The last years of the nineteenth century and the first years of the twentieth century saw an increase in the cultural prominence of the Broadway theater in New York City, propelled partly by New York's increasing importance as a commercial center, which brought new affluence to the city—as well as numerous visitors. It was, of course, a good time for Broadway, where the inherent theatricality of its stage performances (dominated by musicals) was perfectly in tune with the era's thirst for spectacle. Not surprisingly, Orientalist elements were a key feature of turn-of-the-century musical theater, with plays such as *Sinbad* (1891) drawing upon *One Thousand and One Nights* for exotic material. Indeed, the Sinbad story was popular enough that it provided the material for a second stage adaptation of the same title in 1918, this time serving as a vehicle for superstar Al Jolsen, who performed additional songs that were inserted in the program in addition to the main *Arabian Nights*–based story.

If Jolsen songs such as "Rock-a-Bye Your Baby with a Dixie Melody" could be inserted without any relation to the Oriental plot of *Sinbad*, it was also the case that songs with an Oriental motif could be inserted into musicals that did not themselves deal with Oriental themes. For example, the 1912 production *The Lady of the Slipper* (an adaptation of the Cinderella story)[4] contains a Victor Herbert song entitled "Bagdad" that is a genuine classic of Orientalist stereotyping. Among other things, this song became a lasting part of American literary culture by being quoted from by John Dos Passos in both *Manhattan Transfer* (1925) and *The 42nd Parallel* (1930), the latter of which was the first volume in his monumental U.S.A. Trilogy, one of the key works of modern American literature. Dos Passos also quotes the same passage in *Orient Express* (1927), a travelogue that recounts his own journeys through the Middle East in 1921. So Dos Passos had some first-hand experience of the Middle East, and indeed quotes this song with enough irony to suggest that he understands what is going on in the passage.

The passage in question is the following:

> But the women of the harem
> Knew exactly how to wear 'em
> In Oriental Baghdad long ago.

The lines are well chosen, encapsulating in a mere three lines two of the crucial aspects of Orientalist stereotyping: the notion that exotic masculinist havens existed within the harem culture of the Middle East and the notion that the Middle East is an ancient land that was once grand but is now in decay. The two lines immediately before these three read "Girlies gay in silken trousers / Suffragettes no more," both explaining what exactly it is that the women of the harem know how to wear and contrasting these exotic, submissive Eastern women from long ago with modern American women and their contemporary agitation for the right to vote. The song ends with a final summation, emphasizing the mystical glory of ancient Baghdad, but also emphasizing its status as a patriarchal paradise, where women were not only beautiful and submissive, but cheap and plentiful:

> Life was fair and fine in Baghdad
> City fair of mystic spells
> Oh those olden temples golden
> And oh, those spicy garlic smells.
> There they had no alimony
> Divorce? Oh no.
> For the cost of one New Yorker
> You could keep a dozen corkers
> In Oriental Baghdad long ago.[5]

"Bagdad" is a comic song, originally performed in the Broadway show by Dave Montgomery, a comedian who was one half of the then-prominent comedy team of Montgomery and Stone, who had been the original Tin Woodman and Scarecrow of the Broadway adaptation of *The Wizard of Oz*.[6] The song is itself clearly presented in a tongue-in-cheek fashion and not meant to be taken seriously as a description of Middle Eastern history. But the blithe way in which its stereotypes are delivered is typical of the Orientalist imagery that appears in early-twentieth-century American culture, which seems to regard the Middle East as a vaguely amusing source of material without much concern for the material reality of that part of the world. Setting aside the fact that the fantasy Baghdad of this song is a purely masculine utopia that presents women merely as objects intended to provide pleasure to men, there is also the fact that this imaginary vision is not intended as a blueprint for changes that might be needed in contemporary America. It is, instead, presented merely for entertainment purposes, apparently meant to be amusing to both women and men. Indeed, the masculinist fantasy here is so overt that one could see men as the real objects of the joke, though in 1912 this fantasy would surely not have appeared as ridiculous as it does more than a century later.

What is important for our purposes is that this song appears to present a critique of conditions in early-twentieth-century America, suggesting ancient Baghdad as a utopian alternative, even if merely in comic fantasy. In reality, however, the song is merely part of a popular entertainment that is fully committed to the capitalist logic of the emergent consumerist society that surrounds it. That this particular entertainment is based on a well-known fairy tale that itself has strong consumerist resonances is so much the better and merely illustrates the fairy-tale nature of much capitalist marketing.

One way to understand the utopian aspects of the Orientalist craze of the early twentieth century is to appeal to Fredric Jameson's discussion in *The Political Unconscious* of the popularity of romance genres (to which works such as *The Garden of Allah* or *The Lady of the Slipper* would definitely belong) at about this same period in history. Beginning with the question of why nonrealist genres such as romance would remain popular in a routinized capitalist world stripped of magic and reduced by the application of reason to purely instrumental and economic principles, Jameson concludes that such genres remained popular as modern capitalism tightened its grip on American society not despite this routinization, but because of it. In the imaginatively impoverished and routinized world of consumer capitalism, individuals naturally desire something different and less impoverished, making the otherworldliness of romance attractive as a sign of other possible ways of living in and viewing the world. "Romance," Jameson concludes, "now again seems to offer the possibility of sensing other historical rhythms, and of demonic or Utopian transformations of a real now unshakably set in place" (104).

Orientalism, especially in the consumerist form seen in early-twentieth-century American culture, offers this same sort of utopian compensation for the poverty and seeming stagnation of life under capitalism. If Americans view the Orient as a world completely different from their own, then its very existence suggests, if nothing else, that other worlds are possible.[7] There is, then, however problematic and degraded, a definite utopian dimension to Orientalism that contains energies with the potential to move us beyond our habitual ways of thought. In short, Orientalism responds well to the double hermeneutic espoused by Jameson elsewhere in *The Political Unconscious*. For Jameson, any properly Marxist interpretive project must certainly contain a "negative hermeneutic, a Marxist practice of ideological analysis proper." This ideological analysis is essentially the task that Said performs when he envisions Orientalism as something that shackles the Western imagination and places severe limitations on how we can envision the Middle East and its people. However, for Jameson, this ideological analysis "must in the practical work of reading and interpretation be exercised simultaneously with a Marxist positive hermeneutic, or a decipherment of the Utopian impulses of these same still ideological cultural texts" (296). This utopian impulse potentially sets our imaginations free to envision the possibility that our own world might be different than it is, even if it potentially does so at the risk of ignoring the material reality of actual Arabs or others. We will take Jameson's advice to heart throughout this volume, remaining aware of both the limitations that Orientalist ideologies place on certain texts and the utopian energies that strive to move beyond those limitations. For example, if the limitations placed on the representation of the Orient in the West suggest the ideological limitations placed on Western life by capitalism, the continuing fascination with the Otherness of the Orient at least suggests a dissatisfaction with the life offered by capitalism, with at least the potential implication that it might be possible to move toward something better.

Leach's discussion of the use of Orientalist images in early-twentieth-century marketing, however, shows that the particular form taken by Orientalism in America rendered problematic the use of Orientalist images as a form of utopian escape from capitalist routine by rendering Orientalism a *part* of the capitalist routine. The Orient was thus delivered to American consumers in pre-packaged and pre-commodified form—and it is surely the case that many Americans in the early twentieth century knew virtually nothing about the Middle East beyond what they had seen of its use in advertising and marketing.

Marketing the Orient: The East and tobacco

For example, a leading American cigarette brand during the pre–First World War years was "Mecca" cigarettes, buoyed by an extensive advertising campaign that assured potential consumers that those who used the brand were as devoted to it as "Mohammedans" were to prayer. Presumably no one at the time noticed the ominous implication that the cigarettes might be literally addictive. Instead, what was offered was that these cigarettes could bring a world of exotic sensual pleasures to those who consumed them, despite the religious intonations of the advertising. The cigarettes were introduced in 1878 by the Kinney Brothers Tobacco Company, which joined with several other companies to form the powerhouse American Tobacco Company in 1890. This firm would be one of the stalwarts of emerging American capitalism, becoming one of the twelve founding members of the Dow Jones Industrial Average in 1896.

Indeed, the tobacco industry was quite central to the rise of the American consumer culture that Leach describes. Ominously calling cigarettes "the product that defined America," Allan Brandt goes on to declare that

> the rise of national brands of cigarettes was but one indication of the cultural transformation occurring in the early twentieth century. The consumer culture in which the cigarette became so prominent and popular marked the construction of the first truly national, secular culture in American history. (Brandt 55–56)

That producers would so extensively appropriate Orientalist images in their marketing of this new all-American product can be taken as a marker of the thorough entanglement of Orientalism and consumer capitalism in American history.

The success of Mecca cigarettes was no doubt due partly to the clout of American Tobacco—as well as to their marketing savvy, which took such very American forms as packaging baseball cards (as well as cards featuring stars of other sports, such as boxing and billiards) with the cigarettes to increase sales. But ads for the cigarettes featured mysterious-looking turbaned and bearded or mustachioed men to increase their exotic appeal. This marketing, of course, suggests that there was little inherent hostility toward the Middle East at this time and that offering American men a chance to be like Middle Eastern men was considered attractive. These men (and the cigarettes they smoked) were, incidentally, identified as "Turkish," Turkish tobacco having already established a reputation for quality—and Mecca, of course, along with much of the rest of the Middle East, being at this time under Ottoman rule.

In 1911, the assets of American Tobacco were split among that company and several other companies after it was declared a monopoly in violation of anti-trust laws. These new companies included Liggett & Myers, which marketed its own Orientalist brand ("Fatima" cigarettes) and R. J. Reynolds Tobacco, which offered an even more important rival with the introduction of Camel cigarettes in 1913. This new brand featured a trademark camel on each package, with pyramids and palm trees in the background, thus deploying some of the most recognizable Orientalist images of the period. It was also accompanied by an unprecedented advertising campaign that even included processions of live camels in selected cities.[8] However, while Camel cigarettes were advertised as employing a blend of Turkish and domestic tobaccos, they actually contained mostly the latter, and their advertising never emphasized the Turkish nature of the cigarettes to the extent that the Mecca brand had. Indeed, the pyramids on the packs suggested that Camels were Egyptian, which was no doubt intentional, given that Egyptian cigarettes were quite popular in the United States at the time.[9] Thus, when the United States and the Ottomans became adversaries in the First World War, the popularity of Camels was able to survive the war, while the popularity of Meccas did not. Meccas (and Fatimas) were soon out of production, while Camels remain among the world's most popular cigarettes more than a hundred years after their introduction, having maintained their association with the exoticism of the East, while somehow escaping any association with Arab anti-Americanism. Indeed, the brand's iconic "Joe Camel" cartoon mascot, despite being the target of much ire among anti-smoking groups for his ability to attract children to smoking, is also among the most recognizable—and most American—advertising images of the twentieth century.

Oriental spectacles in circuses, shows, and expositions

The early-twentieth-century vision of the East as a fantasyland that offers an escape from the mind-numbing routine of day-to-day life under modern capitalism was perhaps best captured in the popularity of "Oriental" spectacles in circuses of the first years of the twentieth century. Though soon to be pushed to the margins by emergent media culture, circuses in the first years of the century still offered Americans one of the major windows into a different world. The 1914 version of the Barnum and Bailey Circus, for example, featured an elaborate procession entitled "The Wizard Prince of Arabia," billed as an "Indo-Arabic spectacle," presenting such attractions as "300 dancing girls" and "250 singers in weird Oriental choruses." The elephants that were still a staple of the circus of the time (and that would remain so for another century) already carried with them a hint of Oriental exoticism, of course, while the "Indo-Arabic" designation of this particular show indicates the way in which the exoticisms of India and Arabia were often rolled into one in the American mind. Meanwhile, the sheer size of the elephants featured in these spectacles helped to emphasize the air of opulence and excess that was key to the fantasy value of Orientalist spectacles in the circus.

There was, of course, a particularly imperial air (but of a specifically American kind) to the circus, which went to great lengths to emphasize the way in which it had scoured the world to bring exotic entertainments back to America. And this collection went beyond the recruitment of talented professional performers: Barnum and Bailey, for example, offered such attractions as a "Grand Ethnological Congress," in which supposedly ordinary members of various "strange and savage tribes" (including Arabs) were put on display like so many exotic zoo animals. In fact, associated animals (such as elephants and camels) were included in this display as well, and were displayed pretty much in the same way as the human participants in the show. Partly, of course, the outrageous Orientalism of such circus displays was merely an attempt to give audiences what they wanted to see, but such displays also played a key role in shaping audience tastes for the strange and the exotic and for categorizing certain cultures of the world as fitting in those categories. Meanwhile, this spectacular display of the global reach of the circus could also be taken as a reminder of the newly global reach of the United States itself. Holly Edwards thus notes the way in which Orientalist imagery around the turn of the century "served as a preface to, or part of, the consolidation of power that Americans sought in the emerging world order of the early twentieth century" (17). As Janet Davis has noted, however, the ideological underpinnings of such circus displays were thoroughly informed by a desire to present American imperialism as fundamentally different in nature from European imperialism. While the taming of the American frontier had, as Richard Slotkin emphasizes, been underwritten by a narrative of the violent conquest of savages (somewhat in the European imperial mode), US expansion beyond North America tended to be couched as an economic battle against savagery, rather than a political or military one. Thus, for Davis,

> Circus and Wild West spectacles framed the new empire within the American exceptionalist tradition. However inaccurately, these amusements defined U.S. expansion as a distinct counterpoint to European formulations of formal empire solely characterized by colonization and military domination, because the nation's acquisition of noncontiguous territory was predicated on an abiding sense of moral "uplift" through economic intervention. (Davis 194)

In short, the ideological groundwork for late global capitalism was already being laid in America even as classic colonialism was still in full sway in Europe.

Circus images tended to portray the Orient as a land of opulence, mystery, and sexual adventure, though some images were more alarming. Some shows, for example, drew from a popular fascination with the British colonial wars against Mahdist rebels in the Sudan—which eventually ended with the subjugation of the rebels in 1898, but which also included the Mahdist victory at Khartoum in 1885, which was one of the most notorious defeats in the history of British colonial armies. That defeat also featured the death of famed British colonial general Charles George Gordon, who would nonetheless be immortalized in British colonial lore—and ultimately in Hollywood film.[10]

Khartoum was something like the British version of the Alamo, combined with the American Battle of the Little Bighorn, the latter of which preceded the fall of Khartoum by a mere nine years and which had already become a key part of the emergent American entertainment industry through its re-enactments in *Buffalo Bill's Wild West*, a circus-like touring extravaganza that had been founded in 1883 by Buffalo Bill Cody and that would eventually include Sioux Chief Sitting Bull himself in its performances. By 1893, incidentally, Cody had expanded his show into *Buffalo Bill's Wild West and Congress of Rough Riders of the World*, which included elaborate performances not only by cowboys, cavalry, and Indians, but also by a variety of exotic figures, including Arabs and Turks.[11] Cody, incidentally, had hoped to have his show included in the 1893 Columbian Exposition discussed above. Rejected by the organizers, he instead set up adjacent to the exposition and ran his own rival show, with considerable success.

Cody was perhaps rivaled in his day only by P. T. Barnum as a self-promoter and organizer of spectacles—and as a harbinger of the consumerist society to come. It is perhaps not surprising, then, that the Barnum & Bailey Circus would pick up on the potential of the Mahdist rebels as images of exotic fierceness. Indeed, by 1897, the circus included a re-enactment of battles between British redcoats and savage Mahdist rebels in a performance entitled "The Mahdi, or For the Victoria Cross." That Americans attending the circus doubtless knew virtually nothing about the terms of the Sudanese conflict was, of course, not a detriment, as it made the conflict seem all the more exotic and all the more adaptable to spectacle form. What was clear was that civilized British soldiers were battling what seemed to be a collection of Muslim fanatics and African savages, in a motif the vague outlines of which could not have seemed more familiar to a country whose national identity had recently been forged in its own battles against supposedly savage foes, battles that had already been made the stuff of spectacle by Buffalo Bill.

Of course, the cultural position of the circus (like the flowering of musical theater) at the beginning of the twentieth century was almost immediately threatened by the rise of film, a medium that is ultimately much better suited to consumer capitalism, because it involves performances that can be mass produced, packaged, and widely distributed. At the beginning of the century, nearly one hundred circuses and circus-like menageries were touring the United States, but these would soon be surpassed by thousands of movie theaters, ranging from small, shabby storefronts to elaborate movie palaces.

The Orient and the history of American film

On the other hand, the emergent cinema of the early twentieth century lacked both sound and color, giving an inherent advantage to live performances such as the circus and the musical theater as media for the presentation of Orientalist spectacles. Nevertheless, Orientalist fantasy quickly made its way into the new medium of film as well. Indeed, the new visual medium of film had already begun to exploit the exotic potential of Middle Eastern imagery with recorded performances of belly dancers as early as the 1890s. Particularly popular was a short 1904 film of one "Princess Rajah" performing her "Arabian Chair Dance" as part of the "Mysterious Asia" attraction at the St. Louis World's Fair of that year.[12] Later, the exotic romanticism of *The Sheik* (1921) and *Son of the Sheik* (1926) made their young star Rudolph Valentino one of the sensations of the silent film era—though he had already died of peritonitis (at the age of thirty-one) by the time the second film premiered. Other major stars were featured in Orientalist silents as well, such as Douglas Fairbanks, Jr., as the swashbuckling hero of *The Thief of Bagdad* (1924), based on Ahmed Abdulla's 1924 novel, which was itself loosely based on materials from *One Thousand and One Nights*. Indeed, "Oriental" sources have provided material for any number of Western films, which built on their exotic appeal to sell tickets to audiences who otherwise knew very little about the Middle East. For example, the story "Ali Baba and the Forty Thieves" alone has been adapted numerous times, including as a Popeye the Sailor cartoon, not to mention multiple feature films.

If silent film lacked some of the resources for the production of spectacle that were available to the circus or the Broadway stage, it is also the case that movie theaters themselves—as a way of attracting audiences—began to take on an air of spectacle in the 1920s. And Orientalism was at the center of this marketing phenomenon as well, especially after visions of the mystery, antiquity, and opulence of the East were given a boost by the popular fascination with the hunt for ancient Egyptian artifacts in the early 1920s. For example, archaeologist Howard Carter became an icon of popular culture when his efforts in the Valley of the Kings in the years just after the First World War received considerable coverage in the American press. There was particular excitement over Carter's search for the tomb of Tutankhamen, which then became one of the inspirations for the opening of Grauman's Egyptian Theater in Los Angeles in 1922. In one of history's great archaeological moments, Carter in fact discovered the intact tomb on November 4, 1922, only two weeks after the opening of Grauman's Egyptian Theater, which became such a success that it subsequently inspired a string of imitations around America. Like all of the early "movie palaces" that proliferated across America during this period, this theater was designed to provide a properly exotic, escapist setting in which audiences could view the products of the new Hollywood Dream Factory. When the Orientalist *Thief of Bagdad* premiered there in 1924, for example, the event included a parade of live elephants. The long-term success of the theater (renovated in 1998 and still in use today) indicates the close connection between the fantasy elements of Orientalism and the fantasy elements of Hollywood film.[13]

The coming of sound brought even more opportunity for bringing the romance of the Orient to the big screen. Of course, the coming of sound in 1927 was soon followed by the stock market crash of 1929, so the first decade of sound film occurred mostly during the Great Depression, when escapist entertainments were much in demand. In addition to *The Garden of Allah*, many films of the 1930s featured Orientalist images and themes. Indeed, *The Garden of Allah* star Marlene Dietrich had already carved out a niche for herself in films with exotic Eastern settings—roles for which she was presumably well suited because of her own status as a foreign import. Indeed, Dietrich immediately embarked on such roles after being recruited to come to Hollywood from her native Germany by director Josef von Sternberg (himself a recent German import who had directed Dietrich in her breakthrough German film—shot simultaneously in English- and German-language versions—*The Blue Angel* shortly before). Dietrich's first American film was the romantic adventure *Morocco* (1930), for which she won an Oscar nomination. *Morocco* plays heavily on the atmosphere of Oriental decadence in its setting, famously featuring Dietrich (as cabaret singer Amy Jolly) performing a song in a man's suit, during which she provocatively kisses another woman. Such gender-bending scenes were, of course, highly unusual at the time, though Hollywood films were a bit more daring before the installation of the Production Code in 1934. Still, such scenes were also greatly enabled by the exotic North African setting, where aberrant behavior is only to be expected—much as the decadent atmosphere of Rick's Café Américaine was clearly meant to be at least partly a result of its setting in Casablanca a little more than a decade later.

Dietrich and von Sternberg scored another major success (and moved even further east) with *Shanghai Express*, the top-grossing American film of 1932. In this film, the Oriental exoticism of the setting is played up in a number of ways, most of which contribute to an overall sense of a foreign land steeped in decadence, immorality, and political instability. It isn't the Middle East, but it is the East, and by the terms of Orientalism, one East is as good as another.

At one point, for an extra exotic touch, we even see a camel beside the train that is the film's main setting as it prepares to depart Beijing for the three-day journey to Shanghai.[14] Later, when one passenger complains about a delay in the movement of the train (stopped when a farmer's cow balks while crossing the tracks), another explains, "You're in China now, where time and life have no value." At another point, Henry Chang (Warner Oland), who turns out secretly to be the leader of a band of Chinese rebels, explains that he is half white and half Chinese, but isn't proud of the white half and would rather be all Chinese. Shocked, an American passenger interrogating him asks, "What future is there to being a Chinaman? You're born, eat your way through a handful of rice, and you die."

The year 1932 also saw a two-pronged attempt to bring the mystery of the Orient to bear on the newly emergent Hollywood horror film, the genre having been initiated the year before with the success of *Dracula* and *Frankenstein*. The latter made actor Boris Karloff such a popular draw that Hollywood was looking for new ways to employ his ability to project an air of strange menace. They found several such ways in 1932, when Karloff starred in three major horror films. In *The Old Dark House* (directed by *Frankenstein* director James Whale), Karloff plays a dangerous drunken butler without any particular Orientalist implications. Orientalism was in full force, however, when Karloff was employed as Imhotep, the rogue (and definitely menacing) Egyptian mummy unearthed by British archaeologists in *The Mummy*. This film allowed both the mystery and the antiquity of Egypt to be used to good atmospheric effect in the horror film. Indeed, this use was so effective that it spawned an entire horror franchise that is still producing films today.[15] Meanwhile, also in 1932, Karloff was employed in the even more Orientalist *The Mask of Fu Manchu*, though here Karloff, as the title character, embodies not only the decadence of the East but a variant stereotype generally applied only to East Asian Orientals—that of the brilliant, but misguided scientist/intellectual.

The Mask of Fu Manchu, despite being a film from MGM, a major studio that seemed concerned with its image as a purveyor of "quality" entertainment, did little to update or challenge the array of Asian stereotypes that had informed the character's earlier pop cultural incarnations (he originates in the stories and novels of British writer Sax Rohmer, beginning in the years just before the First World War) as the epitome of intellectual evil. Fu Manchu certainly has his savage inclinations, but he is a highly intellectual figure, more mad scientist than crazed heathen. In fact, Fu Manchu holds doctorates from Edinburgh, Cambridge, and Harvard. He is ultra-intelligent and very adept at science and technology, though his followers (who seem to derive from a variety of ethnic and geographic origins, including Middle Eastern ones) are depicted in a more conventionally Orientalist fashion as hordes of superstitious believers in all sorts of mysticism, which he, of course, uses to manipulate them to do his bidding.

Most notoriously, Fu Manchu appeals to the baser instincts of his followers in this film when he exhorts them to "conquer and breed! Kill the white man and take his women!" The courageous, resourceful white people triumph, of course, as bravery and virtue trump intellect and education—even though they are a bit handicapped by constantly having to protect the film's lone white woman from being carried off by Orientals. Then again, this sort of thing works both ways, and white men are also in danger of being seduced by the exotic sexual wiles of Oriental women in the film. *The Mask of Fu Manchu* features lots of pre-Code Oriental debauchery, and much of the film is Orientalist claptrap at its worst: sneaky, cowardly, but potentially murderous Asians slink about the screen, so untrustworthy that even Fu Manchu employs black security personnel for his own protection. One of the film's most Orientalist figures is Fu Manchu's daughter, Fah Lo See (Myrna Loy), who is beautiful and seductive, but cruel and conniving as only an Oriental woman could be. She loves to toy with white men, luring them to destruction with her exotic sexual wiles, thus enacting a number of both Orientalist and sexist stereotypes. Meanwhile, enacting an entirely different array of Orientalist stereotypes, the obsequious gap-toothed Chinese servant in the final scene (a sort of Asian Stepin Fetchit, but slimier) is a classic bit of Hollywood racism.

The Mask of Fu Manchu triggered some protests, as when the Chinese embassy in Washington registered a formal complaint against the film's anti-Chinese racism. In general, however, the film provoked little negative reaction, partly because its Orientalism was not all that unusual within the cultural climate of the 1930s, where insidious Asian villains (or just hints of Asia as a locus of all sorts of perversions) populated a variety of genres, including pulp magazines and the emergent genre of science fiction, as when the Fu Manchu–inspired Ming the Merciless became the arch-enemy of pulp science fiction hero Flash Gordon in 1934.[16]

Such Oriental villains draw to an extent on the thrill factor associated with consumerist Orientalism, but in their depiction of Orientals as Evil Others they represent something of a throwback to the colonialist Orientalism of the nineteenth century. Slightly later, von Sternberg himself (sans Dietrich) showed a combination of Orientalisms, while also combining Middle Eastern and Chinese motifs in *The Shanghai Gesture* (1941), which presents the city of the title as a mysterious place of decadence and corruption and as a gathering place for rogues and adventurers from around the world—much as Casablanca would so famously be portrayed a year later. Indeed, Shanghai is explicitly identified in the film as a modern-day Babel, making its connection to Middle Eastern decadence quite clear. The Orientalist stereotypes in which *The Shanghai Gesture* trades tend to conflate China with the Middle East in other ways as well. The male "protagonist" is the fez-wearing Doctor Omar (Victor Mature), whom one of the other characters describes as an "Arabian," and who appears to be a Muslim, given that he at one point yells "Allah is great!" when in crisis. On the other hand, he himself later claims that, while he was born near Damascus, his father was an Armenian tobacco dealer. He doesn't wish to talk about his mother, except to say that "she was half French and the other half is lost in the dust of time. . . . In short, I'm a thoroughbred mongrel. I'm related to all the earth." He then ends with the well-known quote from the Roman playwright Terence: "Nothing that's human is foreign to me." The charming Omar is a smooth talker with the ladies, but he is depicted as a shady character, not to be trusted. At one point he claims, as he prepares to join a card game, that he cheats at everything but cards. Even his "doctor" title appears to be bogus: he himself admits at one point that he is a doctor "of nothing." Female lead Poppy Smith (Gene Tierney) refers to him as a "Persian poet," having earlier asked him if he was any relation to "the poet Omar," clearly meaning Omar Khayyám. He responds by quoting Khayyám, showing his familiarity with the poet. And, for a final Orientalist touch, the film features Ona Munson as Madame Gin Sling, the mysterious and deadly Oriental woman.

Sometimes considered to be the first film noir, *The Shanghai Gesture* laid the groundwork for Orientalist motifs to play an important role in film noir as a whole, often serving as a sort of shorthand code for decadence, corruption, and strangeness. Shanghai remains key, as in Orson Welles's *The Lady from Shanghai* (1947), a film that (not coincidentally) famously ends in a bizarre funhouse setting in San Francisco's Chinatown. And it is not for nothing that, when Humphrey Bogart's Philip Marlowe finds a dazed and drugged Carmen Sternwood (Martha Vickers) at a scene steeped in murder and pornography in *The Big Sleep* (1946), the young woman is dressed only in a Chinese robe. Nor is it a coincidence that the greatest of all neo-noir films, Roman Polanski's *Chinatown* (1973), chooses to foreground L.A.'s Chinatown as part of a constellation of images referring back to the dark world of film noir proper.

By this time, all sorts of Hollywood productions had gotten mileage out of the use of Orientalist stereotypes. Clearly, as in the classic Orientalism described by Said, there was an element of self-definition here, as American popular culture, deprived of a real Western frontier where white men could assert their dominance, sought to make Americans feel good about themselves via an array of cultural products in which women and nonwhite men were portrayed as inferior. The Western, as elaborately explained by Richard Slotkin, was chief among these products, and Native Americans were the chief scapegoats, but the Middle East did its part as well.

Such products, however, did not have the establishment of a positive image for the dominant group in American culture as their central purpose. Instead, they primarily served as popular entertainment and as a method of alleviating the strains, first of the Great Depression, and then of the Second World War. But these cultural products were also thoroughly commodified, designed to be packaged and sold, to sell tickets and generate income. Consider, for example, the 1940 film *Tin Pan Alley*, about a pair of sisters (played by Alice Faye and Betty Grable) who are vaudeville performers in the years just before the First World War—at a time when Orientalist marketing was at its peak. Perhaps it is not surprising, then, that one of the key production numbers in the film is an elaborate Orientalist spectacle in which Faye and Grable (backed by a bevy of supporting dancers) dance and sing to entertain their husband—a fat, indolent sheikh who clearly enjoys vast wealth and is stipulated to have 1,000 wives. This scene is particularly telling in its stylized pairing of hints of exotic Oriental sexuality with images of Arab excess and wealth.[17] However, the two wives played by Faye and Grable seem so alluring that the sheikh finally decides to cut back on his excesses and to declare his intention to get rid of all of his other wives, keeping only the two of them. Meanwhile, the whole number is performed to the music of a song called "The Sheik of Araby,"[18] which was originally written in 1921 and inspired by Valentino's film *The Sheik* from that same year. The song and the production number surrounding it clearly convey a number of potentially harmful stereotypes about the Middle East, but they do it without any noticeable rancor and in a spirit of innocent (or perhaps ignorant) good fun. Indeed, the song has subsequently been performed by such luminaries as the Beatles and Fats Domino, without any sense that there might be something offensive about it.

The cartoonish representation of Arab culture in *Tin Pan Alley* points toward the almost inevitable use of stereotypical images of Arabs in, well, cartoons. Indeed, Orientalist images can be found in numerous places in American cartoons for kids, as in the 1940 Looney-Tunes offering "Ali-Baba Bound,"[19] perhaps made especially offensive to Muslims by featuring Porky Pig as the main character. The presence of such images in children's culture is in itself a fascinating topic, given that one would expect impressionable young viewers to be especially susceptible to absorbing such stereotyping as part of their worldview. Such examples also indicate the way in which music is especially effective at subtly conveying Orientalist messages that might otherwise be more obviously unacceptable. Music is also one of the contemporary art forms that has most effectively been globalized in recent years, so it is especially central to our arguments in this volume.

"Ali-Baba Bound," for example, prominently features the song "Girlfriend of the Whirling Dervish," which first appeared in the seemingly light musical comedy *Garden of the Moon* (1938) and subsequently became a well-known novelty song, covered by a number of different artists. It is a song that is intentionally silly, detailing the amorous adventures of the unfaithful girlfriend while the dervish himself is too busy "dervishing." Still, its participation in the appropriation of the religious figure of the Sufi dervish as a figure of cartoonish fun (which has helped to make the whirling dervish a stock image of comically frantic activity in American pop culture) is part of a general pattern of disrespect for Islam as a religion. The same song was used again two years later as the opening music to the cartoon "Case of the Missing Hare," in which Bugs Bunny outwits and upstages a befuddled Arab magician by the name of Ala Bahma.[20] And the song has been recorded numerous times, including as late as 1991 by Bette Midler. Such Orientalist songs were frequently used in classic Hollywood films, without any obvious malicious intent, even if such imagery clearly contributes to the negative and harmful stereotyping of Arabs and Muslims.

Animation is, of course, the perfect venue for portraying Orientalist stereotypes, as animated images can easily be produced as pure simulacra, with no original model in reality. Disney, for example, has long used stereotypical imagery from other cultures in its films. The singing, hookah-smoking caterpillar of *Alice in Wonderland* (1951)[21] is a classic example of Orientalist imagery in cartoons that are ostensibly meant for children, while Orientalist images reach a new height in Disney's notorious animated version of *The Jungle Book* (1967). Here, however, the film Americanizes its British colonial source material in Kipling to the extent that the most problematic racial stereotypes are aimed not at the "Oriental" protagonist Mowgli, but at African Americans. In particular, as Booker notes, the film overtly codes its apes and monkeys as African American, an association that has a long and baleful legacy in the discourse of American racism, a fact that is further exacerbated in *The Jungle Book* by the fact that the ape king sings suggestively of his desire to be human, claiming that "an ape like me" can be human, too, with just a hint of training—reinforcing the standard racist notion that African Americans are subhuman simian creatures simply seeking to pass themselves off as human. (*Disney* 30)

And it was Disney animation that produced what is perhaps the *locus classicus* of Orientalism in contemporary American popular culture, the 1992 film *Aladdin*, which introduces us to an Arab world that is overtly described as savage, primitive, and brutal. Islam is essentially absent from the film—except in ways (such as the prominent presence of a genie) that young American viewers are not likely to connect to their source in the Quran. Genies, for example, had by 1992 become stock figures (albeit in modified form) of American popular culture, generally with no reference to the jinn that is mentioned in the Quran. *Aladdin* was widely criticized by Arab American groups (and by other American critics) for features such as the racial coding of its characters, with the "good" characters, while still Arabs, having straight noses and entirely Western features, while its villains have exaggerated "Arab" features (such as darker skin and large hook noses). And yet criticisms of the film did not prevent it from pulling in over half a billion dollars at the box office, nearly 60 percent of which (significantly) came from outside the United States. Indeed, despite lukewarm protests and calls for bans, the film was quite successful in much of the Arab and Muslim world. It certainly did nothing to slow down what was a burgeoning presence of Disney in that world, a presence that has continued to grow to this day as Disney extends its global empire further and further.

Booker, speaking of *Aladdin*'s impact on young American audiences, notes that the film conveys no stereotypes about Arabs that were not already prominent in American culture at the time, but argues that "this fact only makes the stereotypical depiction of Arabs in the film all the more troubling because it presents young viewers with attitudes they are all the more likely to accept due to the fact that they are likely to see these attitudes reinforced elsewhere" (*Disney* 56). One could argue, of course, that this goes even more for young *Arab* viewers, who are treated to a film in which their culture is denigrated, while Western values (and looks) are celebrated. In any case, *Aladdin*, like most of Disney's animated films, seems charming and lighthearted, which makes the images it conveys seem less offensive. It's just a cartoon, so cultural critics (and Arab Americans) should just get over themselves and stop taking it so seriously.

The use of music in the film (a key to the success of all of Disney's animated films) is especially effective in making its negative stereotyping of Arabs seem like harmless fun. Indeed, most of the film's basic Orientalist ideas are put in place at the very beginning, in the film's notorious opening song, entitled "Arabian Nights."[22] The song begins by exoticizing the Arab world through describing it as a "faraway place" roamed by caravans of camels, then finally announcing, famously and cheerfully, "It's barbaric, but, hey, it's home!"[23]

The Orientalism of the biblical epic

In 1998, DreamWorks attempted to reproduce some of the magic of *Aladdin* with *The Prince of Egypt*, an animated version of the Moses story that features some of the most lavish animated images produced to that time. Banned as offensive in some Muslim countries, *The Prince of Egypt* looks back on classical biblical epics such as *The Ten Commandments* (1956) and does little to update their black-and-white moral coding of good Israelites versus evil Egyptians, with the pharaoh, of course, functioning as a typical Oriental despot. However problematic this subject matter might seem for a children's film, the link between children's animation and the biblical epics of the 1950s is a natural one. Children's animation relies heavily upon spectacle to catch and hold the attention of young viewers, which also makes it an excellent venue for Orientalist imagery. But film in general began to rely more on spectacle in the 1950s, as filmmakers sought to produce new kinds of colorful big-screen imagery that could not be effectively duplicated on the small black-and-white screens that had suddenly invaded homes all over America. Westerns, for example, began to depend more and more on panoramic views of the Western landscape as a resource, while some of the most memorable spectacle-based films were the series of biblical epics (such as *The Ten Commandments*) that emerged during this period.

The Egyptians of films such as *The Ten Commandments* made perfect Oriental heavies, and it took very little sleight of hand to transfer the same stereotypes to the Romans as the films shifted to New Testament material with films such as *Ben-Hur* (1959), a film that tells the story of Jesus Christ but squeamishly refrains from showing his face on the screen. The first film actually to show that face was Nicholas Ray's *King of Kings* (1961), a film that features the Roman puppet king Herod as the principal Oriental villain. Here, though, perhaps the most memorably Orientalist scene is the one in which Herod's stepdaughter Salomé performs a seductively Oriental dance, then demands the head of John the Baptist on a platter as payment for her efforts, showing just how cruel and capricious Oriental temptresses can be.[24]

Salomé in *King of Kings* is played by teenage American actress Brigid Bazlen, marketed at the time as the next Elizabeth Taylor. But the next major Oriental temptress in American film would be played by Taylor herself in the title role of *Cleopatra* (1963), a spectacle film that, at the time, was the most lavish and expensive film ever made. The film also solidified the status of the Egyptian queen as perhaps the central image of the seductiveness and potential power of Eastern women in all of Western film. Indeed, though a real historical figure, Cleopatra is by now much better known, at least in the West, for her depictions in Western culture than for her real historical presence. Cleopatra, in fact, has been memorialized as a figure of irresistible sexual charm in Western culture at least since Shakespeare's *Antony and Cleopatra* (1607), with her most influential visual representation in the West being provided by the performance of Taylor in Joseph L. Mankiewicz's 1963 film. Taylor's makeup in the film is clearly intended to highlight her famous eyes, though of course it also echoes the heavy use of eye makeup by women in the real ancient Egypt. Meanwhile, though this film does rely heavily on Cleopatra's (and Taylor's) sexual charm as a motif, it is not in general as Orientalist as one might expect—though the heavily orchestrated Afro-Oriental spectacle with which Cleopatra makes her initial entrance into Rome is perhaps the single best example in Western culture of an association between the famous Egyptian queen and spectacle in general.[25]

Incidentally, one of the most spectacle-oriented forms in American popular culture is professional wrestling, in which wrestlers essentially play characters (often specifically designated as good or evil) who then perform simulated wrestling matches for the entertainment of live and television audiences. Perhaps the most evil of all of these characters was Edward Farhat, the Michigan native who performed as a wild rich Arab from Syria known as "The Sheik" from 1949 to 1998. As with most professional wrestling villains, The Sheik made a point of fighting dirty so that audiences could enjoy rooting against him, but he also stirred the animosity of impatient crowds by performing stunts such as delaying the starts of matches while he knelt on a prayer rug and prayed to Allah. The career of The Sheik was pure entertainment theater and thus partakes very much of the consumerist sort of Orientalism we are discussing here, but, by attempting to encourage and capitalize upon anti-Arab sentiments in crowds, he also drew upon the more adversarial colonialist form of Orientalism, as did the vilification of ancient Egyptians or corrupt Middle Eastern potentates in biblical epics such as *The Ten Commandments* and *King of Kings*.[26]

The Orientalism of *Star Trek*

Meanwhile, the title role of Jesus Christ in *King of Kings* is played by Jeffrey Hunter, an actor who, just three years later, was cast as Captain Christopher Pike, the main protagonist of the first (unsold) pilot to the now-legendary television series *Star Trek*. After a second pilot, *Star Trek* would eventually hit the airwaves in 1966, now with William Shatner as Captain James Kirk in the ostensible lead. *Star Trek*, with the diverse multiracial crew of the starship *Enterprise* as the most obvious example, is well known as a series that broke new multicultural ground. And its casting of the African American actor Nichelle Nichols and the Japanese American actor George Takei was indeed a milestone for American television. In some ways, however, its most important emblem of diversity was the first officer Spock (Leonard Nimoy), a half-Vulcan, half-human hybrid who nevertheless became the series' most beloved character. Spock essentially functions as a walking denial of Orientalist stereotypes. Though he is clearly coded as the Other, he is an Other who serves as a model for what humans should strive to be, rather than a model of what humans should strive to avoid. He is rational, dependable, consistent, and virtuous, clearly meant to be more intellectually advanced than his human counterparts in the series. His portrayal is thus essentially the opposite of Orientalist stereotyping.

Interestingly enough, though, representations of the Middle East were so thoroughly saturated with Orientalist stereotypes that the rejection of stereotyping and the devotion to "infinite diversity in infinite combinations" that reportedly drove creator Gene Roddenberry's vision of *Star Trek* did not initially appear to extend to the Middle East. For example, the initial failed *Trek* pilot (starring Hunter) features a plot in which intellectually advanced (but physically weak) aliens attempt to persuade Captain Pike to remain on their planet to serve as breeding stock to help produce a new race of humans that they can observe for their amusement. To this end, they deploy a human woman, Vina (played by Susan Oliver), they have already conscripted by making her appear to Pike to be the embodiment of various fantasy images of feminine desirability, with the goal of encouraging him to remain on the planet in order to breed with her. Tellingly, one of these images is that of a green-skinned "Orion slave-girl," in which guise

Vina performs a seductive belly dance, accompanied by Middle Eastern music (actually an original composition by Alexander Courage).[27] Belly dancing, of course, is the classic Orientalist image of the exotic sexuality of Eastern women, and *Star Trek* seems to have no qualms about employing the image. These Orion slave-girls reappear several times in the Trek franchise as images of exotic sexual availability and feminine submission, usually performing a similar dance to similar music.

This music incidentally provides a direct lineage back to the turn-of-the-century exhibitions discussed above. In the episode "Whom Gods Destroy," an Orion slave-girl dances to a version of the music that is also included on Vol. 5 of the Star Trek Soundtrack Collection, with the telling title "Arab Hootch Dance."[28] The resonances of this title go back to the 1893 World's Columbian Exposition, where "Little Egypt" performed to an early version of a song entitled "The Streets of Cairo," which would subsequently come to be associated with the sexually provocative form of "hoochie coochie" dancing. (The term "belly dancing," though possibly coined in the United States in conjunction with the 1893 World's Columbian Exposition, was not widely used for some time.)

Alien women are often targets of Orientalist representation in the original *Star Trek*. In the episode "Elaan of Troyius," for example, the imperious title character (played by French-Vietnamese actress France Nuyen) is a virtual embodiment of Oriental feminine threat. In the episode, we learn that, if the tears of an Elasian woman touch a man's skin, he will become her enraptured sexual slave forever. Meanwhile, the men of Elas are characterized as "vicious and arrogant," so Orientalist stereotypes are extended to both sexes in the episode. On the other hand, despite her aristocratic birth and inherent sexual power, Elaan functions in the episode essentially as a sexual bargaining chip: a member of the Elasian royal family, she is being married off (in a deal with the full support of the United Federation of Planets) to the ruler of the planet Troyius to cement a peace treaty between the two planets. In the course of the episode, Elaan attempts to enslave Kirk with her tears, but Kirk's devotion to the *Enterprise* is such that he becomes the first man ever to resist an Elasian woman's tears, impressing Elaan so much that she falls in love with him—and seems quite intrigued by his threat to spank her at one point. In any case, though modeled by name on Helen of Troy, Elaan is clearly presented as an exotic Oriental woman, dangerous but tameable. Among other things, her dress and makeup are modeled after the iconic image of Cleopatra—emblazoned on the popular American consciousness by Elizabeth Taylor only a few years earlier as Hollywood Orientalist shorthand for exotic, sexy, mysterious, and powerful.

Recent trends in American representations of the Middle East

Later incarnations of the *Star Trek* franchise would be a bit less Orientalist—and *Star Trek: Deep Space Nine* (1993–99) even featured a half-Arab actor (Siddig El Fadil, later changed to Alexander Siddig) as the station's chief medical officer, Dr. Julian Bashir. In the meantime, Arabs in Western popular culture remained confined primarily to roles such as seductively undulating women and comically threatening men—as in the well-known scene in *Raiders of the Lost Ark* (1981) in which Indiana Jones is menaced by a seemingly dangerous black-garbed, sword-wielding Arab, only to gun down (with seeming boredom and exasperation) his overmatched Eastern foe with his trusty revolver, demonstrating the superior firepower of Western technology.[29] The 1972 attacks at the Munich Olympic Games had also helped to introduce the figure of the Arab terrorist—in films such as *Black Sunday* (1977)—but the representation of such figures in American popular culture would reach new levels after the first Gulf War (1990–91) and events such as the first bombing of the World Trade Center (on February 26, 1993) helped to usher in a whole new array of works (especially films) featuring the figure of the fanatical Muslim jihadist, as in Edward Zwick's *The Siege* (1998). The image of the Muslim terrorist became such a stock item in the 1990s that it even came in for comic treatment in films such as James Cameron's *True Lies* (1994). However, this focus on Muslim terrorism would gain considerable force (and stridency) after September 11, 2001, which would lead to a bevy of new films, some of which—such as Paul Greenglass's *United 93* (2006) and Oliver Stone's *World Trade Center* (2006)—were directly about the events of that day, and others of which—such as Sam Mendes's *Jarhead* (2005) and Kathryn Bigelow's *The Hurt Locker* (2008) and *Zero Dark Thirty* (2012)—were directly about the subsequent "war on terror," including the second Gulf War. In addition, a number of post-9/11 films—such as Peter Berg's *The Kingdom* (2007) and Ben Affleck's *Argo* (2012)—dealt with Muslim terrorism or the political situation in the Middle East in general. Even a film such as Stephen Gaghan's *Syriana* (2005)—in which the biggest villains are American oil companies in collusion with the US government—still puts the requisite stress on Arab treachery and corruption, while including an essentially gratuitous appearance by Muslim suicide bombers.

We would argue, however, that films such as these represent a different phenomenon than the consumerist current of American Orientalism that ran roughly from Barnum and Bailey's Circus and the world expositions of the late nineteenth century through the original *Star Trek* at the end of the 1960s and

Raiders of the Lost Ark at the beginning of the 1980s. Films about terrorism and related topics respond to specific events and to a particular situation involving military, economic, and political interactions of the United States with the Middle East. They thus resemble the Orientalism detailed by Said in relation to French and British colonialism. The current of American Orientalism that we have been discussing in this chapter (and on which we focus throughout this volume), on the other hand, grows out of a more symbolic and imaginary interaction between the United States and the Middle East in which American consumers have (until recent years) thought of Islam and the Middle East mostly in stock stereotypical images that work well in advertising and entertainment, even if they provide little in the way of real understanding.

The kind of cultural imperialism that Said describes certainly exists—and has certainly been fed in the past few decades by Orientalist images in the American media that are very much of the colonialist kind described by Said.[30] Indeed, some of the most prominent representations of the Middle East in recent American culture—such as the television series *Homeland* and *Tyrant*—have sometimes been spectacularly Orientalist in the colonial mode. But there are also signs of a slow, but significant mainstreaming of Arabs and Muslims in American popular culture that works against Orientalism altogether. And we believe that this trend is actually aided by the consumerist form of Orientalism, which ultimately makes boundaries between East and West hard to maintain. With the two cultures converging, it is difficult to maintain Orientalist binaries, even of the consumerist kind.

For example, in a 2016 Amazon Original television series, *Goliath*, we are presented with the spectacle of an evil American defense contractor that makes huge profits by producing weaponry (much of it illegal) that is then used to wreak havoc in the Middle East. This series might thus still depend upon a classic good versus evil binary, but the protagonist, played by Billy Bob Thornton, displays virtually none of the characteristics of the conventional hero, other than being on the right side in a legal battle against the defense contractor. Nevertheless, it is clear that the American corporation (really a multinational corporation) is at the evil pole, with virtually no redeeming features, while the people of the Middle East are presented as innocent victims of this corporate evil, though none of them actually appear as characters in the series. At one point, however, we are shown pictures of the maimed bodies of victimized Arabs, and it is clear that any terrorism involved in this series is being perpetrated *against* Arabs, not *by* them. The pictures are striking enough, in fact, that the judge in the case does not allow them to be introduced as evidence, because they would be "unduly prejudicial" in creating a negative image of the corporation. Thornton's character wins the case anyway, and the jury awards a huge settlement to his client, the son of a man killed while involved in illegal weapons research for the company.

Though *Goliath* garnered a Best Actor Golden Globe nomination for Thornton, it is still a relatively minor product of the American Culture Industry. However, one of the most visible recent products of that industry also suggests the mainstreaming of Arabs. The critically acclaimed *Mr. Robot*, a techno-thriller series that debuted on the USA network in June of 2015 and that continues to air as of this writing, features Egyptian American actor Rami Malek in the lead role of Elliot Alderson, another decidedly anti-heroic (but very sympathetic) hero, who is, among other things, a socially dysfunctional drug addict. Elliot is a computer security engineer by day and vigilante hacker by night. There is no indication that he is an Arab,[31] but much was made (in a positive way) of Malek's ethnic background when he won the Golden Globe and Primetime Emmy (among other awards) for Best Actor in 2016. The same awards also went to the show itself, which was created and written by Egyptian American Sam Esmail, who has said in an interview with BBC Xtra, a talk program on the BBC's Arabic service,[32][33] that the show was inspired by the role played by hackers and online social media in the 2011 Egyptian Revolution. As in *Goliath*, the villain is an evil corporation (literally called "Evil Corp" in the series, though this is apparently filtered through Elliot's perception, while the real name is actually "E Corp").[34] Esmail also says in this interview that his background as an Arab American influenced his creation of the character of Elliot as an alienated outsider. Meanwhile, the "fsociety" hacker group that Elliot joins in order to take on E Corp features a young Muslim woman, the daughter of Iranian immigrants, as one of its key members, though the series refreshingly makes little of this fact, presenting hijabi hacker Shama "Trenton" Biswas (Sunita Mani) as just another member of the group, rather than as an exotic add-on. On the other hand, Mr. Robot himself (the apparent leader of fsociety, played by Christian Slater) tells Elliot in the second episode of the first season that the meek-seeming Trenton has a fierce side, suggesting that she has a bit of "Allahu Akhbar" in her. The reference here to the stereotypical mantra of Muslim terrorists might seem to be Orientalist, but the fsociety hackers are themselves cyber-terrorists, and Mr. Robot clearly means the remark as an ironic compliment—while the fact that Mr. Robot is actually a figment of Elliot's troubled imagination also complicates the issue.

This more positive treatment of Arabs in recent popular culture evolves, we believe, from the consumer Orientalist tradition of treating the Middle East as part of the vast image bank that global consumer capitalism (and, now, its cultural arm, postmodernism) can draw upon to do its work. After all, the free flow that marks our current global system inevitably makes Arabs more familiar and less exotic, making Orientalist representations of any kind hard to maintain. This is not, of course, to say that Orientalisms of both the consumerist and colonialist kinds are not still alive and well, just that they are beginning to weaken. Indeed, there is at least one major American cultural form that still thrives on consumer Orientalist imagery in particular. This form is the music video, in which Orientalist imagery draws upon the long legacy of consumerist Orientalism, but which is not well suited for more politically motivated anti-terrorist Orientalism. The next chapter looks at the use of this kind of Orientalism in Western music videos.

2

"Shake Ya body like a Belly Dancer": Orientalism in American Music Videos

During her 2014 "On the Run" tour, American (and global) megastar Beyoncé stirred up considerable controversy due to her use of a sample from Egyptian star Umm Kulthum's classic "Inta Omri" ("You Are My Life") during a near-naked performance of her song "Naughty Girl." Tamara Wong Azaiez, for example, complained that the performance was disrespectful to Umm Kulthum, a revered figure in Arab cultural history. More generally, Azaiez felt that, in this performance, "Beyoncé is exoticizing Arab music to show what she thinks the Arab world is—a region of dark-haired beauties serving the needs of men. This is insulting to Arabs everywhere." This sort of appropriation of the supposedly exotic sexuality of Arab women is nothing new, of course, just as the general appropriation of images from Arab culture has a long (if not so distinguished) history in the Orientalist discourse of the West. Beyoncé's appropriation of Umm Kulthum, however, might not be quite as simple (or as offensive, at least in an Orientalist sense) as it first appears. Beyoncé's music in general employs an eclectic array of appropriations from a variety of sources—as when, in this same song, she references Donna Summer's notorious 1975 disco megahit "Love to Love You Baby." And Beyoncé's influences are international—as are her popularity and the reach of her much-hyped live performances, which have taken her to the Middle East and other Muslim countries, though sometimes with substantial controversy. In addition, Beyoncé has expressed[1] an enthusiastic admiration for Arabic music, though she names Lebanese star Fairouz, rather than Umm Kulthum, as a particular personal favorite. Moreover, Beyoncé's career is deeply connected to hip-hop culture, in which the sampling of the works of other artists is a crucial technique, though the extent to which this sampling is culturally specific to hip-hop rather than merely another example of postmodern pastiche is of course debatable.

In any case, though from an Egyptian point of view it might be sacrilege to say so, one might argue that Beyoncé, at least in terms of global visibility, popularity, and influence, is a far bigger star than Umm Kulthum ever was. Thus, her "borrowing" of Umm Kulthum's music might be legitimately regarded as a compliment that introduces Umm Kulthum's music to a vast new audience, even if in a context that might have shocked the late Egyptian singer and certainly would shock many of her traditional fans. Umm Kulthum, of course, has a special status in Arab culture, but this status, which makes her a figure of both authority and tradition, also makes her a target of Arab musicians who would choose to challenge tradition and authority. Mark LeVine thus notes that the Palestinian-Israeli heavy metal band Khalas opened their first album with an "instrumental metal version" of "Inta Omri," as a way of being intentionally provocative and transgressive (118). Beyoncé seems to have no such subversive intention, though her appropriation of Umm Kulthum from a position of relative cultural power (as opposed to the marginal status of a band like Khalas) has its own special problems.

Such positionality within structures of power cannot be ignored, but Beyoncé's use of "Inta Omri" might be legitimately regarded as an example, not of simple one-way cultural appropriation, but of the kind of transnational flows that have increasingly come to characterize the music industry in recent years. Thus, while Beyoncé's borrowing from Donna Summer might seem more appropriate within the sexually charged atmosphere of her "Naughty Girl" performances—and while it might seem more appropriate for one African American star to borrow from another—one might also note that Lebanese singer Myriam Klink seems to be channeling Summer's overtly sexual panting and moaning in the notorious 2017 song "Goal," performed with Jad Khalife and quickly banned from Arab television, then later removed from YouTube.

Images thus circulate in late global capitalism very much the same way commodities have always circulated in capitalism as a whole. Indeed, the real problem with Beyoncé's appropriation of Umm Kulthum—and one might say the same for her participation in Coldplay's use of overtly Orientalist images from Indian culture in "Hymn for the Weekend" (2015)[2] —might not be its Orientalist disrespect for any particular other culture but its postmodernist treatment of any and all images from any and all cultures (including American culture as much as Arab culture) as mere commodities, available for selection as from a cafeteria menu, then plugged in wherever wanted, without any serious consideration of the source of the image or of the way the image functioned in its original cultural context.[3]

"Shake Ya Body like a Belly Dancer" 65

Figure 2.1 Guest performer Beyoncé in all-out exotic Eastern mode in the music video for Coldplay's "Hymn for the Weekend" (2015) (screen capture).

The music video for Shania Twain's 1998 hit "That Don't Impress Me Much"[4] illustrates this cafeteria-style method of appropriation especially well. Here, the exotically dressed singer hitchhikes through a desert landscape, but refuses offers of rides from a menu of American-style macho men who seem to expect her to be thrilled to have a chance to partake of their charms—and their various forms of macho transportation. The men include a biker, a trucker, a fifties-style greaser in a cool car, and a he-man in a jeep. The line is, perhaps not surprisingly, topped off by a black-clad Arab on a spirited Arabian stallion. To complete the convergence of Arab and American macho images, Twain waves the Arab off just as she had the Americans, this time singing, "What do you think, you're Elvis or something?"[5]

Of course, there is a long history of the appropriation of images from Eastern culture for marketing purposes in the West (and music videos are essentially commercials for the performers who make them). This history suggests that the videos for songs such as "Hymn for the Weekend" use the images for their impact as exoticized spectacle much in the same way they were earlier used in the Barnum and Bailey Circus. Music videos, though, have their own legacy in terms of such images, in a phenomenon one might see as beginning with the Ray Stevens novelty song "Ahab the Arab" (1962), for which Stevens recorded an accompanying video[6] when he re-recorded a slightly modified (but equally Orientalist) version of the song in 1995. This song (which Stevens has said in interviews was inspired by his childhood reading of *The Arabian Nights*) centers on an illicit love affair between the title character (described as "the sheik of the burning sand") and an exotic, sexually charged Arab woman named Fatima, who belongs to the local sultan and who is so exotic that she has "rings on her fingers and bells on her toes and a bone in her nose." She sits in a tent, soaking in decadent luxury, snacking on fruits and generally indulging her appetites, which include candy bars and cola, but which mostly include nightly clandestine trysts with Ahab, who comes furtively riding across the desert on his trusty camel Clyde to slip into her tent, despite the dangers involved at the hands of the sultan.

As trite and silly as it might appear, "Ahab the Arab" was a big hit for Stevens and was subsequently covered by several other artists. It was also, in 1962, received without controversy—partly, no doubt, because it is so obviously nonserious, but partly also because audiences at the time were not particularly concerned about such ethnic stereotyping, especially of Arabs, who were only a tiny blip on the American cultural radar at the time. Of course, Orientalist images had been around for some time and were well known—thus the effectiveness of the song, which plays with these images, seemingly without any awareness that there are real Arabs existing in the world whose lives might be impacted by such stereotyping (as when American oil companies felt it was acceptable to exploit Arab oil as a resource to which Americans had a natural right, until the local powers-that-be began to exert their ownership, especially beginning in the 1970s).

Arabs became a bit more real (and somewhat less of a joke) to Americans with the coming of the 1974 oil embargo, but stereotypical images of Arabs (now sometimes with a slightly more rancorous edge) remained a significant segment of the iconographic fund upon which the American Culture Industry could draw. Sometimes this imagery was still employed primarily for humor, but it also came increasingly to be used for atmospheric effects, especially with the rise of music videos as an important cultural form. The visual imagery in such videos is largely designed to create a certain mood and to enhance the impact of the music, but the images need to be easily recognizable, so that this effect can be immediately achieved. There is little time in a work as brief as a music video to build a pattern of imagery.

Since the 1980s, when the rise of the MTV cable network gave music videos a much more effective distribution platform, images related to Middle Eastern culture have been of three principal types. First, some images are employed simply to produce an air of exoticism. Particularly prominent in music videos employing this type of imagery are motifs deriving from ancient Egyptian culture (pyramids, pharaohs, the Sphinx), which serve as a form of Middle Eastern imagery, even though the ancient Egyptians were not, of course, Arabs. Indeed, ancient Egyptian motifs are particularly effective because they can produce some of the same effects of exoticism (especially exotic sexuality) as Arab imagery, but without all the nasty baggage associated with real Arabs, given that ancient Egyptians no longer exist and thus don't have to be dealt with in the real world. Ancient Egypt can thus be more easily rendered a seemingly neutral source of material for the construction of Western music videos or other pop cultural artifacts. But ancient Egypt and the modern Middle East seem often to be conflated in the Western mind, just as Orientalism in general has tended to homogenize the "Orient." As Rowe has noted, "the obsession with ancient Egypt" in American culture dating back to the nineteenth century can itself be seen as a "displacement of modern Egypt" ("Arabia Fantasia" 64).

The second type of popular Orientalist video draws more specifically on the eroticism of the exotic Eastern woman, with belly dancing featuring as a particularly prominent motif.[7] Finally, a number of recent Orientalist videos have drawn upon the common perception that Westerners have of the Arab world as a locus of obscene wealth (mostly from oil). These videos, especially in hip-hop culture, often treat this wealth in an admiring way, however, viewing "Arab money" as just another version of the fantasy bling with which that culture frequently attempts to associate itself. And, of course, videos employing images of the latter kind often include images of the former kind as well: one of the things obscene wealth gives one access to is exotic sex. In addition, it is worth noting that these images of exotic sexuality and excessive wealth are also often associated with ancient Egypt in American popular culture, combining all three of the basic types of Orientalist music videos.

"Walk like an Egyptian": Exoticizing (and commodifying) Egypt

One of the most popular music videos ever produced using ancient Egyptian themes was "Walk Like an Egyptian" (1986),[8] by the girl group the Bangles. Comically playing on a well-known pose from reliefs found inside ancient Egyptian pyramids, the video seems harmless enough, though it is certainly always problematic to have fun at the expense of another culture. In this case, the culture involved no longer exists—though this argument ignores the fact that there are present-day Egyptians who might view these artworks as a key part of their cultural heritage and thus might take offense at this use of the imagery. The video is straightforward and amusing, relying on a simple one-shot visual joke— of a kind that might be found in something like a GEICO commercial. The song is also catchy—and in fact stayed on *Billboard* magazine's hit charts long enough to become the number one most popular song of 1987.

The lyrics of the song, written by Liam Hillard Sternberg, are almost nonsensical, adding to the nonserious tone of the song. They do suggest, however, that walking like an Egyptian might be a form of celebration and escape from routine, as when they refer to school children doing the Egyptian walk when they get out of school or when they depict the Egyptian walk as a relief from the difficulties of life. Perhaps the most interesting stanzas in the song, however, come at the end seems to suggest a series of stereotypical images of (mostly Oriental) repression:

> All the Japanese with their yen
> The party boys call the Kremlin.
> And the Chinese know (oh whey oh)
> They walk the line like Egyptians.
>   All the cops in the donut shop say
> Ay oh whey oh, ay oh whey oh
> Walk like an Egyptian.

These lines are apparently not meant to suggest anything serious, yet the first suggests images of uptight Japanese businessmen, devoting their lives to the pursuit of money. The second is a reference to the then still-extant Soviet Union, which in Reagan-era America was perhaps the central stereotypical image of a repressive society. Finally, the reference to China (both a classic Eastern locale and a Cold War image of communist repression) is a bit harder to decode, because it seems to depict them as slavishly following the party line, but doing so like Egyptians. This line seems to turn the rest of the song on its head, suggesting that walking like an Egyptian is an image of walking like the lines of slaves who famously built the Egyptian pyramids and other monuments—though one could square this line with the rest of the song by viewing the Egyptian walk as a form of resistance, as a means of dealing with an otherwise repressive life of slave labor, linking ancient Egyptian slaves with those kids suffering through a long day at school, the Japanese oppressed by capitalism, or the Soviets and Chinese oppressed by communism. The final reference to cops in a donut shop is similarly doubly coded, suggesting the cops as images of authority who make others walk the line, but also depicting them in a donut shop, a stereotypical comfort zone where they can perhaps lighten up and relax.

If some of the images in this song seem contradictory, no one really minds—and few have seemed to notice. Indeed, the contradictions in this song replicate one of the central contradictions in Orientalism itself, in which the Orient is depicted both as a land of soul-crushing repression and as an exotic realm of adventure and romance that offers relief from the tedium day-to-day life in routinized bourgeois Europe.[9] This contradiction might reveal some of the contradictions in the ideology of colonialism itself and thus be potentially troubling, but in the lighter, more commodified world of consumerist Orientalism inhabited by this song, it seems right at home. It's pure rock and roll in its postmodern pop mode. Have some fun, act silly, and take your images from anywhere you want: it will help you cope with the repressive nature of day-to-day life, wherever you're from.

In any case, the real key to the success of the song's music video, which is mostly just a performance video interspersed with shots of various people (mostly on the streets of New York) attempting to "walk like Egyptians,"[10] is the band's front-woman Susanna Hoffs, who exudes a sort of sly sexuality during her vocals that, given the subject matter of the song, cannot help but partake at least a bit of the stereotype of the mysterious Oriental woman with arcane, forbidden sexual knowledge.[11] Particularly crucial here are the close-ups of Hoffs's dark eyes, glancing from side to side, almost unavoidably reminding viewers, even if unconsciously, of Cleopatra, the central figure in the iconography of ancient Egyptian feminine sexuality—and one whose sexual allure prominently featured her heavily made-up eyes. Cleopatra is well enough known as a sexual icon that any music video that relies on feminine sexual allure and that refers to ancient Egypt in any way almost inevitably evokes her, however indirectly, though it is also the case, as Joseph Boone points out, that ancient Egypt is sometimes symbolically associated with "absolute hedonism" in a more general sense (171).[12] Ancient Egypt is also, of course, closely associated with spectacular displays of wealth and ornamentation, making ancient Egyptian imagery perfect fodder for the culture of our hyperreal society of the spectacle.

Perhaps the best example of a video that evokes Cleopatra, hedonism, and spectacle all at once is the one for Katy Perry's 2013 pop hit "Dark Horse."[13] Unlike those of "Walk Like an Egyptian," the lyrics of this song have nothing to do with ancient Egypt whatsoever. But the video itself is conceived as an elaborate spectacle, virtually the opposite of the low-budget simplicity of the Bangles video. The Perry video begins with on-screen text that identifies the action as occurring in Memphis, Egypt, "a crazy long time ago," again indicating that the video is not to be taken too seriously—but also suggesting a lack of respect for the antiquity of ancient Egypt. The camera then zooms in on Perry, reclining on a luxury barge on the Nile. Perry then begins to sing in close-up, arms bent in the Egyptian walk pose, eyes in full Cleopatra makeup, but wearing a white wig bearing blue hieroglyphs, presumably to make the effect even more exotic.

The scene then cuts to her in a more conventional dark Cleopatra wig, sitting on a throne in an elaborately colored robe, attended by near-naked male slaves, their skin died blue, again presumably for exotic effect. As the video proceeds, Perry is shown in various exotic getups, with the image of her on her throne, dripping in wealth, remaining central, as various suitors bring offerings to her, generally drawing her displeasure and swift retribution—all with a decidedly comic tone. The song, basically, is about an exotic woman who offers extreme pleasure, but also extreme danger, punctuated by repeated warnings, such as "So you wanna play with magic? Boy, you should know whatcha fallin' for" and "don't make me your enemy." At one point, rapper Juicy J, a featured performer, interjects further warnings, including a suggestion that she might "eat your heart out, like Jeffrey Dahmer," a reference to the notorious serial killer who was known for literally eating the hearts (and other organs) of his victims.[14]

The lyrics never specifically mention Egypt or Cleopatra or the Orient, but the Cleopatra imagery is obviously apt, Cleopatra serving as one of our culture's prototypical images of this kind of alluring, but dangerous woman. This video simply latches onto the iconic status of Cleopatra as a quick shorthand method of conveying its theme, with the comic treatment indicating a self-awareness of how stereotypical it all really is. After all, such appropriations of Eastern imagery in Western music are rampant in contemporary Western popular culture—one might recall Madonna's Super Bowl performance again, or Perry's own appearance as a Japanese geisha (to indicate a stereotypical image of feminine submissiveness) to open the 2013 American Music Awards.[15][16]

Both of these latter performances also play on the notion of the Orient as a locus of splendor and spectacle, though perhaps the most spectacular music video ever produced in this mode was the 1992 video for Michael Jackson's "Remember the Time,"[17] one in a series of videos (the 1983 "Thriller" is perhaps the best example) in which Jackson and his production team attempted to elevate the music video to a new level of artistic achievement, drawing inspiration from cinema—before the form settled into today's schema, in which music videos, however innovative, are more akin to television commercials. The video for "Remember the Time" runs for nine minutes and sixteen seconds, even though the official recording of the song itself runs exactly four minutes. The remaining five minutes plus is filled with spectacle evoking the splendors of ancient Egypt. The song itself is a simple nostalgic love song in which the singer reminds his beloved of the time when they first fell in love. It again has nothing to do with Egypt, except to employ ancient Egypt as an image of past glories. The sumptuous video itself employs images of ancient Oriental excess combined

Figure 2.2 Katy Perry decked out as a Cleopatra-like Egyptian queen in her 2013 music video for "Dark Horse" (screen capture).

with images of contemporary American excess that include a cast headed by movie star Eddie Murphy, as a pampered pharaoh, and supermodel Iman, as his bored queen. The plot, such as it is, involves the pharoah's various attempts to find someone who can entertain the queen—with Jackson predictably being the one who succeeds in doing so (a bit too much so, for the pharoah's taste), with an elaborately choreographed performance of the song. This performance also includes numerous other supporting performers, including a group of rather contemporary (if stereotypical) veiled women with whom he dances at one point, thus collapsing historical periods and combining ancient Egypt with the modern Arab world. Indeed, most of the "ancient Egyptian" dancers in the video appear rather contemporary, while neither their dancing nor Jackson's singing and the accompanying music draw upon ancient Egyptian culture in any way—except for occasional moments when the dancers briefly assume a mock version of the Egyptian walk pose.

The overall effect is to create an atmosphere of both richness and nostalgia, but it is a peculiarly postmodern form of nostalgia devoid of emotional depth. It is a *performance* of nostalgia, rather than the genuine longing for a lost past that informs true nostalgia. The images of ancient Egypt, meanwhile, are merely employed in a mode of pastiche to create the desired effect, without any real sense of their original historical context or meaning. Egyptian queens were figures of great feminine power, for example, and are often presented as such in music videos—but are usually shown as exercising this power in such a comically capricious and petulant manner as to make them anti-feminist stereotypes. A sort of sexual exoticization of Egypt—as perhaps exemplified in Flaubert's description of the dancer and courtesan Kuchuk Hanum, a favorite example of Said—was key to the high Orientalist discourse of the colonial period. In the period of late capitalism, however, this exoticization has largely been replaced by a commodifying tendency that renders Egypt more accessible and less threatening, a mere source of material for pastiche.

This sort of pastiche is, for Fredric Jameson, perhaps the central compositional strategy of postmodern art, which frequently borrows both the style and the content of earlier works from various periods. Pastiche, for Jameson, is similar to parody, except that it does not engage the styles or works being imitated in any sort of critical dialogue. It is

> the imitation of a peculiar or unique, idiosyncratic style, the wearing of a stylistic mask, speech in a dead language. But it is a neutral practice of such mimicry, without any of parody's ulterior motives, amputated of the satiric impulse, devoid of any laughter and of any conviction that alongside the abnormal tongue you have momentarily borrowed, some healthy linguistic normality still exists. (*Postmodernism* 17)

Jameson, however, emphasizes the temporal aspect of this phenomenon, seeing it as a manifestation of a particular kind of nostalgia that amounts to a "random cannibalization of all the styles of the past" that reduces the past to a sort of cafeteria menu of spectacles, a collection of images stripped of context and disconnected from any genuine sense of the participation of these images in the historical process.

Music videos that draw upon imagery from ancient Egypt often meet this description well: in many cases (as in "Remember the Time"), the pastness of ancient Egypt is a crucial point. However, the exoticism of ancient Egypt is even more important, and an examination of these videos adds an important element to Jameson's conceptualization of postmodern pastiche, which now can be seen to be borrowing images not just from the past of a given culture, but also from other cultures—again, though, with little appreciation for the original context or significance of those images. As Said has so vividly described in *Orientalism*, this kind of cultural appropriation is far from innocent, given the uneven power relations that have informed the encounter between the East and the West for the past several hundred years (and given the particularly vexed relationship between the United States and the Middle East in the present day). And it is no more innocent in its contemporary consumerist form than in its classic colonialist form, though the power relations involved are now more economic than political.

For Jameson, the context-free borrowing from the past that he associates with postmodern pastiche indicates a loss of historical sense that significantly weakens the utopian energies of postmodern culture and deprives that culture of the ability to mount any meaningful opposition to the power of late capitalism, becoming, in fact, merely the "cultural logic" of late capitalism itself. When those borrowings draw material from *other* cultures, past or present, and when those other cultures have historically been exploited by the culture doing the borrowing, then this lack of acknowledgment of the historical context of the source would seem to be especially problematic, even if it is problematic in somewhat different ways.

One could argue, of course, that ancient Egypt is by now part of the historical heritage not only of modern-day Egypt but of modern America.[18] Generations of American schoolchildren have certainly studied it that way, though in an oddly ahistorical sense that establishes little in the way of a direct historical narrative that leads from ancient Egypt to the modern Western world, that narrative somehow only starting with ancient Greece. Then again, Martin Bernal has presented an extended and spirited (if controversial)[19] argument for a direct historical link between the civilizations of ancient Egypt (and Phoenicia) and ancient Greece that somewhat fills in this gap.[20] Bernal's narrative has never become mainstream in the American cultural imagination, of course, and one could in any case argue that regarding ancient Egypt as a direct historical predecessor to modern-day America is simply another case of cultural appropriation, of conscripting another culture's heritage to make Americans feel that their own heritage is richer. Still, considering ancient Egypt or Phoenicia to be a direct historical predecessor to modern Western civilization does at least have the virtue of undermining the Orientalist binary opposition between the East and the West.[21] Unfortunately, the exoticization of ancient Egypt in most American music videos that feature its imagery tends to produce the opposite effect and to create a sense of ancient Egyptian culture as the Other to modern American culture, rather than as the predecessor.

Belly dancing, the Orient, and the lure of sexual exoticism

One of the images from Middle Eastern culture that appears most often in Western music videos is that of the belly dancer—the very personification of the notion of the exotic Oriental woman.[22] For example, one of the biggest hits of 1999 was Christina Aguilera's "Genie in a Bottle"[23] which propelled the eighteen-year-old singer to stardom—partly for her impressive singing, but also for how fetching she looked dancing and undulating in a series of bare-midriff costumes. None of these costumes look especially Oriental, yet, given the title and lyrics of the song, they inevitably recall the popular Western vision of the costuming of belly dancers or harem girls. And, in the popular American imagination, this sort of costuming was already associated with genies as well. After all, the best-known female genie in American popular culture to this time was "Jeannie," the character portrayed by Barbara Eden in the popular television series *I Dream of Jeannie*, which ran on NBC from 1965 to 1970 (pretty much during the same time period as the original *Star Trek*). One of the keys to the success of the series was the belly-dancer costume worn by the lovely Eden, which combined with Jeannie's submissive attitude toward her (American male) "master" to make her an effective image of the mysterious Eastern woman (in this case Persian, rather than Arab)—who has almost unbounded sexual power, but who is nevertheless slavishly devoted to the pleasure of the man who dominates her. The effect, meanwhile, is only increased by Jeannie's seeming naiveté, which adds to her air of sexual submissiveness and to the sense that her master is fully in control of her sexuality.

Aguilera's "Genie in a Bottle" draws on all of these same formulas to achieve its sexy success, using the implied motif of the sexually compliant Oriental woman to enhance a video that is already charged with erotic energies through both the visuals and the lyrics. The song is about a young woman who promises to bring vast amounts of sexual pleasure to the man who finally succeeds in convincing her to release her virginity to him. To achieve this success (in an obvious reference to the famous technique for releasing genies from the containers that hold them), Aguilera announces, "you have to rub me the right way," which can be taken as a metaphor for treating her with the proper respect, but which carries a powerful sexual innuendo suggesting that skillful foreplay is the key to finally convincing her to consent to intercourse. And when that intercourse happens, the video promises (via the genie imagery), it will be magical, especially powerful because of all the pent-up energy that will finally be released—like a genie being released from a bottle (or a lamp) after centuries of confinement.

The belly-dancer motif that is alluded to only obliquely in "Genie in a Bottle" has been used much more directly in a number of other videos. The belly dancer, in fact, joins the Cleopatra figure as the two most common images of Oriental eroticism in American music videos. For example, R. Kelly's video "Snake" (2003)[24] includes a variety of stock "Middle Eastern" images, such as camels and tents in the desert—but also includes a cobra and a snake charmer, which would be much more common in Indian culture, though of course Arab and Indian culture are often confused in American culture, especially where belly dancing is involved—and belly dancing is definitely the central referent in this video. Kelly goes through the video in a variety of mock Arab costumes, which basically consist of standard gangsta-style hip-hop clothing supplemented by head coverings that are apparently meant to resemble those worn by Arabs. The video features one central (African American) dancer in a belly-dancer costume, though her dancing is only vaguely reminiscent of authentic belly dancing. There are also scenes in a large tent in which a crowd of people (mostly African American) is entertained by a group of dancers in similar costumes, but also dancing in a style that only vaguely refers to belly dancing. They do, however, clearly enact what Shohat and Stam have called "the imaginary of the harem," which frequently reflects "a masculinist utopia of sexual omnipotence" (161). Indeed, the sexual innuendo in the song is very clear, as Kelly urges the woman dancer to "move your body like a snake,"[25] which could refer either to dancing or to sexual intercourse, the latter of which is further indicated when he later assures the woman that "I love the way you work your chocha," "chocha" being Caribbean/Latin American slang for the female genitalia.[26]

Speaking of Caribbean culture, the musical aspects of this song have essentially no Middle Eastern elements (other than an occasional passing reference), though the rhythmic structure is vaguely reminiscent of reggae, one "third-world" rhythm apparently being as good as another. In reggae culture, especially in the "dancehall" version, the musical accompaniment, or "riddim," to a popular song might be widely borrowed and used in other songs to the point

Figure 2.3 Belly dancer in exotic garb from the music video for R. Kelly's "Snake" (2003) (screen capture).

that it becomes a virtual genre in itself, somewhat like the sampling that occurs in American hip-hop or even the memes that propagate through the internet. Indeed, "Snake" was reminiscent enough of reggae that it provided the basis for a particular dancehall riddim known as "Baghdad," referencing the Middle Eastern imagery of the "Snake" music video.

Belly dancers are such stock images of exotic feminine sexuality that one needs only to dress women dancers in belly-dancer costumes and a music video is automatically invested with sexual energy—even if the dancing involved has virtually nothing to do with authentic belly dancing. Akon's "Bananza (Belly Dancer)" (2004)[27] is an especially overt example of the use of belly-dancer costuming to create an air of exotic sexuality. Accompanied by music that includes a speeded-up electronic version of an Oriental strain, Akon urges the "ladies" to "shake ya body like a belly dancer," that apparently being the sexiest way a woman can move. These movements are illustrated by a series of African American dancers in costumes that seem like modernized versions of belly-dancer costumes (one with an iconic python around her neck), while their actual dancing, highly sexualized, also seems like a sort of modernized (and generally speeded-up) version of belly dancing, with some decidedly African intonations added in. Indeed, the dancing in this video is an especially good example of not only belly dancing itself, but also the postmodern appropriation of belly dancing to generate the sort of sexual atmosphere with which belly dancing is widely associated.

One might say the same for Jason Derulo's "Talk Dirty to Me" (2014),[28] a song all about the allure of exotic women from around the world, the point of the lyrics being that one doesn't need to share a common language to communicate during sex with such women. "Talking dirty," in fact, is clearly coded in the video as a reference to this sort of nonverbal sexual communication, to letting one's body do the talking during sex. The music itself includes a repeated Middle Eastern refrain that makes it clear that Middle Eastern women are especially high on the list of exotically sexual women, even though the video itself includes no women who seem clearly Middle Eastern. The video consists basically of a series of scenes of Derulo dancing and singing, intercut with scenes of dancing women, two of whom are clearly meant to be performing belly dances, even though the dances are again not very authentic. One of the women seems to be dressed as a belly-dancer version of a Native American (with perhaps a hint of Brazilian, or even Polynesian) woman, including a feathered headdress, which makes no sense at all, but which combines two different stock images of exoticism. The other is a woman in an Indian-style costume, so that the film includes both types of "Indian" women: brown and exotic.

Figure 2.4 Belly dancer from the music video for Jason Derulo's "Talk Dirty to Me" (2014), clearly designed to look as exotic as possible (screen capture).

That this song and video engage in an obvious dialogue with the image of the exotic Middle Eastern woman can be seen in the fact that it was chosen for a Coke Studio Middle East performance designed to highlight the intersection between Arab music and Derulo's style of American music.[29] Here, Derulo performs his song in tandem with sexy Lebanese pop star Maya Diab, though Diab is not dressed in a belly-dancer outfit. Moreover, when Derulo is thrust into the context of the real Middle East and its supposedly exotic sexuality, he has to clean up his risqué lyrics—and even change the title of the song, to merely "Talk to Me." Moreover, the inserted guest performance by rapper 2 Chainz in the original song (which actually includes the song's most obscene lyrics) is missing entirely from this performance.[30]

Arab images, Arab money

Despite the rapper's Arabic-derived stage name, Wiz Khalifa's "Work Hard Play Hard" (2012)[31] doesn't rely on Orientalist imagery. It is, however, typical of an important trend in hip-hop culture in the way the lyrics consist almost entirely of Khalifa bragging about how much money he has—including lines such as "I got so much money I should start a bank." Given the prevalence of stereotypes about how rich Arabs are, it should then come as no surprise that these stereotypes often intersect with hip-hop culture.

In "Arab Money" (2008),[32] American Muslim rapper Busta Rhymes (who in a later remix was accompanied by an all-star guest cast that includes such figures as Diddy, Akon, and Lil Wayne) brags about having so much income that he is "gettin' Arab money," which, among other things, allows him to get "Middle East women."[33] The music video includes a number of images of wealth, though it is, in fact, rather mild—focusing mostly on things like luxury cars and indulgent food. And the actual Arabs in the video are in modern, Western dress, with no camels in sight. Still, many in the Arab world found the song offensive, and it was even banned in some places, such as the UAE—after the song specifically mentions Dubai as a locus of such expensive real estate that one could spend twenty million on a mere loft. Iraqi Canadian rapper The Narcicyst recorded a song entitled "The Real Arab Money" in response, declaring the Rhymes song racist and pointing out that not all Arabs are rich, that there is much suffering in the Arab world (especially in places such as Iraq and Palestine), and that flashy Dubai is not representative of that world or of places such as his ancestral home of Basra, Iraq.

The stereotypes of Arab wealth mentioned in the song are enduring ones, however, and have, in fact, been in place throughout the engagement of American popular culture with Arab culture—and in the elaborately costumed Oriental splendor of the Barnum and Bailey Circus. The reaction of The Narcicyst to "Arab Money" indicates the problem with such Orientalist imagery, which appropriates Eastern culture for the entertainment of Western audiences, with no consideration of the original context or meaning of such images, while ignoring the difficult reality of life for so many in the Middle East.

This same problem often persists, even in the work of Western artists who have some claim to an Eastern cultural heritage. We are thinking, for example, of the Westernized commodification of Arab pop music in the case of the Beirut-born Canadian singer Sari Abboud, who tellingly performs under the stage name "Massari," which means "money" in Levantine Arabic. Massari has made his Arabic heritage a big part of his self-marketing, and with some success—he is quite popular in the Middle East, even though his videos do anything but celebrate traditional Arab or Muslim culture. This marketing also means that Massari has a potential claim to the use of Middle Eastern imagery in his music and videos, much in the way that one might argue the incorporation of belly dancing into her performances is legitimate for the Lebanese-Colombian performer Shakira.[34] Massari also sometimes incorporates Middle Eastern influences into his actual music, though in a relatively minor and secondary way. Indeed, while Massari has identified the traditional Syrian singer George

Wassouf as the greatest influence on his music, that influence is rather hard to detect in Massari's actual work. One of Massari's earliest hits, "Be Easy" (2005),[35] shows very little Middle Eastern influence of any kind, for example, and basically features a series of suggestions that Massari is living the high life, which apparently includes driving a flashy yellow Lamborghini and drinking lots of Dom Perignon champagne. It of course also includes consorting with a stream of attractive women, with whom the video is liberally populated. The women (largely African American) are engaged in a variety of activities, including dancing in ways that might sometimes be identified as belly dancing— in costumes that clearly allude to conventional Middle Eastern belly-dancer costumes, though they are not authentic versions of such costumes. Most of the dancing and costuming, however, are entirely Western and might be at home in virtually any R & B video, though there are specific elements of the Caribbean "Dutty Wine" dance as well. The Middle Eastern references are just there to add a bit of spice, a suggestion of the extraordinary, presumably authorized by Massari's ethnic heritage, with the Caribbean references just thrown in for good postmodern transnational measure.

Massari's most extensive and overt use of Orientalist imagery occurs in the video for "Shisha" (2012),[36] which features a guest performance by rapper French Montana, an Arab American hip-hop artist who was born in Morocco, but moved to the United States at the age of thirteen. Here, both Massari and Montana play on their Arab identities in a song about smoking hookah (for which "shisha" is another name). Hookah here becomes a symbol of decadent pleasure, which is the real subject of the video, which also features Massari tooling about in his trademark yellow Lamborghini and repeated references to alcohol consumption. It again includes the obligatory complement of scantily clad women dancers, typically in costumes that allude to Middle Eastern belly-dancing costumes (though generally dancing in a more modern, Western style), while the (African American) female lead struts through the video looking as exotic as possible, draped in chains and shown in several scenes walking with a pet lion on a leash. Leading the lion seems an image of her power, but the chains she wears (however light and decorative) are surely an emblem of sexual bondage and submissiveness. This video, in fact, is mostly about sex, however ostensibly it might be about shisha. In fact, it essentially equates the two, making the shisha a sort of exotic Oriental apparatus for the enhancement of sexual pleasure. Meanwhile, the actual dancing of the women in the video again includes elements of the Dutty Wine, while the lyrics of the song specifically mention "wining" as a sort of seductive activity.

The video begins with a multiracial group of near-naked women sitting in a circle, their backs to a hookah setup, looking drugged out and sucking on hookah pipes the phallic significance of which is rather obvious. This ultimate image of sex-and-drug-charged Oriental decadence is then followed by a fade-out into a shot of an urban clock tower, somewhat reminiscent of the Abraj Al-Bait clock tower, one of the key landmarks in Mecca. This tower, which features a luxury hotel run by the Canadian Fairmont Hotels chain, caters to pilgrims to the nearby Grand Mosque, or Masjid al-Haram, the holiest site in all of Islam. The tower itself is thus an excellent example of transnational flow. One of the tallest buildings in the world, it is part of a complex developed by the Saudi Bin Laden Group, but was designed by a German firm. It is very Western in design; however, it features an Islamic spire topped by a stylized crescent that sits atop its traditional tower clock that might have come from nineteenth-century Europe, except that it itself sits atop a huge skyscraper. This combination of elements marks the building as a quintessential example of the mash-up style of postmodern architecture. The somewhat vulgar high-tech lighting that illuminates the building makes it appear even more postmodern—almost like something from Las Vegas. Indeed, however much a part of the hajj tradition it might be, this building is in itself an image of the victory of modernity over tradition; it was built (controversially) on the site of the Ajyad Fortress, an eighteenth-century Ottoman fort that was demolished in 2002 to clear the way for the new building complex, drawing protests from Turkey.

The Wikipedia entry for the song "Shisha" originally identified the tower in the video as Abraj Al-Bait. However, there are clearly differences in detail between the real Abraj Al-Bait and the tower in the video, which in fact appears to be the Palace of Culture and Science in Warsaw, Poland, a fact that Wikipedia (as of this writing in January 2018) now reflects. It might well be that the tower is meant to evoke Abraj Al-Bait, though it is not clear why they would not use the real Abraj Al-Bait. If one assumes that the tower is indeed the one in Warsaw, though, other interesting connections arise. This building, whose architecture is modeled on that of the "Seven Sisters" skyscrapers in Moscow (built as a display of Soviet pride and capability), was constructed in 1955 to honor Joseph Stalin, and was indeed originally named the Joseph Stalin Palace of Culture and Science. The building, then, was essentially intended as a monument to communism—though many in Poland initially resented it as a sign of the domination of their country by the Soviet Union. Today it houses a variety of facilities (such as a multiplex cinema and offices for various companies), marking its complete incorporation into the global system of late capitalism. Indeed, somewhat like Abraj Al-Bait, this tower has also recently had high-tech lighting added, so that it can be illuminated in various patterns and colors, making it a spectacular display of the kind on which late capitalism thrives. Whatever the intentions of the makers of the video (and we suspect that they just liked the way the tower looked and thought it was reminiscent of a hookah), the inclusion of this tower in the video thus serves as a reminder that Orientalism is not the only form of East-West binary opposition that has been prevalent in Western culture in recent decades. Indeed, during the Cold War years of 1945–91, the central such opposition was that between American capitalism and Soviet communism, though it is far from coincidental that the stereotyping of Soviet communism in the Cold War rhetoric of the West was reminiscent of the discourse of Orientalism in so many ways.[37] In addition, it might also be noted that the strength of these Cold War antipathies was so strong that certain areas of Eastern Europe (such as Lukashenko-dominated Belarus) remain among the areas of the post–Cold War world that have actually been least penetrated by American popular culture.

To make things even more interesting, the next fade-out in the video is to a shot of the striking Burj Al Arab hotel in Dubai, built (on an artificial island) to resemble the sail of a ship and essentially designed as an ostentatious display of wealth and power. By now it is clear that this tower imagery (which rhymes with the central tower in the hookah apparatus itself) is meant to be phallic in nature (as, for that matter, is the Lamborghini), contributing to the overall air of sexuality that pervades the video. But there is more than sex at stake in the images of these towers. If one reads the first tower as an image of the incorporation of the former Soviet bloc into global capitalism, then surely the Dubai tower (and the video also includes several shots of the striking Dubai skyline)[38] can be taken as an image of the incorporation of the Middle East into the late capitalist system in recent years. Thus, within seconds, the video presents suggestions (with no hint of irony or critique) of the ways in which both forms of Eastern Otherness have now been incorporated into the global system of late capitalism, one of the central characteristics of which is a breaking down of all boundaries and oppositions, enabling the free flow of capital and the free exchange of commodities.

If, as does Jameson (and as do we), one regards postmodernism as the cultural logic of late capitalism, then it should come as no surprise that this video is so postmodernist in its orientation. Within the first few moments of the video, the sacred and the profane, the Eastern and the Western, the ancient and the modern, the communist and the capitalist are all thrust together in a fragmented barrage of complex and contradictory imagery, almost impossible to decode or

Figure 2.5 Two exotic women with a phallic hookah apparatus in the music video for Massari's "Shisha" (2012) (screen capture).

map. This sudden barrage creates a cognitive confusion such as one might get from excessive hookah smoking—especially as the video consistently hints that the hookahs on display might contain something stronger than tobacco. Then again, this sort of combination of diverse images from a wide variety of sources without any real reasoning behind it is typical of postmodernist art, which is highly fragmented, never asking the viewer to pull the pieces together into a coherent whole as, say, a modernist collage might do.[39]

The song "Shisha" itself really has very little to do with Middle Eastern culture, except for the central shisha reference, which would seem to be simply another Orientalist attempt to employ the exotic cultural associations of the Middle East to create an air of decadent and indulgent sexuality. Massari and Montana are essentially Western artists who happen to have been born in the MENA region and who employ Orientalist images not as an expression of cultural pride in their origins, but simply as pre-packaged tools that they can use to help sell their own product—which is the sense their audiences derive of being transgressive and sexual in ways that escape the boredom and confinement of day-to-day life under late capitalism. But of course, in the best postmodern mode, this seeming cry of protest, while it does contain a faint gesture of utopian longing for something beyond capitalism, does not perform any sort of real critique of the capitalist system. Instead, it assures us that capitalism offers one opportunities to experience great wealth, great sex, and great mind-altering intoxicants. If a couple of poor Arab immigrants such as Massari and French Montana can make it big while living it up in this way, why can't we all?

Of course, viewers of the video are not likely to be so simple minded that they assume from watching it that they too can have the women and the Lamborghini and the bling if they will just ignore the rules, party hard, smoke shisha, drink wine, and let all the good things come to them. But viewers might well develop fantasy associations that allow them to experience a few moments of vicarious pleasure amid the otherwise dreary nature of their daily lives. "Shisha," in fact, is driven by a pure ideology of consumerism, made all the more objectionable by the fact that women (and animals such as lions) are among the commodities available to be consumed, in addition to the shisha and the alcohol, the gold chains and the Lamborghini.

Rapper (and former stripper) Cardi B's 2017 megahit "Bodak Yellow" attempts to reverse the gender politics of this sort of imagery, while relying just as centrally on Orientalist images as codes for wealth and decadent power. The song is basically just one long boast about how rich and sexually powerful the singer has become now that she's a star, and the accompanying video[40] makes extensive use of Orientalist images to drive that point home. It begins with a shot of the Dubai skyline—now virtually synonymous with wealth and excess, then cuts to a shot of Cardi B in veiled desert garb, shot from below as if she might be up on a camel, a hint that is reinforced immediately by another cut to a caravan of camels moving through the desert. A quick shot of a snarling (but leashed) cheetah, then back to Cardi B performing the song in her desert garb (with face veil removed), with a camel standing nearby (but not too nearby). Then back to the veiled Cardi B, again shot from below to suggest that she is now up on the camel. Then we see a shot of her lounging haughtily in what looks like a black latex outfit near (but not too near) the cheetah. More cuts between the camels and the cheetah including some shots of Cardi B actually atop a camel. Other scenes going forward show a sort of decadent desert dinner party at which a presumably rich and powerful Arab drinks wine with a hookah nearby, showering Cardi B with jewels and what appear to be American $100 bills. Cardi B, though, would clearly have us believe that she is fully in charge of whatever transactions are underway. Even an Arab man, presumably accustomed to dominating women, is no match for her sexual power. No victim of sexual exploitation, she is, as she declares in the song, "a boss," not a "worker." The video then ends with another flurry of camel shots as the camel train finally moves off into the distance in the desert.

Importantly, the lyrics of "Bodak Yellow" have nothing whatsoever to do with Arabs or the desert or camels or cheetahs. The imagery is used in a completely gratuitous way, stripped of context—in the mode that Jameson associates with postmodern pastiche. It is certainly the case that videos such as those for "Shisha" and "Bodak Yellow" could be seen as collapsing the hierarchical binary opposition between the East and the West on which Orientalism (and colonialism) once thrived. This does not, however, make such videos automatically subversive or progressive. After all, late capitalism itself collapses these oppositions, which are, in fact detrimental to its global operations—just as they were once beneficial to the operations of colonialism.[41] We have come a long way from "Ahab the Arab," which treats Arabs as exotic (and vaguely ridiculous) Others, to "Shisha," which conscripts motifs from Arab culture as images of coolness, wealth, and masculine power that can be used to enhance the existing Western roster of such images. "Bodak Yellow" perhaps goes even further in attempting to use such images to convey a sense of *feminine* power. We would argue, though, that the real power being celebrated in these videos is the power of money, and specifically of capitalism. It is significant, then, that a similar celebration of luxury and wealth can increasingly be found in the songs and video clips produced in the Arab world itself, where popular music has increasingly come in recent years to resemble the popular music of the West. Such cultural tributes to the power of capital are, in fact, crucial to the convergence of the Arab and American pop music industries in recent decades. We examine this phenomenon more closely in the next chapter, via a survey of the contemporary Arab pop music industry—and especially of the video clips that have become such a crucial component of that industry in the twenty-first century.

3

I'd Like to Sell the World a Coke: Arab Pop Music and Pop Music Video Clips

Despite a thoroughgoing suspicion of many kinds of music in some interpretations of Islam, music has long been a prominent part of Arab culture. Popular singers such as Egypt's Abdel Halim Hafez (1929-77) have become venerated figures, rubbing elbows with kings and presidents. Moreover, despite a special skepticism toward the propriety of women singing or otherwise performing music in public, women singers such as Egypt's Umm Kulthum (1898-1975)[1] and Lebanon's Fairuz (1935-) have been among the most admired, respected, and even revered figures in modern Arab culture. The same might also be said for Lebanon's Sabah (1927-2014), though Sabah's controversial public persona also made her a more direct predecessor to today's sexy Arab pop singers. Perhaps, then, it is no surprise that music has been such a crucial component of the now-decades-old explosion in the production of popular culture in the modern Arab world. In addition to its own importance as a cultural form, music—in the form of music videos (generally referred to as "video clips" in the Arab world)—has also been central to the rapid growth of Arab satellite television. Walter Armbrust, in fact, argues that "in quantitative terms one could say that video clips dominate Arab satellite television," with as many as one-fifth of the channels on Arab satellite television broadcasting video clips at any given time (231).[2]

In any case, video clips (often featuring female pop singers in sometimes rather risqué costumes and situations) have been a particularly popular component of the Arab music business, though such clips have also come in for considerable criticism, especially among more conservative Muslim critics who see many of the performances of women in video clips as inappropriate and immoral. Patricia Kubala discusses the claims by some Egyptian critics that video clips are a threat to the moral fiber of the nation. Similarly, Armbrust entitles his essay on video clips "What Would Sayyid Qutb Say?" not only in reference to the Egyptian Muslim Brotherhood leader from the 1950s and 1960s, but also in more general reference to the widespread disapproval of video clips among conservative Islamic elements of Middle Eastern culture. As Armbrust further notes, traditionalists might object to video clip culture on two different fronts. For one thing, "the intrinsic commercialism of videos inevitably invites scorn from cultural gatekeepers, who almost uniformly condemn them for lack of artistic merit" (232). More importantly, Armbrust argues that video clips tend to be centrally about sex, thus drawing more ire from conservative elements.

On the other hand, the fact that sexy pop singers such as Lebanon's Elissa, Nancy Ajram, Myriam Fares, and Haifa Wehbe or Egypt's Ruby and Sherine have remained wildly popular despite such (often quite harsh) criticisms can be taken as a sign of the power of modernizing forces in Arab culture, forces that are by no means overmatched by the power of Islamic conservatism.[3] The polished recordings (and video clips) of modern Arab pop stars are clearly influenced by both Western recording technologies and Western musical and visual styles.[4] Moreover, in addition to serving essentially as advertisements for the stars who appear in them, video clips often show their stars living romanticized and luxurious Western lifestyles, which increases the fantasy effects and thus the auras of these stars, but also represents an implicit endorsement of such lifestyles. This materialist aspect of video clips understandably reinforces the concern of some in the Arab world that the clips are undermining traditional Islamic values. And they no doubt do carry with them a certain suggestion that Western modernity (i.e., capitalism) brings with it wealth, luxury, and fun—not to mention sexual gratification—unavailable in a strictly traditional Muslim (or, for that matter, Christian) climate.

The Palestinian poet and political scientist Tamim al-Barghouti, for example, complains that the world represented in Arab video clips has little to do with the world of ordinary Arabs:

> Video clips are full of half-naked, well-sculpted women, and rich, handsome young men in convertibles, chasing and flirting with one another against backgrounds of European green, or extravagant mansions. Poor streets and simple clothes appear as relics, folklore, or exotic eye-catchers; the music, the choreography, and the lyrics are as foreign to such backgrounds as a Victorian Orientalist is to a mosque. (226)

Importantly, however, Al-Barghouti argues that the scenes in these video clips do not represent a straightforward imitation of the West. Instead, for him, they represent a genuine expression of the worldview of an Arab elite psychologically damaged by the colonial past into desiring to be like the West but feeling they cannot succeed because of their natural inferiority.

Al-Barghouti certainly has a point about the distance between the lifestyles represented in Arab video clips and the lifestyles of ordinary Arabs. On the other hand, he fails to note that a similar gap exists between the lifestyles represented in American music videos and the lifestyles of ordinary Americans. Even country music videos, for example, supposedly based on the "authentic" lives of down-to-earth real folk, project a distorted and idealized version of the lives of such folk—to the extent that they even bother to try, given that recent "country" music and its videos—say, from Shania Twain to Taylor Swift—are often indistinguishable from pop music and its glossy videos. Al-Barghouti, writing for a volume published in 2010, also perhaps fails to appreciate the impressive technical advances made in Arab video clips in recent years, as well as the transnational flow of talent and ideas that make it increasingly difficult to make a strict distinction between Arab video clips and Western music videos.

In any case, video clips have certainly helped to put Arab music on the international map, partly because the aesthetic of this particular art form is itself especially international. It is also especially postmodern, and the frenetic, quick-cut editing style associated with music videos is a central example of the fragmented form that Fredric Jameson has seen as a key characteristic of postmodernist culture. It is not for nothing that E. Anne Kaplan has identified music videos as a quintessentially postmodern form, partly because of their thoroughly commercialized nature. Video clips are thus a perfect illustration of Jameson's argument that postmodernist art is the kind that is produced when cultural production "has become integrated into commodity production generally" (*Postmodernism* 4). Video clips are also a key locus of innovation in the visual arts: many up-and-coming film directors, for example, have honed their craft in making music videos, including such luminaries from around the world as Spike Jonze, David Fincher, Michel Gondry, and Tarsem Singh. The same is becoming true in the Arab world, where rising Lebanese feature film director Nadine Labaki has also had a successful career directing video clips for stars such as Ajram. In video clips, the stakes are much lower than in a feature-length film, making it feasible to give chances to unknown directors or to attempt daring aesthetic experimentation. Such experimentation is also a key characteristic of postmodernism in general, where

> the frantic economic urgency of producing fresh waves of ever more novel-seeming goods (from clothing to airplanes), at ever greater rates of turnover,

now assigns an increasingly essential structural function and position to aesthetic innovation and experimentation that is produced when culture itself has become completely commodified, artistic creativity becoming simply a part of the general rage for innovation and new product development that is a crucial component of late capitalism. (Jameson, *Postmodernism* 4–5)

For our purposes, however, perhaps the most crucial characteristic of postmodern culture per Jameson is its international reach. For Jameson, postmodernism is the culture of a late capitalism that is nearing global dominance, the culture that arises when the long historical process of global capitalist modernization is nearing completion. This theorization of postmodernism as the "cultural logic of late capitalism" provides a compelling framework within which to understand the similarities between American music videos and Arab video clips, since both are now part of the same global postmodernist culture.

Relevant here is Jameson's argument that the principal compositional strategy of postmodern art is a form of pastiche that involves the borrowing and recirculation of styles and techniques from previous works of art. According to Jameson, postmodernist artists tend to regard the works of the past as a sort of tool kit from which they can pick and choose the aspects that they believe will be effective in their own work—almost like choosing items from an à la carte cafeteria menu. However, as Booker has argued (writing about postmodern film), this situation does not imply that postmodernist artists are not creative and original, but only that their creativity lies principally in their inventive use of styles and techniques originally developed by others, rather than in developing their own unique styles (*Postmodern* 188).

If postmodern artists can borrow the styles of any time period without concern for the original historical context, then it is also the case that artists any*where* should be able to borrow styles that emanate from anywhere else. From this point of view the gradual convergence of aesthetic styles in various art forms around the globe is not only understandable, but inevitable. If music videos are indeed a quintessential postmodern form, then one might expect that this convergence might especially apply to video clips. This is also the case, of course, due to the internationalization of the music industry itself. Performers, producers, and video clip directors freely float from one national context to another, partly because styles translate so easily from one country to another, but also partly because the Culture Industry that provides them with employment is itself so international. Though the Arab music industry is rapidly becoming more mature and established, some major stars of Arab music have recorded for companies whose ultimate ownership is American, as when Ajram recorded for EMI Arabia, a subsidiary of the Western entertainment conglomerate—though EMI has now virtually withdrawn from its Middle Eastern operations.[5] Even culture companies that seem purely Arabic tend to be *pan*-Arabic. The Arab world's largest entertainment company, for example, is the Riyadh-based Rotana, owned primarily by Saudi Prince Al-Waleed bin Talal and involved in a variety of enterprises, from hotels to television stations. Rotana is a particularly big player in the Arab music business, at various times listing on its roster of recording artists such stars as Lebanon's Elissa, Wehbe, and Marwan Khoury; Egypt's Sherine and Tamer Hosny; and the UAE's Ahlam. But even Rotana is partly owned by the American entertainment conglomerate 21st Century Fox, itself a spinoff of the international conglomerate News Corp.

One of the rising forces in the Arab recording industry is Platinum Records, a subsidiary of the Saudi-owned (but Dubai-based) satellite television powerhouse Middle East Broadcasting Center (MBC). Platinum is home to a number of up-and-coming younger stars from around the Arab world, including Palestine's Mohammed Assaf, Bahrain's Hala Al Turk, and Egypt's Carmen Suleiman, all three of whom got their big breaks in the music business via appearances in music competition shows on MBC. Among other things, Platinum features a sub-label, Platinum Independent, that specializes in producing content in English, with the hope of making it marketable to Western audiences, thus increasing the transnational flow of culture between the East and the West. Meanwhile, MBC has a British CEO and reportedly has employees from sixty-five different countries ("MBC's CEO").

The Arab video clip as a cultural phenomenon

If anything, the video clip industry is even more international than the music recording business itself, perhaps partly because the largest venue for the viewing of such videos is now the website YouTube, which is easily available around the globe. YouTube has, in fact, perhaps been as important as satellite television in popularizing Arab video clips, especially among Arabs in diaspora around the world. The site provides a venue through which artists can attain (and maintain) high visibility, making both their newer and their older clips easily available to a wide audience around the world. Video clips for the recordings of top Arab stars can quickly mount into the millions of views on YouTube. Saad Lamjarred's 2015 catchy pop megahit "Lm3allem" ("The Master,"[6]) reached 100 million views

Figure 3.1 A group of dancers in a postmodern pastiche of traditional Moroccan garb in the video clip for Saad Lamjarred's hugely popular "Lm3allem" (2015) (screen capture).

within three months and, as of this writing, now has almost 600 million views, making it the most viewed Arab video in the history of YouTube. The highly colorful, comically frenetic video features Lamjarred and a number of dancers in what might best be described as postmodern pastiches of traditional Moroccan costumes, including brightly colored, crazily patterned djellabas—with the addition of American-style sneakers.

Lamjarred, incidentally, also scored a major hit in 2013 with "Mal Hbibi Malou" ("What's Wrong with My Love"[7]), which now has over 200 million views on YouTube. His 2014 song "Enti Baghya Wahed" ("You Want Someone,"[8] audio only) won the Murex d'Or[9] for "Best Arabic Song"—even without the promotional aid of an official video clip. In 2017, Lamjarred's clip for "Ana Machi Sahel" ("I'm No Fool,"[10]) won the Arab Nation Music Award for the most viewed Arab video clip of the past year, with over 100 million views. And, in 2018, Lamjarred's video clip for "Ghazali" ("Gazelle"),[11] which features another postmodern amalgamation of images ranging from camels to Michael Jackson, was another immediate YouTube hit, drawing more than fifty million views in its first month on the site. Lamjarred is also another example of the importance of televised competition shows for launching musical careers in the Arab world. He first gained attention when he placed second on the 2007 edition of *Superstar* (the forerunner of the current *Arab Idol*), even though his somewhat gawky appearance on the show didn't entirely foretell his later success.

Still, while Lamjarred might be the biggest Arab video star, the phenomenon of Arab video clips remains most directly associated with the careers of sexy female pop stars. The career of Ajram (a Lebanese Christian who is one of the biggest stars never to record for Rotana and never to remain attached for long to a single recording label) is particularly indicative of the crucial role of sexy video clips in the careers of many female stars in the Arab world. A relative unknown when the video clip for "Akhasmak Ah" ("We Might Quarrel, but I Won't Leave You," 2003[12]) was released, Ajram became a star overnight as a result of her sexy dancing and singing in the clip, during which she appears to be channeling Egyptian film legend Hind Rostom, the "Marilyn Monroe of the Middle East" (Cestor 104). On the other hand, by American standards, Ajram appears rather sweet and wholesome—though her most popular YouTube clip "Ma Tegi Hena" ("Won't You Come Here," 2014[13]) is perhaps her most sexually suggestive, even including scenes of bondage.

One of Ajram's most interesting (and most Western-inflected) video clips is the one for "Hassa Beek" ("I Feel You," 2017[14]), which overtly plays upon her double image as a wholesome wife and mother, as well as a glamorous and sexy star. Shot entirely in black and white (and thus highlighting Ajram's piercing blue eyes less than usual in her clips, though they are still striking, even in black and white), the clip begins like an American film noir, with film-noir-style credits on the screen (in English) as a character played by Ajram enters the office of a private detective who has apparently found evidence of her husband's infidelity. Then the director yells "cut," and we are on the set of the film, where it becomes clear that Ajram is playing an actress who is performing in this film noir. The clip blurs fiction and reality to an extent, but especially blurs time periods. The black-and-white cinematography and allusion to film noir give much of the clip a feel of something from the American 1940s or 1950s, but much of it also seems quite modern, though there are no signs of overtly contemporary technology, and the actress played by Ajram drives a Ford Mustang from the 1960s. Most of the costuming and set design is also indeterminate in terms of its placement in time.

The plot (like the lyrics) is quite simple: Ajram's glamorous actress is involved in an on-set flirtation with a handsome man (perhaps the producer) who is involved in making the film noir. Meanwhile, the man's pretty (but less glamorous) wife is home with their son, feeling lonely and neglected. In the end, however, the man declines to become romantically involved with the actress and returns to his wife. The catch, of course, is that both the actress and the wife are played by Ajram, who thus projects a double identity that is indicative of her complex public persona, while at the same time embodying the fragmentation of identity that observers such as Jameson have associated with postmodernism.[15] The geographical setting is indeterminate as well. The director of the film noir speaks to his actors in Arabic (and Ajram's singing is in Arabic), but all of the

Figure 3.2 Title frame of the video clip for Nancy Ajram's "Hassa Beek" (2017), clearly designed to mimic the opening title of an American film noir (screen capture).

signs that we see during the clip are in English, and a scene of the son's birthday party (sans dad, who doesn't show) features the singing of "Happy Birthday" in English—though that would certainly not be uncommon in the Arab world these days.[16]

The video clip for Ajram's "W Maak" ("And with You," 2017[17]), from the same album as "Hassa Beek," is similarly postmodern and similarly echoes American culture. It is structured around Ajram and several other young women featured in the clip watching the 1954 American instructional film *Toward Emotional Maturity*, designed to counsel young people (especially young women) on how to keep their emotions in check. The film contains little in the way of plot, other than vague suggestions that these young women might not be fully following the advice in the instructional film. Meanwhile, most of the scenes take place in very American-looking settings, such as a bowling alley and a 1950s-style soda shop/restaurant. Perhaps the most postmodern aspect of the video, however, is its mixture of materials from different time periods. In addition to the echoes of the 1950s already noted, there is a 1980s feel to some of the scenes, such as one set in a video arcade, yet there are also scenes featuring contemporary technology, such as cell phones. Meanwhile, the clip also features a particularly interesting form of postmodern pastiche. Visually, it is clearly modeled on a commercial shot for the Zhivago clothing line in Australia by Dale Alexander Bremner—but there is a good reason for the resemblance. Bremner also served as the cinematographer for the video clip for "W Maak." Thus, instead of borrowing the style of another artist, clip director Leila Kanaan apparently simply hired the artist to replicate his own style. Finally, like so many Arab video clips, this one features product placements for specific sponsors, in this case Damas jewelry and the British cosmetics brand Rimmel.

Figure 3.3 Screen capture from the video clip for Nancy Ajram's "W Maak" (2018), showing the performer beside a Western-style Wurlitzer juke box.

Video clips have also been crucial to the career of Fares, whose provocative dancing and flying mane of hair are particularly photogenic and who perhaps shows more skin (and cleavage) than any other major woman singing star in the Middle East. The costuming and set designs of her video clips are among the most modern and Western of all Arab video clips, as in "Eih Elly Byehsal" ("What's Happening," 2008[18]), in which Fares undulates atop a speeding, high-powered motorcycle as a colorful, psychedelic background streams behind her, then later dances in skin-tight silvery pants that reflect explosions of light off her wriggling derriere. Yet Fares's video clips are also particularly postmodern, mixing a variety of different cultural elements. In the clip for "Kifak Enta" ("How Are You?," 2015[19]), for example, she performs a relatively traditional-sounding Arabic song while dancing about in a brilliantly colored ultra-American-looking bare-midriff outfit that looks like it came from a Hollywood vision of California in the 1960s. Meanwhile, most of the performance takes place on a Beirut rooftop, replete with pigeon cages and satellite dishes, though the clip also includes an indoor scene in which the fourth wall is broken, showing the video crew at work fanning mist and sprinkling confetti about Fares as she performs.

The video clip for Fares's "Aman,"[20] the title track for her 2015 album, provides perhaps her most interesting combination of different cultural elements. Here Fares performs a very traditional song in a relatively traditional vocal style (and in classical Arabic), but backed by hard-driving electronic dance music of a kind that one might find in a contemporary dance club. Meanwhile, the entire video consists merely of a sequence of shots of Fares dancing and singing in a variety of costumes amid a spectacular array of digital special effects that enhance the club-like feel of the song. However, these costumes are quite interesting, ranging from a simple white modern gymnast's leotard to a variety of highly exotic costumes, generally featuring some sort of elaborate veil, mask, or head-covering in what appears to be designed to enhance her allure as a vague fantasy of the exotic Oriental woman. There's even a bit of belly dancing. Meanwhile, none of the facial coverings featured in the clip seem designed to indicate modesty. Rather, they seem designed to titillate, drawing attention to Fares's mesmerizing dark eyes, which seem filled with sexual promise. On the other hand, the costumes appear more medieval than specifically Middle Eastern. Some of them do, however, have a vaguely Andalusian feel, which enhances the Oriental effect—and which is entirely appropriate, given that the song Fares sings, electronic dance music backup notwithstanding, is a classic from the Andalusian *Muwashahat* music tradition. Actually entitled "Lama Beda Yetathana" ("When He Started to Sway") the song is more than 500 years old and has been performed by any number of legendary Arab singers, including Fairuz and Syrian male singer (and former muezzin) Sabah Fakhri. This clip thus combines the East and the West, the old and the new, in particularly overt ways.[21]

The video clips of Wehbe also rely in a particularly overt way on the sexuality of the performer. As Cestor notes, Wehbe has been a particularly controversial figure, the subject of "crude jokes as a result of her participation in private concerts for Saudi princes" (105). But Cestor also suggests that Wehbe has become "an idol for the young and the leading trendsetter for Arab pop singers" (105). It is certainly the case that physical appeal (as conveyed through video clips and otherwise) is particularly crucial to the success of Wehbe, who is now an established and award-winning television actress as well as pop singer.

Figure 3.4 Myriam Fares in an exotic facial covering in the video clip for "Aman" (2015) (screen capture).

Her video clips, though, remain central to her reputation for sexiness, as when she plays a sexy jewel thief (stealing prominently displayed Zhouraib jewelry) in the clip for "Ezzay Ansak" ("How Could I Forget You," 2012[22]). Her clips are also a big part of her reputation for audacity and modernity in style. She even performed her 2014 English-language song "Breathing You In" in a clip (directed by Palestinian American Tarik Freitekh[23]) that featured shots of spacecraft and of a NASA logo (and American dancer Casper Smart as a guest star)—as if to emphasize her status as an emblem of Westernization and modernization in the Arab world.

By 2018, however, Wehbe song "Touta" (2018, "End of the Story"[24]) is performed in Arabic and apparently signals the end of Wehbe's association with Freitek, which had long been foregrounded on social media such as Instagram. Its video was released on Wehbe's YouTube channel under her own logo. In it, Wehbe enacts the advice given in a book (written in English) on how to deal with breakups.

Wehbe's status as a state-of-the-art performer also informs her selection in 2017 to be brand ambassador for the MBC-run gaming app WIZZO, beginning with her starring role in a promotional trailer for the military video game *Invasion*.[25] While this and other aspects of Wehbe's recent career seem to want to announce their modern, Western flavor, other songs and clips by Wehbe seem specifically designed as a fusion of Eastern and Western styles—as is done quite overtly in her disco-style collaboration with French DJ David Vendetta,

Figure 3.5 Haifa Wehbe works out in a Western-style outfit with added Eastern-style belly dancer's coin belt in the video clip for her song "Touta" (2018) (screen capture).

"Yama Layali" ("So Many Nights," 2010[26]). However, Wehbe performs this sort of cultural fusion more subtly (and perhaps more effectively) in the video clip for "Baddi 3ich" ("I Want to Live," 2005[27]), which also makes a strong political statement. The clip opens to the playing of Western-style electronic dance music that will provide a backbeat to the entire song. Credits identify the singer simply as "Haifa"—no last name needed, given her status in the Arab world. Cut to a scene in a mysterious forest, with masked dancers lying on the ground beneath a sort of chrysalis; a figure within the chrysalis begins to move as if trying to find its way out. The dancers awake and reach upward as the figure emerges luxuriantly from the chrysalis, greeted in apparent celebration by the dancers in a primal scene of wakening and birth. The figure, of course, is Haifa, who launches into the song a declaration of her desire to be allowed to go where she wants, be who she wants, and live her life her own way. Throughout the video, her long black hair flies wildly as she undulates in a low-cut clingy silken garment of which traditionalists in the Middle East would no doubt strongly disapprove. As if in recognition of that inevitable disapproval, the scene quickly turns threatening, and Haifa seems to be struggling against various forms of constraint throughout the video clip. Having emerged from the chrysalis, she seems in constant danger of being re-contained; she seems constantly in danger of being enclosed, suffocated, yet she refuses to submit to the shadowy shapes that surround and seem to want to engulf her as she moves through a sort of underworld. She looks alarmed, but determined, refusing to be intimidated or dissuaded. At last, she reaches a ladder that seems to offer a potential way out. She climbs upward, soon emerging from the underworld, her garment magically changing from white to red—the traditional color of love and passion and sexual liberation. She is now in a new world, surrounded by a bed of flowers. Relieved, she releases her grip on the ladder and falls backward into the flowers, then rises from them in triumph as raindrops fall upon her contented face, symbols of life and fertility surrounding her.

The music of "Baddi 3ich" remains Western and contemporary throughout—and to that extent the cry for individual freedom in the song seems to suggest that a key to such freedom lies in Western-style modernization. Yet the images have a dreamlike, surreal, otherworldly quality that makes it hard to identify them with any particular culture or locale. The images combine with the lyrics, though, to make the song a clear feminist anthem, especially in a Middle Eastern context in which so many forces try to limit the ability of women to live on their own terms. It's a declaration of independence by one of the Middle East's most independent performers, though the overall texture of the video clip suggests

Haifa's understanding that independence for an Arab Muslim woman is an ongoing struggle. Still, though this particular song and video were produced by Rotana, by the time of "Breathing You In" Wehbe had broken with that entertainment powerhouse and moved instead to Freitekh's American-owned operation in what can be taken both as a sign of her own independence and as a key sign of globalization in Arab pop music.

"Baddi 3ich" is something like an Arab version of Cardi B's "Bodak Yellow," stripped of the vulgarity and boasting. It is also stripped of the competitive vibe that runs throughout "Bodak Yellow," in which Cardi B seems to see her success as a victory over other (possibly envious) women, addressed consistently in the song as "bitches" and "hoes." Cardi B simply declares herself a winner, a victor over everyone she has encountered. Haifa declares herself a sister in the struggle who just wants the right to pursue that struggle in her own way. Cardi B boasts of her ability to manipulate men with sex. Haifa says nothing about sex at all, but her sexuality dominates the screen. It is part of who she is; if you don't like it you don't have to look. Cardi B employs an array of Orientalist images to support her claims to wealth and power; Haifa uses culturally neutral images, perhaps (especially when combined with the sound of the music) with a slightly Western intonation, but there is no proud proclamation that she has conquered this other culture and made it her own or indication that her mastery of Western music has made her superior to others in the East. Haifa invites (but does not command) other women to follow her; Cardi B taunts the women she claims to have left in her dust.

"Baddi 3ich" is an exemplary cultural fusion that draws energies from multiple sources without showing disrespect for any of them and makes a strong personal political statement without disparaging the politics of others. The camels, cheetah, and cartoonish rich Arab of "Bodak Yellow"—like the scimitars, camels, and belly dancers of R. Kelly's "Snake" music video—are objectionable partly because they have been ripped out of their original cultural context and then used in a context that is dramatically foreign (and would be morally repugnant) to that original context. The astronauts, spacecraft, and NASA logos of the "Breathing You In" video clip are borrowed from American culture and then used in a cultural context that is perfectly compatible with American culture—because it's all really part of global capitalist culture. In both cases the borrowed images represent a use of pastiche as a sort of shorthand to produce a particular atmosphere, whether it be of exotic sexuality in the case of Kelly or Cardi B or twenty-first-century modern sexual openness in the case of Wehbe. But when Kelly and Cardi B dress like mock Arabs, it is a joke, a travesty;

when Wehbe dresses like a modern woman, unashamed of her sexuality, she is just being who she is. She is not mocking Western women for how they dress or act. Kelly's and Cardi B's use of Arab imagery seems fake and contrived, and is certainly inauthentic. In fact, given the legacy of Orientalism, it would be hard to imagine any way they could use that imagery effectively, given the nature of their videos. On the other hand, Wehbe's use of modern Western imagery, contaminated by no such Occidentalist legacy, seems perfectly appropriate and effective already—and certainly not offensive to Westerners. It is, in fact, not a case of cultural appropriation at all. It is simply an example of the global culture of late capitalism, a culture of which Wehbe is herself a part.

Of course, Wehbe's unashamed demand for autonomy in a sexually charged video such as "Baddi 3ich" is precisely the sort of move that has made video clips so controversial in the Arab world. Cestor, for example, notes the criticisms by al-Barghouti that "music videos reveal the desire of Arabs to submit to Western style, undermining the achievements of Arab music, which for a long time remained relatively immune to Occidental acculturation" (104). But even videos that seem self-consciously to go for a more Middle Eastern style can cause controversy for their reliance on feminine sexual allure. The video for Fares's 2008 song "Moukanoh Wein" ("Where's His Place"[28]) is relatively simple, primarily featuring Fares singing and dancing in an almost postapocalyptic desert-like landscape. The performance, especially the dancing (some of it on camelback), which many viewed as excessively provocative, drew considerable criticism in the Arab world, though some of the criticism was good-humored. Lebanese drag queen Bassem Feghali performed a parody of Fares's song from the same album, "Moush Ananeya" ("I Am Not Selfish"), at the 2008 Lebanese Murex d'Or awards show, dressed as Fares in the clip for that song, though largely imitating her dance moves from "Moukanoh Wein." Emphasizing the crucial role played by a certain part of Fares's anatomy in those moves (and in both clips), Feghali wore inserts to give him a huge ass and changed the lyrics to declare the commercial value of having such a prominent posterior.[29]

The fact that Arab video clips are underwritten by the ideology of late capitalism can further be seen in the extent to which they are used to market, not merely the performers in the clips, but other products as well. Product placement is at least as common—and possibly even more overt—in Arab video clips as in American music videos, as when Ajram shows off her Damas jewelry in clips for songs such as "Elly Kan" ("All That Was," 2007[30]). This clip was made in conjunction with Ajram's major endorsement deal with Damas, a Dubai-headquartered company that claims on its website to be the Middle East's "leading international jewellery [sic] and watch retailer."[31] Damas jewelry, in fact, features in a number of Ajram's video clips, including the one for her 2006 song "Ana Yalli Bahebak" ("I'm the One Who Loves You"[32]), portions of which were spliced into a Damas TV ad. Not to be outdone, Elissa has performed in a series of commercials for the Saudi L'azurde jewelry company, including a two-minute extended spot in which, due to a mix-up, she is nearly forced to perform her hit song "Hob Kol Hayati" ("Love of My Life") without the accustomed adornment of her L'azurde jewelry, but is saved at the last minute through the intervention of a handsome benefactor, bringing her lost necklace in the nick of time.

Incidentally, Elissa's 2014 clip for "Hob Kol Hayati" ("Love of My Life"[33]) is also a virtual Samsung commercial—including a self-referential gimmick in which, within the video, we see that she has been watching the lyrics clip of the song on YouTube via her Samsung Note phone. Samsung phones, in fact, feature prominently in a number of Elissa's video clips, as when the clip for the 2013 single of "Te3ebt Mennak" ("I'm Sick of You"[34]), features a Samsung Galaxy S4 phone as a major element of the clip.[35] This clip, incidentally, was clearly influenced by Britney Spears's 2004 music video for "Everytime,"[36] thus serving as a key example of such influences.

Fares's video clips, however interesting they might sometimes be, are also not above dipping into the purely commercial, as when the clip for "Nifsi Aoulhalak" ("I Wish I Could Say It to You," 2015[37]) basically stars Fares's famous flying hair, again backed by electronic dance music, but now enhanced by Wella hair

Figure 3.6 Elissa uses her Samsung phone in the video clip for her song "Hob Kol Hayati" (2014) (screen capture).

care products, which are prominently featured in the clip. It is, of course, no accident that Fares at the time had a lucrative endorsement deal with Wella, a German company headquartered in Switzerland whose products are distributed worldwide, including in the Middle East.

Elissa has converted her considerable fame into marketing might in other ways as well, including the filming of a number of commercials for Pepsi, both for airing in the Middle East and for distribution worldwide. In 2006, for example, she appeared in a series of commercials that featured both her and American singing star Christina Aguilera. One of these commercials,[38] in fact, features the two singers apparently performing in a number of different countries (including Brazil, Russia, Japan, and India),[39] while another features the two hacking into the videoscreen at a World Cup soccer match to hawk Pepsi.[40] In an interesting East-West reversal, however, Christina appears as a belly dancer in the commercial (perhaps in an allusion to her "Genie in a Bottle" video), while Elissa appears in the one European locale. In any case, the theme is clear: Pepsi wants to emphasize the international nature of their brand and the fact that it is cool to drink Pepsi no matter where in the world you live.

Pepsi and their chief rival Coca-Cola are among the most iconic of all international brands, and both are fond of emphasizing their international reach—as in Coke's famed "I'd Like to Buy the World a Coke" ad from 1971.[41] That reach has long been intertwined with the reach of American popular culture, and Pepsi in particular has employed high-profile pop-culture icons to promote its products, as in their use of Michael Jackson in their television ads of the mid-1980s—during the same period in which Jackson was central to a We Are the World campaign that might have been sincere in its desire to fight world hunger, but that also emphasized the growing globalization of American popular culture.

In recent years, the Coca-Cola company has invested in internationalization through pop culture via its sponsorship of the "Coke Studio" television franchise. Beginning with Brazil in 2007, the Coke Studio franchise moved to Pakistan and India, and then on to the Middle East, where it was broadcast on MBC for three seasons from 2012 to 2014. The original versions of the Coke Studio franchise featured different artists (generally from the same country) who normally perform different styles of music, coming together for a final live performance that involves a fusion of their two different styles. The Middle East version of Coke Studio ("Coke Studio Bel 3arabi") featured some of these same combinations as well, though it was perhaps most distinctive for the episodes in which it featured team-ups between Western artists and Middle Eastern ones.

In one episode, for example, Sherine combined with American rapper Nelly, while Fares appeared with American rapper Flo Rida in another episode. And, as we noted in the previous chapter, one of the more interesting combinations on the show features sexy Lebanese songstress (and game show host and general media personality) Maya Diab performing with American singer Jason Derulo for a heavily censored performance of his risqué song "Talk Dirty to Me." Such occasional squeamishness aside, though, these dual performances generally mesh well, and the message of the show—that music can transcend all sorts of differences—is convincingly delivered.

Meanwhile, if Elissa and, for that matter, Wehbe and fellow Lebanese star Nawal Al Zoghbi have worked extensively with Pepsi, Ajram has worked extensively with Coke, bringing the cola wars into the center of Arab pop culture. In 2004, for example, Ajram made a series of video clips that foregrounded Coca-Cola, while also making literal Coke commercials in conjunction with clips, such as "Oul Tani Kida" ("Say That One More Time," 2004[42]), that are essentially spin-offs and longer versions of the ads. As late as 2014, Ajram was still hawking Coke in an extensive campaign that promoted the drink in conjunction with the World Cup and that also featured Algerian raï star Khaled.

Arab pop stars and the globalization of the music industry

Khaled himself (who performed under the name "Cheb Khaled" earlier in his career and is still better known by that name) began to gain recognition outside of North Africa as early as the late 1980s, solidifying that expansion in 1992 with "Didi,"[43] identified by Shoup as the first "global hit" of raï music (52). Khaled became an even bigger star in 1996 with his huge hit "Aïcha,"[44] in which the singer, performing in both French and Arabic, offers treasures to a woman who responds that what she really wants is to have the same rights as men.[45] Indeed, the ability of so many North African singers to perform in French furthered a cultural exchange that helped singers such as Khaled to gain considerable attention outside North Africa.[46] Indeed, raï, a traditional North African musical form often associated with political protest, has in recent years enjoyed considerable cross-fertilization with Western music (especially reggae and rap music) in general, each enriching the other, though some traditionalists have seen the influence of Western music on raï as a form of cultural (and moral) contamination.[47] Some, of course, might see the recent movement of artists such as Khaled toward more and more commercial forms to be a verification of this sort of contamination, though one might also see it as drawing valuable international attention to Arab music and its artists.

Khaled himself reached full international status with the 2012 megahit "C'est la vie," which was supported by an immensely popular video clip[48] that helped the song to become a major hit in both Europe and the Middle East. With main lyrics in Algerian Arabic and a chorus in French, the upbeat, high-energy dance tune seemed specifically designed for international consumption.[49] As of July 2018, the clip had over 67,000,000 views on YouTube. Shot in an extremely Western, extremely modern style, the video features happy, energetic young people seemingly of every race and nationality, dancing and singing along with the song.

This clip reflects the typical style of its producer, RedOne, the American-based, Moroccan-born producer who has become a leading figure on the global music scene, a phenomenon that is itself a key indicator of the transnational flow of contemporary popular culture. RedOne first became known for his work with Lady Gaga, but he is a powerhouse producer who has worked with any number of major stars, East and West; his background and career epitomize the international flavor of today's music industry, as well as the convergence of cultures we have been discussing throughout this volume. For example, RedOne's 2016 megahit "Don't You Need Somebody" not only features an international array of guest performers, but was supported by a series of different clips produced for distribution in different regions of the world. The version produced for the Arab world in conjunction with MBC's Platinum Records, for example, features a segment in Arabic sung by Saudi performer Aseel Omran,[50] with a number of other Platinum Records stars appearing in the background. The song and its array of video clips are clearly designed to function (and to be marketed) as an instance of global culture.[51]

Along these same lines, one might mention the RedOne-produced "Exotic" (2013[52]) which teams up Cuban American rapper Pitbull (the self-proclaimed "Mr. Worldwide") and Indian singer/actress (and former Miss World pageant winner) Priyanka Chopra in a song that is again specifically intended to participate in the globalization of popular music. Chopra, a former Bollywood star who is now an American television star, is a perfect choice for the video, which features segments of her singing in Hindi, Bollywood-style, but which mostly combines Pitbull's rap with a basic electronic dance music matrix. There is actually very little that is truly exotic about the video—except for its overt emphasis on Chopra's looks, which might be taken as a classic example of the Orientalist presentation of the exotic Eastern woman. Of course, when culture and capitalism go global, the resultant homogenization leaves little room for the truly exotic. Indeed, the lyrics of the song specifically conflate various sites around the globe, including references to "Rio" and Pitbull's declaration that "from Morocco to Mumbai / Bollywood, Hollywood is all about the money. Cash!"

Such team-ups between Eastern and Western artists are becoming increasingly common amid the general globalization of the music industry. Egyptian star Tamer Hosny has recorded a number of video clips with Western artists, including Akon, Shaggy, and Snoop Dogg. His video with Snoop Dogg, "Si Al Sayed" (2013[53]), is particularly interesting because of the way it plays with a number of stereotypes about the Middle East. The title of the song refers to a stock character from Egyptian culture (deriving from Al-Sayyid Ahmad Abd al-Jawad, the patriarch figure from Mahfouz's Cairo Trilogy), a preening, super-macho male who thoroughly dominates and controls the women in his life. In the video (directed by Freitekh), Hosny plays himself as a man who fantasizes about dominating his woman in this way; unfortunately, the woman has other ideas, leading to some lighthearted play with Middle Eastern gender stereotypes, all of which is complicated by the presence of the American Snoop Dogg, whose persona in his own videos is somewhat like that of the Si Al Sayed character, but in a Western context. Indeed, Hosny almost seems to want to assume the Si Al Sayed role in the video to impress his visiting friend Snoop Dogg, so that the video as a whole reminds us that patriarchy is an international phenomenon, even if it is also one that is being increasingly challenged on a global scale. As Snoop Dogg says in one of his lines in the song, "The king is the king, whether East or West." All in all, though, this clip challenges the whole notion that, in personal relationships, men are kings and women are merely supporting players.

Figure 3.7 Tamer Hosny and guest performer Snoop Dogg are joined by a group of female backup dancers in the video clip for Hosny's "Si Al Sayed" (2013) (screen capture).

In another example of East-West fusion, Massari joins Assaf as the two enjoy themselves in the environs of Dubai in the video clip for "Roll with It" (2018[54]). This video is basically a tamed and watered-down version of the one for "Shisha," again drawing upon the reputation of Dubai as a locus for worldly pleasures, but perhaps in a way that would be more widely approved in the Middle East, de-emphasizing the women and the liquor and dropping the shisha. Indeed, only Massari is shown drinking what might be liquor, while the women (fully clad but in Western styles) who do appear are associated only with Massari, not with Assaf; in fact, the only time Assaf appears in the frame with a woman is in a brief shot in which he and Massari ride four-wheelers in the desert; a woman rides behind Massari on his vehicle, while Assaf rides alone.[55]

Assaf came to prominence as the winner of *Arab Idol* in 2013, an event that is chronicled in Hany Abu-Assad's 2015 film *The Idol*, which details the many difficulties faced by Assaf, as a Palestinian, in even getting to the competition. Assaf's victory in the competition was widely celebrated in the Middle East, where he became a sort of emblem of the Palestinian cause and champion of relatively traditional Arab values. By the time of "Roll with It," though, he is hanging with Massari in Dubai and living it up, seemingly having changed his style considerably, though carefully keeping his distance from the all-out decadence of Massari.

In "Roll with It," Massari sings in English (except for an occasional "habibi"),[56] with lyrics about dancing and sex that roughly replicate the lyrics of "Shisha." Assaf, meanwhile, performs entirely in Arabic, though the voice of Palestine here sings with a Moroccan accent that perhaps references the recent pop success of artists such as Lamjarred. The Arabic lyrics form a more conventional love song, as Assaf declares himself a mad lover, addicted to his habibi, but makes no overt mention of sex or, more that matter, of the body of his love. The overt attempt at East-West cultural fusion in "Roll with It" is quite clear. But the song and its video clip also attempt to fuse audiences and styles. Massari seems, by performing with Assaf, to want to strengthen his credibility as an Arab artist; Assaf, by performing with Massari, apparently seeks to increase his appeal to a more cosmopolitan audience by seeming hipper and more modern.[57]

Video clips, self-orientalism, and self-marketing

If "Roll with It" plays with the increasingly stereotypical association of Dubai with wealth and fun,[58] other Arab music videos play with other Orientalist stereotypes. For example, the video clip for "Eb'a Abelny" (2005, "Come See Me Sometime"[59]), by the Egyptian pop star Ruby, centrally depends upon classic Orientalist iconography. Here, the singer undulates via her own epileptic version of belly dancing while wearing a variety of quite revealing costumes that can only be described as postmodern reinscriptions of stereotypical Oriental dancing girl outfits—ranging from one that looks more like a mirrored go-go girl costume (but bearing some Oriental designs) to one in which her seemingly near-naked body is decorated with what appear to be Oriental designs in henna while she toys with a large python draped suggestively around her neck.[60] In the meantime, she performs in front of a series of backgrounds featuring classic Egyptian iconography, but updated with a decidedly postmodern look. For example, much of the video seems to be performed inside a stage set of an ancient Egyptian tomb—but it is most avowedly a stage set that calls attention to its artificiality, and not a real tomb.

In case there was any doubt about whether this video was just another case of postmodern pastiche of ancient Egyptian culture (albeit emanating from Egypt itself)—or whether it might be a straightforward declaration of Egyptian cultural pride in the illustrious past—Ruby followed this video clip in 2007 with a clip for the song "Mesheet Wara E7sasi" ("I Followed My Heart"[61]) that is even more blatantly postmodern (and self-orientalizing).[62] The song itself is pure electronic dance music, while Ruby's varied costumes are now mostly quite Western in appearance, and she is at points even accompanied by two women in Western dress playing violins. Pyramids, the Sphinx, and other ancient Egyptian iconography still reside in the background as Ruby performs the song (though now her dancing is more Western and has almost nothing to do with belly dancing). And now the ancient Egyptian icons are even more obviously stylized and artificial, mere postmodern simulacra and not authentic images.

One could, of course, argue that such videos represent a defiant resistance to the appropriation of Egyptian culture by the West. And the on-screen text that appears near the end of the clip (somewhat like an advertising slogan) might appear to support this reading: "Egypt is the source of civilization and the destination of the future," attributed to Sherif Sabri, the director of this video clip (and all of Ruby's clips). However, given the nature of the music and of the clip (and given the fact that this text is in English[63]), the implication of the video seems to be clear: however glorious its past, Egypt now needs to be thinking about moving into the future, with the future defined as Western-style modernization (and this video presented as evidence that Egypt can be just as modern as any nation, however much other cultures might associate it with antiquity). The slogan also serves as a sort of advertisement for Egyptian tourism, inviting Westerners to come visit. The video, then, is not a sign of resistance to the kind of thoroughgoing capitalist modernization (and commodification) that Jameson associates with postmodernist culture. It is, instead, an open declaration of an intention to participate in the postmodernist, global world of late capitalism. Ancient Egypt is here just as commodified as in Western videos, made just as much into a sort of visual advertising slogan.[64]

Arab music videos can appropriate and commodify other cultures as well. An excellent example can be found in the video clip for Wehbe's "Enta Tany" ("You Again," 2010[65]), in which the Lebanese singer performs in a world filled with a mixture of ancient Greek and ancient Roman images. No need to distinguish between the two, because every sort of image is fungible fodder for the postmodern, just as everything *Eastern* is interchangeable in the classic Orientalist view. Along these lines, one might note Egyptian Hisham Abbas's clip for "Habibi Dah" ("This Is My Love," 2001[66]), which features a guest performance by Indian singer Jayashree and which is filled with images from Indian culture. Similarly, Ahlam's performance of "Talqah" ("Bullet," 2016[67]) is accompanied by a clip that is filled with images from Indian culture—and that was made in conjunction with MBC's marketing push for its new Bollywood channel.

For our purposes, one of the most interesting examples of this sort of pastiche in Arab video clips can be found in Abbas's team-up with fellow Egyptian Hamied El Shaeri for "Einy" ("My Eye," 1997[68]). Here, in what is actually an extended dream sequence, the two singers dress throughout as American gangsters amid a barrage of stereotypical character types from American popular culture, set on a brightly colored street that looks like a postmodern pastiche of a street from a film set. This sort of cultural borrowing matches, in an Occidentalist way, the Orientalism of Western videos such as "Walk Like an Egyptian" or "Dark Horse." One could argue, in fact, that the entire phenomenon of Arab video clips represents a sort of Occidentalist cultural borrowing. But this situation also clearly demonstrates the difference in power relations that exists between Orientalism and Occidentalism, not only in terms of the historical realities of colonialism and late capitalism, but in terms of the realities of global popular culture, in which American culture exerts a far more powerful force than does Arab popular culture. Stock images from Hollywood film are easily recognizable to Arab audiences, but the reverse is not the case; in the West, only a very limited range of images (belly dancers, pyramids, camels, deserts) is available to indicate "Arabness."

The Ruby clips mentioned above, of course, indicate that Arab artists are not above playing on this limited range of images in their own video clips. Belly dancing is particularly important in Ruby's clips. However, when she broke onto the scene with her first video, for "Enta 3aref Leih" ("Do You Know Why," 2003[69]), in which she belly dances throughout, the performance was met with considerable controversy and criticism in the Middle East, though it also drew a great deal of positive attention. Here, Ruby writhes her way through the streets of Prague in a variety of colorful costumes (mostly Oriental, but one that is entirely Western) that make the European city (and its inhabitants, who seem oblivious to her presence in their midst) seem relatively drab in comparison. It is almost as if Ruby is in color, while the city and its inhabitants are in black and white. The implication seems clear: Ruby, the Oriental woman, is invested with a vitality and a sexual energy that are lacking in Europe, in what would appear to be a direct reinscription of the Orientalist stereotype of Europe needing to draw upon the exotic energies of the Orient to re-invigorate itself.

As with Ruby's later videos, then, the question that immediately arises is whether the video reclaims this belly-dancer imagery for the Middle Eastern culture from which it originally arose or whether the video simply performs the same kind of commodifying postmodern pastiche of that imagery that is found in Western videos. Is this a case of an Oriental woman defiantly seizing control of her own representation, or simply a case of an Oriental woman participating in her own commodification and stereotyping? The answer, of course, is a little bit of both, though Ruby's image seems to have been managed more by Sabry than by Ruby herself, who was, after all, only twenty-two years old in 2003, complicating the issue still further. One could argue that placing Ruby's belly dancing within the context of a European city calls attention to the way in which belly dancing has so frequently been appropriated as an image of feminine sexual allure in the West; Ruby does generally look out of place in the city, perhaps suggesting that the use of belly-dancer imagery in Western videos is inappropriate. Ultimately, however, this video seems to have little subversive force, and it is difficult to imagine this video presenting any real challenge to the stereotypical image of belly dancers as presented in Western videos. If anything, placing Ruby's belly dancing completely outside of Middle Eastern surroundings would seem to be just another example of postmodern pastiche, of the use of images without concern for the original context in which they occurred.

Ruby's follow-up video clip, for "Leih Beydary Keda" ("Why Is He Hiding His Feelings Like This," 2004[70]), again consists of little more than a series of shots of

Ruby singing and belly dancing in a variety of costumes, this time with a very plain background that consists of things such as a screen simply displaying her name. In this video, however, her costumes are entirely modern and Western, and her belly dancing is almost entirely stripped of exoticism. She's just an ordinary, modern girl-next-door, belly dancing in a workout suit, a frilly red dress, and a short-skirted college-girl outfit. Ruby's belly dancing is rather mundane and amateurish in all of her videos. It is the kind of dancing, as Elmessiri notes, that might be "practiced by ordinary girls at home, for fun. This acts to remove the barrier separating daily life from belly dancing—normalization of risqué activity" (166). Ultimately, then, for Elmessiri, Ruby represents not an image of the exotic, hyper-sexualized Oriental woman, but something much more domestic (if equally sexist): she conveys the message that "girls are cute and cuddly, receptive and playful" (169).

This domestication of belly dancing could be seen as striking a blow against Orientalist exotification of belly dancing. However, Elmessiri (who is highly critical of the whole genre of the video clip) sees Ruby's video clips simply as a reflection of globalization and the standardized stripping away of genuine context that accompanies it. Hany Darwish is even more harsh in his criticism of Ruby, to whom he refers as "a porn star who compensates for lack of vocal talent with her physical presence" (261). Recalling director Sabri's background in advertising, Darwish notes that Sabri's advertising campaigns often employed a Westernized version of belly dancing that sought to "remold the Orientalist image of Oriental women by producing European clones" (260). He then argues that Sabri carries the same techniques over into his video clips, especially the ones for Ruby, who simply becomes another commodity for which the clips serve as advertisements. "For Sabri," Darwish concludes, "the female body becomes, unabashedly and frankly, the ideal marketable product" (262).

Darwish, an Egyptian journalist, is certainly correct about the link between video clips and advertisements, though his squeamish horror of the female body might somewhat undermine his analysis—as when he argues that the relatively tame and wholesome (but admittedly still sexually charged) clip for "Leih Beydary Keda" "kills off the imagination of the viewer by presenting him with all the known dramatic ploys of pornography" (262). Of course, what is considered tame and wholesome and what is considered pornographic is a matter of both individual inclination and cultural expectation, but this video seems especially tame even in comparison with other videos by Ruby—and certainly in comparison with some of the videos by Lebanese pop stars such as Wehbe or Fares. One thing for certain, though, is that all of Ruby's videos do appear to market her (and the image of sex-infused wholesomeness that she represents) as a commodity, suggesting that these videos participate in the global system of late capitalism, rather than offering resistance to it.

Along these lines, one might also consider the early videos of Lebanese star Maria Nalbandian (generally known merely as "Maria"), beginning with the clip for "Elaab" ("Play," 2005[71]), which revolves around Maria's auditioning for a television commercial for a line of products with the brand name "Maria." The link between Maria's performance in the video and the marketing of a line of products of the same name thus makes it quite clear that Maria herself is essentially being marketed as a product—complete with its own animé-style logo. The video clip for "Betekdeb Alaya" ("You Lie to Me," 2005[72]) reinforces this same connection. Here, Maria plays a seemingly ordinary schoolgirl, vying for the attention of her sexy male teacher, yet the video is also (inexplicably) filled with images of more products from the "Maria" line, including candies and even the school uniforms worn by Maria and the other girls at the school.

Hala Al Turk and the making of a child star

Such examples demonstrate just how thoroughly the music business really is a *business*, its products inexorably caught up in the commodifying tendencies of the global system of late capitalism. They also show an unbothered acceptance of commodification that seems a bit troubling—especially when this celebration of consumerism is extended to children. Of course, in the music industry (East or West), children themselves can become marketable products, as the case of Maria shows, though Maria herself was twenty by the time her "schoolgirl" videos were released. However, one of the rising stars of Arab music is young Hala Al Turk (often simply billed as "Hala"), from Bahrain, who has been on the scene since she was literally a child. Her recording of "Live in the Moment" (which features main lyrics in Arabic with a catchy chorus in English) was a major hit (2015[73]). Hala's rise to stardom has been fueled, meanwhile, by her popularity on the youth-dominated YouTube, where the video clip for this song (recorded when she was still twelve years old) scored more than twelve million views in three months. As of this writing, the clip has garnered more than 100 million views. What is striking about this entirely wholesome (from a Western point of view) clip is how completely familiar it would look to Western viewers,

Figure 3.8 Screen capture from the video clip for Hala Al Turk's "Live in the Moment" (2015), with the singer joined by a group of backup dancers who might be at home on America's Disney or Nickelodeon channels.

as Hala sings and dances with a well-coordinated group of backup dancers, all looking like ordinary Western teens or pre-teens and wearing informal Western-style dress. As if to emphasize global and cross-cultural communication, one dancer wears a T-shirt reading "A Wonderful World" in English, while another wears a T-shirt reading the same thing, but in Arabic ("3alam jameel").

Hala began appearing on Arab television at the tender age of seven, winning her episode of the children's talent competition show with the interesting mixed English-Arabic name *Star Sghar* ("Little Stars"); she then gained widespread attention when she appeared at the age of eight as a contestant on the (inaugural) 2011 season of *Arabs Got Talent*, in which she advanced through several rounds. *Arabs Got Talent*, an entry in Simon Cowell's global *Got Talent* franchise, provided excellent exposure for the young performer, who recorded her first video clip—for the consumerist fantasy "Baba Nezal Ma3ashah" ("Daddy Got His Salary"[74])—while still eight. That clip, as of this writing, has nearly 120 million views on YouTube. Her Disneyesque 2013 video clip for "Happy Happy"[75] was her biggest YouTube hit to date, with over 350 million views as of this writing. By 2015 she returned to *Arabs Got Talent* as a celebrity guest star, performing "Live in the Moment."

From age seven to age twelve, Hala evolved (under the guidance of her record-producer father) from an adorable little kid, performing simple, kidlike songs in humorously cartoonish video clips, to a polished, professional performer. She has some talent and even more charisma, but she's a manufactured product, crafted by the same kind of Culture Industry machine that cranked out Disney girls such as Britney Spears, Christina Aguilera, Miley Cyrus, and

Selena Gomez. She herself has cited Nickelodeon product Ariana Grande as her most important show business role model. She's apparently a big fan of Justin Bieber as well, performing a rendition of his "Baby" on the weekly MBC news/talk program *Fi Osbu3* ("In a Week") shortly after her run on *Arabs Got Talent*. By the time of her much more elaborately produced 2016 video clip for "Why I'm So Afraid,"[76] a song performed entirely in English, she was looking all grown up, with lots of makeup, her Western-style marketing going full speed ahead. This marketing has, capitalism being what it is, included an appearance in a television commercial for the UAE-based Life 'N' Rich brands of household products—in which she acts entirely in English.[77]

In 2015, Hala received widespread tabloid-like coverage when a photo emerged of her suggestively pressing her posterior against a full-sized poster of a male singer—exactly in the region of his private parts. The English-language version of the Arab news website *Albawaba* Wehbe, none of which has seemed to slow her rise to fame. In fact, you couldn't buy better advertising.

Hala, in short, has established a widespread presence in the Arab media, and her handlers and promoters at MBC have done a good job of keeping her in the public eye, even to the point of airing some of her family's private controversies on the Arab version of the *Entertainment Tonight* (*ET*) entertainment news magazine. Early in Hala's career, her parents divorced, with her father Mohamed Al Turk soon remarrying to Moroccan singer (and former *Arab Idol* runner-up) Dounia Batma. Meanwhile, Hala's biological mother, Mona al Saber, complained that she had been excluded from Hala's life and cut off from all communication with her—all of which made for a lively segment of *ET*.[78] All publicity is good publicity, available to be converted into advertising.

Collectively, the video clips discussed in this chapter demonstrate the extent to which recent mainstream Arab pop music has largely evolved according to Western models. As such, the form in general is thoroughly commodified and commercialized, though there are exceptions—including examples such as Haifa Wehbe's "Baddi 3ich," in which Western-inflected ideas pose political challenges to traditional Middle Eastern ideas. Meanwhile, in the next chapter, we discuss Arab and Arab diasporic rap music, which has also been clearly influenced by its Western predecessors, but which quite often maintains a strongly oppositional energy, suggesting that being influenced by Western cultural forms does not necessarily imply acceptance of dominant Western ideologies.

4

"They Can't Use My Music to Advertise for Coca-Cola": Arab and Arab Diasporic Rap and the Resistance to Postmodernism

The Arab Spring revolutions of 2010 and 2011 were, like all such events, the culmination and confluence of a complex variety of forces and historical tendencies. However, one important triggering event that helped to kick-start these revolutions can be located in the work of the Tunisian rapper Hamada Ben Amor, better known as "El Général."[1] In December 2010, El Général released a song entitled "Rayes Lebled" ("The President of the Country"[2]) that sharply criticized the then Tunisian president Zine El Abidine Ben Ali. This video added fuel to growing protests that soon swelled into revolution. El Général then released a second song, entitled "Tunis Ya Bladna" (2011, "Tunisia Our Country"[3]) on social media, leading to his immediate arrest. He was soon released, but only after pledging to perform no more political songs. Nevertheless, his protest music remained an inspiration for the forces opposed to President Ben Ali, who was forced to flee to Saudi Arabia only a few days after El Général's release. "Rayes Lebled" became an anthem of what came to be known as the "Jasmine Revolution." However, in 2014, El Général released "Rayes Lebled 2"[4] charging that the revolution had not achieved its goals and that conditions in the country had not significantly improved since the ouster of the former president. In a similar way, the rap song "#Jan25" (2011[5]), by the Syrian American rapper Omar Offendum and others (including Iraqi Canadian rapper The Narcicyst), has been seen as an important contribution to raising awareness in the West of the Egyptian Revolution that followed soon after the Tunisian one.[6]

Arab hip-hop, postmodernism, and globalization

Such stories of politicized music, of course, contrast strongly with the situation of much of the Arab popular music discussed in the previous chapter, which has become highly commercialized, often showing a strong influence of Western musical models. The same, of course, is also true to an extent of rap music in the Arab world, though Torie Rose DeGhett is certainly right to emphasize that "rap that belongs to the Middle Eastern and Arab traditions is not to be mistaken for simply homage to or continuation of North American rap but, rather, is a new genre that brings its own purposes and influences to hip hop" ("Record" 95).

Hip-hop is, in fact, quite well established in the Middle East (and, especially, in North Africa[7]), though some Arab rappers are certainly more Westernized (and commercialized) than others. For example, one of the most visible rappers in the Arab world is also one of the least original—and least political—though the latter fact is probably a key to his success in the world of Arab media. We are referring here to Saudi Arabia's Qusai (formerly known as "Don Legend" when he began his career performing in the United States), whose hosting of the television program *Arabs Got Talent* indicates his mainstream status. Meanwhile, the overt product placement of Braun shavers and Pepsi Cola in his video clip for the song "Yalla" (2012[8]) indicates just how thoroughly conscripted within the capitalist system his work really is. Meanwhile, the lyrics of this song (performed half in English and half in Arabic) call for change in a particularly nonmilitant and nonthreatening way, taming the spirit of hip-hop and making it safe for popular consumption.

Qusai seems to want to present himself as a nonthreatening America-friendly Arab, who has released much of his work with English titles. As he puts it in

Figure 4.1 Lebanese singer Farah shown at the end of the video clip for Qusai's song "Yalla" (2012), openly acknowledging the clip's affiliation with Braun shavers and Pepsi Cola.

his song "Salam" (from his 2008 album *Don Legend the Kamelion*), "I represent the Middle East to the fullest—with no bullets." His "message" (or lack thereof) is in many ways epitomized in the collaborative song "Arab World Unite" (2011[9]), produced by Bahrain's DJ Outlaw (Mohammed Hasan) and featuring a collection of different performers from around the Arab world, with Qusai playing the lead role. In this song, released on Qusai's album *The Inevitable Change* (2012), the various performers (alternating between English and Arabic) unleash a continuous stream of clichés, delivering a jumbled announcement of their support for some vague and undefined notion of Arab unity, while many of them also contradictorily announce their pride in their individual nations. The song also contains a vague hostility toward the Arab Spring revolutions as a divisive force in the Arab world. It begins, in fact, with Qusai's denunciation of the revolutions as the work of agitators whose project is akin to that of the devil:

> (2011) what a start
> The year has begun by tearing us apart.
> (Hey, Arabs!) The Middle East caught in the middle,
> (Tempted by) the devil, confusing it with work of a rebel.[10]

These lines contrast dramatically with the support for the revolutions shown in the work of Offendum and El Général (or Libyan rapper Ibn Thabit, whose music helped to topple Muammar Gaddafi). Such rappers are key examples that show the ongoing political power of popular music in the Arab world, however strong the impetus to contain the subversive power of music within the confines of the commercial. This is especially the case with rap music, and Arab rappers (including rappers who belong to the Arab diaspora), taking their cue from earlier American rappers, have often seen their music as a weapon of political activism. Meanwhile, as Hisham Aidi notes, the "rap loop" of communication between the protestors of Tahrir Square and the rappers who performed on "#Jan25" "galvanized youth on both sides of the Atlantic," even as he warns that this effect should not be exaggerated (223). Similarly, Pennycook and Mitchell have seen rap music as lending itself particularly well to transnational flows, arguing that the worldwide vitality of rap music is a key example of "local traditions being pulled toward global cultural forms" (30).

While some Arab rap music has become relatively slick and commercialized (such as the work of Qusai) and other highly commercial Arab musical artists have performed with American rappers (such as Tamer Hosny's collaborations with Shaggy and Snoop Dogg), much contemporary Arab rap retains the political urgency that informed the early growth of American rap music. This is especially the case when rap has engaged with the Palestinian cause, as when artists such as Palestinian Tamer Nafar, British Palestinian Shadia Mansour, and British Iraqi Lowkey have used their music as a platform for delivering pro-Palestinian political messages. And this delivery has been largely successful, gaining considerable exposure in the West, while presenting the Palestinian position in ways that seem familiar to Western audiences otherwise accustomed to thinking of Palestinians as cultural others, or even merely as terrorists. Indeed, as Ted Swedenburg notes, Palestinian rap has arguably "received far more attention in the West to date than any other musical genre from Palestine" (17). Moreover, as Swedenburg further notes, only Palestinian rap that has been devoted to the political struggle for Palestinian liberation has been able to attract any sort of serious critical attention (18). If one views the recent decline of American rap music into formulaic celebrations of ostentatious wealth and illicit drugs within the context of the flagrant sexual objectification of women largely as a consequence of the general commodification of culture under late capitalism, then one can see the work of political rappers such as Mansour and Nafar both as evidence that the process of modernization that leads to late capitalism is less advanced in the Arab world and as evidence of resistance to this process.

Jameson's theorization of postmodernism as the "cultural logic" of late capitalism is centrally informed by an understanding of the long historical process of capitalist modernization that began with the Renaissance and the colonization of the Americas. A central element of this process of modernization is the growing commodification of every aspect of human life, including even those aspects (such as love or the aesthetic) that might at first seem opposed to this reduction of all aspects of social life to various forms of economic exchange. This process, for Jameson, is a hegemonic one within the context of late capitalism, a phenomenon with an inherently global tendency. Indeed, the process of cultural convergence and transnational cultural flow that is the central concern of this volume is crucial evidence of the globalizing tendencies of postmodernism. There are, of course, exceptions to this commodification of culture under late capitalism, and Jameson himself has elsewhere identified certain marginal forms of cultural production as potentially interesting sites of opposition to the global cultural hegemony of postmodernism, producing "authentic" works of culture that are not mere commodities:

> The only authentic cultural production today has seemed to be that which can draw on the collective experience of marginal pockets of the social life of the world system: black literature and blues, British working-class rock, women's literature, gay literature, the *roman québécois*, the literature of the Third World;

and this production is possible only to the degree to which these forms of collective life or collective solidarity have not yet been fully penetrated by the market and by the commodity system. (*Signatures* 23–24)

Rap music (and hip-hop culture as a whole) would at first glance appear to be a key example of precisely this kind of "marginal pocket" of cultural production. In addition, the work of pioneering hip-hop artists such as Afrika Bambaataa and Grandmaster Flash can be seen as a self-conscious effort to explore alternative African American cultural identities that avoid conscription by the mainstream culture.[11] Hip-hop would then be a legitimate example of the kind of "subculture" famously described by Dick Hebdige in relation to phenomena such as British punk culture, particularly in its role as a way for young African Americans to seize control of their own cultural identities.[12] Of course, as Hebdige has noted, even the most radical subcultures have a tendency to fall into the gravitational well of commodification presented by the mainstream: "Youth cultural styles may begin by offering symbolic challenges, but they must inevitably end by establishing new sets of conventions; by creating new commodities, new industries, or rejuvenating old ones" (96). In short, the very countercultural forces that were originally meant to oppose the dehumanizing and spiritually impoverishing power of the system of capitalist commodification themselves tend to be co-opted by that system and to become a part of it.

The process of mainstreaming that Hebdige describes in relation to subcultures in general provides an excellent framework within which to understand the path taken by American hip-hop from its roots in the streets of the Bronx in the 1970s, to the angry and highly political (but also widely popular) output of key rappers and rap groups of the 1990s (Tupac, Public Enemy, N.W.A.), to the branching of more recent rap into slickly commercial work (Jay-Z, Diddy, Kanye West) on the one hand and crassly commodified vulgarity (2 Live Crew, Lil Wayne, Plies) on the other.[13] Many vectors are at work in the subsequent process of the depoliticization (and increased commercialization) of American hip-hop, though surely the best way to understand the overall history of the mainstreaming of rap music is provided by Jameson's reminders of the tendency of *all* culture to become commodified in the postmodernist era of late capitalism.

In some cases, American political hip-hop has expressly attempted to establish cultural connections to the Middle East (in addition to the obvious African connections), as in the case of Lakim Shabazz, whose 1990 song "The Lost Tribe of Shabazz"[14] draws upon the Nation of Islam doctrine that Shabazz, an ancient prophet from Mecca, led his primal tribe out of the Arabian peninsula and into Africa, to become the ancestors of modern African American Muslims.[15]

The lyrics of this song combine with the visual images of its music video (which juxtapose images from ancient Egypt and the contemporary Muslim world with images from modern [African] America) to suggest that African Americans (and especially Black Muslims) have deep cultural roots in the Muslim world of the Middle East and North Africa and thus maintain important contemporary connections to those societies as well. Indeed, the key element of the song, repeated many times, is the line "*Our* people will survive America," which is accompanied by cuts between African Americans and Middle Eastern images such as Arabs on camels in the desert. The "our" is emphasized to make clear that the song is trying to make common cause between Arabs and African Americans.

Such connections—along with such facts as the important influence of the Nation of Islam and its offshoot, the Five Percenters,[16] on the evolution of American hip-hop—also help to explain why the entire hip-hop lifestyle has proved attractive to young Arab Americans in the past few decades, and Arab American hip-hop itself has involved some of the same variants as African American hip-hop, with young Arab Americans often identifying with African American culture as arising from a cultural position similar to their own. Thus, while Arab diasporic rappers in America such as Offendum have retained a strong political connection to the Arab world, performers such as French Montana have exploited their Arab roots to make themselves seem more colorful and exotic, all the while bragging about their vast incomes and their prowess with women in a mode as debased as that of any contemporary African American rapper.[17] For example, in addition to his performance in support of Massari in "Shisha," Montana is also featured on the video clip "A.W.A." (2014[18]), by the Algerian-born rapper Lacrim. "A.W.A." stands for "Arabs with Attitude," echoing the well-known American gangsta rap group N.W.A. ("Niggaz wit Attitude"). But this song and clip otherwise have very little to do with the politically charged music of N.W.A. In his sequence in the video, Montana brags about his wild hip-hop lifestyle and about how he gets "Ayrab money." He also declares himself a "fly rich young nigga," aligning himself with both Arab and African American ethnicity and culture, but in a way that surely has little to do with genuine political solidarity in the struggle.[19]

Rappers of the Arab diaspora

In addition to Arab American (or Muslim American rappers) there are several important Arab rappers who live in the West but who deal primarily with cultural identities and political issues in the Arab world and whose principal audience is therefore located in the Arab world. Diasporic Arab performers such as Offendum and Mansour thus not only follow in the footsteps of politically engaged American rappers but also look back on the important tradition of diasporic Arab poetry known as *Shi'r al-'Arabī fī al-mahjar*. With Gibran Khalil Gibran serving as the best-known example in North America, the poets of this diaspora emigrated from the Arab world (mostly to the Americas and especially from Syria and Lebanon) from the late nineteenth to the mid-twentieth centuries. While these poets generally remained permanently abroad, they retained a strong sense of connection to their Arab roots, and their poetry was extremely popular and highly respected in the Arab world.

Offendum, whose family originally came from Syria, was born in Saudi Arabia (in 1981), but moved to the United States at an early age.[20] He grew up in Washington, DC, and was educated (in architecture) at the University of Virginia, where he began to perform as part of the hip-hop duo The N.O.M.A.D.S, along with Sudanese American rapper Mr. Tibbz. After graduation, Offendum moved to Los Angeles, where he worked as an architect for a decade. He now dedicates much of his time to his creative pursuits as a rapper, poet, and designer, as well as to his efforts as a political activist—which are extensively integrated into his artistic work. Offendum overtly identifies as both an Arab and an American and has stated in an interview that his development as an artist was crucially affected by the 9/11 bombings, which he felt placed him under special scrutiny as an Arab living in America, giving him both the opportunity and the responsibility to speak out against misrepresentations of Arabs (Davy). This phase of his career culminated in the release of his first album, *SyrianamericanA*, in 2010. Here, Offendum raps in both English and Arabic and draws upon elements of both Eastern and Western culture—as when the chorus of the track "New Orient" employs a speeded-up sampling of Nina Simone's classic "Feeling Good" (1965) or when "Damascus" quotes lines from Syrian poet Nizar Qabbani's "Damascene Poem."[21]

Such allusions are a big part of what DeGhett sees as the "scholarly eye" with which Offendum seeks to "convey the complexity of Arab-American identity" ("Hip-Hop Academia").[22] Indeed, the songs of Offendum's initial album are already both highly intellectual and highly political, addressing issues related to the immigrant experience in America and to relations between the United States and the Middle East. However, he has gained his greatest visibility (and has clearly grown as an artist) from his reactions to the 2011 Arab Spring uprisings and to the subsequent spread of these uprisings to Syria. The video clip for the collaboration "#Jan25" features a series of segments of Al Jazeera's televised coverage of the Egyptian Revolution, and the song itself begins with a portion written and performed by Offendum, the first line of which is a reference to the classic 1970 Gil Scott-Heron song "The Revolution Will Not Be Televised." This reference links the revolutionary spirit of the January 25 revolution in Egypt to the one that informed 1960s political activism in the United States (especially the Black Power movement), and the song then moves into what is essentially an homage to the "spirit of resistance" of the Egyptian people in the face of oppression, a spirit that Offendum has identified in another interview[23] as similar to the spirit that animates hip-hop itself.

Not surprisingly, given his Syrian background, Offendum has been particularly strident in his support for the Syrian Revolution and his opposition to the regime of Syrian president Bashar al-Assad. In the video for #Syria (2012[24]), a sort of companion piece to #Jan25, news footage from the Syrian revolt provides the background to Offendum's English-language rap in support of the revolution, punctuated by the Arabic slogan of the revolution, "Alsha3b Yureed Isqaa6 al-Nithaam" ("The People Want to Overthrow the Regime"), which the crowds in the footage chant and which Offendum repeats. At the end of the song, however, Offendum switches to Arabic and raps the words of the protest anthem "Yalla Erhal Ya Bashar" ("Hurry Up and Leave, Bashar"), which has been attributed to Ibrahim Qashoush, who was found murdered, his vocal cords ripped out, after having performed the song at a protest rally in the Syrian city of Hama.[25] The song's lyrics pull no punches in their impatience to see the end of the Bashar regime:

> Bashar, you liar,
> Fuck you, and fuck your rhetoric.
> Freedom is now at the door
> So go.
> Maher,[26] you coward, you agent of Satan,[27]
> The Syrian people will not be humiliated.
> So go.
> Bashar, fuck you and fuck anyone who cheers you on.
> To tell the truth, I'm disgusted to even look at you.
> So go.
> Bashar, enough stalling.
> If you come to Hama, your blood will flow.
> Your atrocities are not forgiven.
> So go.

Unfortunately, Bashar did not go, and the Syrian Revolution did not achieve its ends, developments Offendum addresses in his 2015 song "Crying Shame."[28] Here, Offendum expresses his frustration at events in Syria and at the seeming inability of Syrians to find a viable solution to their political morass, fragmented into competing factions and united only by "our ability to seek the wrong advisors" or to move beyond the legacy of colonialism, meanwhile trying the find ways to blame all their problems on Israel. But he also has harsh words for the Western media, which depict conditions in Syria in a way that makes the inhabitants there look cartoonishly unable to handle their own problems, fanatically devoted to seeking extreme and violent solutions. Noting the "patronizing marathons of half truth on the news," he suggests to Americans (referring to Bashar's violent attacks on his own people) that "if Obama bombed America, you'd probably be extreme too."

Offendum has been very active in collaborations with other Arab rappers, especially his close friend and associate Yassin Alsalman, the Iraqi Canadian journalist and rapper who has generally performed under the name The Narcicyst (generally now abbreviated as "Narcy.") In addition to #Jan25, Offendum and The Narcicyst have performed together extensively. In 2007, for example, Offendum and The Narcicyst combined with Arab diasporic rappers Excentrik and Ragtop to form the collective Arab Summit on the mixtape *Fear of an Arab Planet*, whose title directly references the American political hip-hop classic album *Fear of a Black Planet* (1990), by Public Enemy, a group that has

Figure 4.2 Syrian American rapper Omar Offendum performs in the video clip for his song "Crying Shame" (2015).

been particularly influential on Arab hip-hop culture in general.[29] These titles derive from the notion of white Western fear of the Other, whether the other be black or Arab.

The Narcicyst has also identified directly with African American culture. In the video clip for his song "P.H.A.T.W.A." (which appears on his self-titled 2009 album, along with such tracks as "The Last Arabs," which features Offendum), Narcy walks through an airport and complains to his African American friend that, at least in airports, Arabs are now more marginalized than blacks.[30] "Iraq is the new black," says the rapper in this song.[31] Then again, The Narcicyst has also engaged in dialogue with African American hip-hop culture in "The Real Arab Money," his angry response to African American (Muslim) rapper Busta Rhymes's "Arab Money," which we noted in Chapter 2.

In addition to Offendum, The Narcicyst has also collaborated with numerous other rappers from the Arab diaspora. For example, in "Hamdulillah" (also from the 2009 self-titled album, then again featured on the soundtrack to the 2015 film *Furious 7*) he teams up with Mansour, widely known as "The First Lady of Arabic Hip Hop." "Hamdulillah" makes references to Palestine and Iraq, but is one of Narcy's least political tracks, serving largely as a hymn to humility and brotherly love.[32] Mansour herself serves as a backup artist on an unusually large number of songs, often singing rather than rapping, and switching freely between Arabic and English in her performances.

Hip-hop culture in general tends to be especially collaborative, but Mansour's frequent appearances as a "featured" artist on the recordings of others point toward the especially collaborative nature of Arab diasporic rap. Indeed, this form of musical production often operates via a collective mode of production similar to that associated by Hamid Naficy with the "accented" cinema of diasporic filmmakers, including Palestinian ones. Similarly, Arab diasporic rap is often produced via the "interstitial" mode of production that Naficy also associates with accented cinema. According to Naficy, "it would be inaccurate to characterize accented filmmakers as marginal, as scholars are prone to do, for they do not live and work on the peripheries of society or the film and media industries. They are situated inside and work in the interstices of both" (46). Of course, music is less expensive to produce than are films, so the production of Arab rap music can be more informal and marginal than the production of feature films, but it is certainly the case that the leading Arab diasporic rappers are actually quite well known, even if in a more limited circle of followers than those who listen to the top mainstream pop stars, East or West.

Mansour is probably best known for the 2011 single "Al Kufiyyeh 3arabeyyeh" ("The Kufiyyeh Is Arab"[33]), in which she declares the traditional kufiyyeh scarf to be an Arab cultural tradition—in angry response to her discovery that an American company was manufacturing and marketing kufiyyehs as Israeli symbols. Her point, of course, is really much larger than the kufiyyeh itself and has to do more with the general appropriation of Arab (especially Palestinian) culture by an Israel that otherwise has often seemed determined to eradicate that culture. In this song, incidentally, Mansour is supported by a featured performance by African American rapper M-1 of the politically engaged rap duo "dead prez."

Mansour, who was born in England and has lived there all her life, nevertheless strongly identifies with the Palestinian cause and has focused on it in much of her work. This sense of belonging to two different cultures might explain the particularly international scope of her work—and especially of her collaborations. In addition to her work with The Narcicyst on "Hamdulillah," she has been backed by Offendum on her song "Lazem Netghayar" ("We Have to Change," 2013[34]). Here, using the Israeli destruction of Palestinian culture as a key example of man's inhumanity to man, Mansour urgently calls for human beings to change the way they treat each other so that we can all move together into a better future. But Mansour also criticizes Arab societies for their own stubborn resistance to change, declaring her determination to continue to fight for the liberation of Palestine from Israeli oppression and the liberation of the Arab world from the shackles of its own backward mindset.

One of Mansour's most effective performances as a featured artist occurs in her backing of black British rapper Logic on "So Serious" (2011[35]), a politically charged declaration of righteousness that includes a number of Palestinian images. She has also collaborated multiple times with Chile's Ana Tijoux, who is herself an inherently international artist, having been born in France while her Chilean parents were there in exile during the Pinochet regime in their home country. For example, in "Somos Sur" ("We Are the South," 2014[36]), Tijoux raps in Spanish and Mansour appears as a featured artist rapping in Arabic. The song is an expression of international anti-imperial solidarity, as is emphasized in the accompanying video clip, which features both Chileans and Palestinians dancing and wearing traditional costumes (including, in the latter case, kufiyyehs). Mansour's work also connects with Latin America via her appearance as a featured artist on the song "Too Much,"[37] by Lowkey (born "Kareem Dennis," in Britain, to a British father and an Iraqi mother). This song expresses solidarity with Venezuela and (especially) Cuba as objects of US neo-imperial domination.

Tamer Nafar and DAM: Palestinian rap

Nevertheless, Mansour's principal focus remains on Palestine, as is certainly the case with Nafar, the pioneering rapper who began rapping at the end of the 1990s, when the form was still extremely marginal in the Middle East. Nafar was initially inspired by American rap and was a particular fan of Tupac Shakur during his early engagement with rap.[38] Originally loosely aligned with Zionist rapper Subliminal and rapping in Hebrew, as well as in English and Arabic, Nafar has seemed to grow more coherent in his political position over time, beginning largely in the antiauthoritarian spirit of hip-hop but then moving into a more specifically pro-Palestinian mode. Nafar's best-known work has been produced as part of the rap group DAM (Arabic—and Hebrew—for "blood"), which consists of Nafar, his brother Suhell, and their friend Mahmoud Jreri. Initially producing a variety of kinds of songs, DAM first drew major attention with their single "Meen Erhabi" ("Who's the Terrorist?"[39]), which responded to the beginning of the Second Intifada in September 2000 and which featured each member of the group rapping one verse, with each verse centering on the typical characterization of Palestinians as terrorists and arguing that the Israelis who have taken the Palestinians' land are the true terrorists. This song drew major attention in the Western media and led to a European tour for the group. The song's Arabic lyrics include a controversial comparison of Palestine's Israeli occupiers to both Nazis and rapists, reading in English translation as:

> Democracy?
> Actually, it's more like Nazism!
> Your countless raping of the Arabs' soul
> Finally impregnated it,
> Gave birth to your child.
> His name is Suicide Bomber.
> And then you call him a terrorist?

In 2003, Nafar was featured in the documentary *Channels of Rage*, which detailed his break with Subliminal over political differences and ended with the outbreak of the Second Intifada. In 2006, DAM recorded a formal album, *Ihdaa* ("Dedication"), which increased their global visibility and led to performances at music festivals around the world. They were also prominently featured in the 2008 documentary *Slingshot Hip Hop* (directed by Palestinian American director Jackie Salloum), which examines the Palestinian hip-hop scene, clearly placing the group at the center of that scene.[40] A number of other Palestinian rappers also appear in the documentary, including Mohammed Farra and his group Palestinian Rapperz (PR), Mahmoud Shalabi, female duo Arapeyat, and singer-rapper Abeer Zinati.

Much of the work of Nafar and DAM is (understandably) angry and strident, motivated by a desire to speak out for the Palestinian cause, though, as Swedenburg argues, they (as well as other Palestinian rap groups, such as Ramallah Underground and G-Town) also deserve respect for their facility as rap artists, apart from their political message (23). Nafar and DAM have also sometimes turned to humor to deliver their message in a lighter vein, as in the song "Mama I Fell in Love with a Jew"[41] which appears on their second album, *Nudbok Al Amar* ("Dabke on the Moon," 2012). Meanwhile, in a recent solo effort, Nafar has responded to the endorsement of the products of Israeli company SodaStream (whose machines allow the home preparation of carbonated drinks and are manufactured in Israeli-occupied Palestinian territory) by American actress Scarlett Johansson with the humorous song (performed in English) "Scarlett Johansson Has Gas" (2014[42]).

Nafar also stars in the 2016 film *Junction 48*, declared by celebrity cultural critic and philosopher Slavoj Žižek, in April of 2016, to be "the best film of the last twelve months." Directed by award-winning Israeli director Udi Aloni (who also directed the 2002 documentary *Local Angel*, which featured DAM, as well as the video clip for the DAM song "Innocent Criminals"[43]), *Junction 48* was co-written by Nafar and Oren Moverman. The film's protagonist, Kareem, is a Palestinian rap star played by Nafar and is clearly based on many of Nafar's own experiences. The film is in many ways reminiscent of the 2002 Eminem vehicle *8 Mile*, though it is also strongly rooted in the special experience of Palestinians living within Israel. For example, the confrontations of Kareem and his friends with Israeli police and Palestinian drug dealers are a key element of the film. Meanwhile, Kareem's girlfriend Manar (played by Samar Qupty) is also a crucial character, and a chief concern of the film is her special experience as a Muslim woman. For example, in one sequence, she allows her likeness to be used on a poster advertising an upcoming hip-hop concert, leading her family to threaten her with physical violence if she undermines their "honor" by performing in the concert, which she ultimately does not do. The liberation of young Palestinians, the film makes clear, will require a victory over both Israeli prejudice against Arabs and the Arabs' own prejudice against anything that threatens their conventions and traditions.

This incident from the film is clearly based on one, related in *Slingshot Hip Hop*, in which Zinati was scheduled to perform in a high-profile concert

Figure 4.3 Tamer Nafar and Samar Qupty perform in the 2016 film *Junction 48*.

with DAM, but was forced to withdraw after her cousins threatened her and her parents with violence should she appear in the concert. This kind of experience is typical of the prejudice sometimes faced by women rap performers in the Arab world. When an interview (primarily in Arabic) with Mansour was posted by Samar Media,[44] many of those who responded in the comments thread complained angrily (in Arabic) about what they saw as the impropriety of a woman doing what Mansour does. One comment declared threateningly to Mansour that "if Saladin were alive today you wouldn't live for one more second. Here you are following the Jews and the Christians with the shit you are doing and you want Palestine to be victorious?" Another commenter simply declared, "You are a hypocrite and an apostate," while another advised her that she would be better off to veil herself. Another, commenting on Mansour's status as the "First Lady of Arab Hip Hop," simply stated, "First Lady of Whores," while another adopted the same approach, proclaiming that "Palestine needs real fighters and not a whore."

Given this situation, it is perhaps not surprising that Nafar, like *Junction 48*, has made women's rights a key concern of his work, in addition to his concern with the Palestinian situation. Thus, in his Arabic spoken-word video "Bafakir Ar7al" ("Thinking of Leaving," 2017[45]), Nafar complains of being hassled at the airport merely because he is Palestinian, as well as mocks Arabs for boasting about how "we invented this and we invented that," when in fact their main invention was boasting about how "we invented this and we invented that." Further, he excoriates Arabs for being so proud of their honor while locating their honor primarily in a millimeter of skin between a girl's legs. Meanwhile, when Palestinian singer Mohammed Assaf (a darling of Palestinians since his victory in the 2013 season of *Arab Idol*) declared in an interview on the Egyptian talk show *Al Mataha* that he would never allow his sister to sing in public because of his culture's "traditions," Nafar responded with an angry open letter to Assaf, noting it is difficult to criticize the "Cinderella from Gaza," given his popularity among Palestinians:

> Like the Palestinians who were united for the first time in the streets of Gaza, the West Bank, the Diaspora, the Refugee Camps and inside of '48 to support Muhammad [*sic*] Assaf, we ask Assaf to join us on the same streets to encourage that girl from Yemen, Gaza, Morocco, Jordan and al Lyd—that girl who is dreaming to sing, dance, write and perform in *Arab Idol*! We as Palestinians must fight the Israeli Apartheid and the Gender Apartheid. My dream is to march hand in hand, a woman holding a man's hand against any separation wall. It is not reasonable to walk separately and ask for unity at the same time! (cited by Žižek from the "DAM Palestine" Facebook page)

Perhaps the most striking engagement of Nafar and DAM with women's issues in Palestine occurs in the 2012 song "Law Arja3 bil Zaman" ("If I Could Go Back in Time"), with a video clip directed by Salloum and featuring backup vocals by Amal Murkus.[46] This song tells the story of a young Palestinian woman whose family attempts to force her to marry her cousin. She refuses, and instead plans to travel to the airport and flee the country, seeking freedom. However, she is intercepted by her father and brother, who take her into the woods, shoot her in the head, and bury her in a shallow grave. Narrated using the innovative technique of beginning with the scene of her burial and then moving backward in time to her early years as an innocent young girl, the song makes powerful points about the ongoing problem of honor killings in this part of the Arab world. While DAM has undergone some criticism for this song and clip (and for this gender-oriented aspect of their recent work in general) as a potential distraction from the urgent problem of Israeli persecution of Palestinians,[47] "If I Could Go Back in Time" is, in fact, a highly effective reminder that the Palestinians can never be free as long as they continue to oppress their own women, Israelis or no Israelis. And, while the song and clip focus only on one specific problem among many, such focus is typically a strength of political art, especially such brief works, as opposed to full-length academic studies.

Lowkey: Fully engaged rap

Given Nafar's interest in both women's rights and Palestinian rights, it is not surprising that he has sometimes collaborated with Mansour. Mansour's collaborators Logic and Lowkey, incidentally, have also frequently worked with each other, further demonstrating the collaborative nature of Arab and Arab disaporic rap. Logic, for example, teamed with Lowkey to found "New World Order" (later "People's Army"), an organization of artists devoted to promoting political activism in support of various causes. Lowkey and Logic have also both performed live and recorded together. Lowkey, meanwhile, has emerged as perhaps the most articulate and politically sophisticated of all the rappers of the Arab diaspora. He began rapping as a teenager and has developed an extensive body of work that is informed by a strong sense of his dual British and Iraqi heritage—and particularly of the historical relationship between Britain and Iraq (and the Arab world in general). As he says in his song "Cradle of Civilisation" (included on the 2011 album *Soundtrack to the Struggle*, which culminated the first phase of his career as a rapper), though he has lived his entire life in Britain, "Still I feel like an immigrant, an Englishman amongst Arabs and an Arab amongst Englishmen"[48,49]). Here, Lowkey directly echoes the poem "Counterpoint: On Edward Said," by famed Palestinian poet Mahmoud Darwish. Speaking of Said, an Arab who spent most of his life in the West, working in English, Darwish writes: "He says: 'I am from there, I am from here, / but I am not there, I am not here.'"

"Cradle of Civilization" is a lament for the suffering of modern-day Iraqis, a declaration of Lowkey's sense of connection to the ancestral place he has never seen, and a reminder that Iraq (and especially Baghdad) "will always be the cradle of civilization." In addition to such acknowledgments of his Iraqi background, Lowkey has been strongly engaged with the Palestinian cause, as in the song "Long Live Palestine"[50] included on *Soundtrack to the Struggle*. This song was followed by a collaborative "sequel"—"Long Live Palestine, Part II"[51]— that is not on the album but that was released in conjunction with Part I as an EP in 2009. Here, Lowkey leads an international group of artists expressing support for the Palestinian cause (in English, Arabic, and Farsi). This group includes The Narcicyst, Mansour, and members of DAM, as well as Lebanese-Syrian rapper Eslam Jawaad, Iranian British rapper Reveal (Mehrak Golestan), Iranian rapper Hichkas (Soroush Lashkary), and American rapper Hasan Salaam. Among other things, Salaam's segment of the song includes lyrics that nicely deconstruct the logic of Orientalism:

> There's no such thing as the Middle East.
> Brother they deceiving you.
> No matter where you stand,
> There's always something to the east of you.

Lowkey's political concerns go beyond the Arab world—and beyond Britain. He has largely espoused an internationalist perspective, rejecting nationalism of all sorts and regarding nations as artificial constructs. Much of the rhetoric of his music (as well as his numerous interviews) is directed at the global power of American imperialism, which he sees as both military (he has repeatedly emphasized the number of military bases the United States has around the world, including in Britain) and cultural. For example, in one interview,[52] he notes that he originally became interested in rapping (at about the age of twelve) under the influence of American culture, even going so far as to rap in an American accent, because he associated American culture with quality and high achievement. Later, though, he switched to his own heavily British, working-class accent, and has not looked back, though he has often collaborated with some of the more politically engaged American rappers. He has also, in recent years, begun to rap more and more in Arabic. In fact, Lowkey has often identified commercialized American rap music as a tool of American cultural imperialism, despite the fact that rap music has so often been seen as a countercultural form. In "Obama Nation" (also on *Soundtrack to the Struggle*), perhaps Lowkey's most strident critique of American policies, the rapper notes that Obama has "Jay-Z on speed dial."[53] Elsewhere, Lowkey notes in an informal presentation,[54] "Hip hop at its best has exposed power; it hasn't served power.... What's being rammed down our throats as hip hop: is it challenging power, or is it serving power? We have to question: when the US government loves the same rappers that you love, you have to ask yourselves whose interests are those rappers serving?"[55]

Lowkey begins "Obama Nation," with a prologue that emphasizes the fact that his target is not the American people, but the system that governs them. In the midst of the song, he notes that "I'm not anti-America; America is anti-me." The rest of the song is a thorough dismissal of US president Barack Obama as a lackey of the system who has done virtually nothing to quell injustice in the United States, while meanwhile, if anything, stepping up the violence of America's attempts to dominate the rest of the world. The angry (but often funny) lyrics also emphasize that Obama's skin color has been of little consequence in a nation that remains avowedly racist both at home and abroad:

> Afraid of your melanin
> The same as it's ever been
> That ain't gonna change
> With the race of the president.
> I see imperialism under your skin tone
> You could call it Christopher Columbus syndrome.

Lines such as "The American dream only makes sense if you're sleepin'" and "America is capitalism on steroids" are clever and entertaining, but also biting, and there is no mistaking the bitterness and anger that lie behind this song. Meanwhile, the repeated play on the similarity between "Obama nation" and "abomination" and use of lines from "The Star-Spangled Banner" as a background to the song's repeated hook do not detract from the force of its critique of America's bloody and interventionist foreign policy, a course that the Obama administration did little or nothing to curtail. On the other hand, Lowkey also acknowledges the roots of his art in American rap when he notes near the beginning of the song, "Their politics took my voice away/But their music gave it back to me."

In "Obama Nation Part II"[56] Lowkey is joined by M-1 and black British rapper Black the Ripper in an equally strident critique. Here, for example, M-1 raps that Obama is a "neo-colonial puppet, white power with a black face." The song also includes a repeated refrain sampled from Lupe Fiasco's "Words I Never Said": "Limbaugh is a racist, Glenn Beck is a racist / Gaza strip was getting bombed, Obama didn't say shit." Black the Ripper is even more pointed in his criticism of African Americans who join the establishment:

> You're just another puppet but I'm not surprised
> Look at Colin Powell and Condoleezza Rice.
> They didn't change shit, house nigga's fresh off the slave ship.
> You'll all burn in hell even Michelle, Obama Nation.[57]

In "Terrorist?,"[58] again from *Soundtrack to the Struggle*, Lowkey addresses the stereotypical characterization of Arabs and/or Muslims as terrorists, arguing that the American and British militaries have committed far more destructive acts of terrorism than any Islamic fundamentalists. In the video clip for this song, Lowkey plays both the part of an accused terrorist being interrogated in a grubby Abu Ghraib-type prison and the part of his clean-cut, bespectacled interrogator. As the song proceeds, the lyrics are supplemented by text displayed on the wall behind them and by visuals of various violent acts perpetrated by the West upon other parts of the world. The message could not be more clear.

Beginning in 2012, with his career in high gear, Lowkey took a four-year break from rapping (announcing that he was taking the time off to pursue his studies), but in 2016 he returned with a vengeance, quickly releasing two tracks that responded to the perceived crisis caused by refugees from the Arab world (especially Syria) coming to the West in increasingly large numbers. In "Children of Diaspora"[59] Lowkey, with the vocal support of Mai Khalil (who had also appeared on some of his earlier tracks), mocks the Western fear of the Other as based on racism and ignorance. He cites specific cases (Anthony Walker, Stephen Lawrence, and Mark Duggan) of British immigrants who were killed by those driven by this racist fear, as well as several African Americans (Emmett Till, Tamir Rice, and Alton Sterling) who were also killed, apparently with racist motivations. In addition, he notes the struggles that children of diaspora have faced in order to get by in the white-dominated West, noting in particular Michael Jackson's attempts to lighten his skin and minimize his nose, until he ended up doing "what they did to the Sphinx." He also approvingly cites those who have stood up to racism with acts of resistance or defiance, such as Malcolm X, and defends Gabby Douglas, the American Olympic gymnast who refused to place her hand over her heart when "The Star-Spangled Banner" was played during the 2016 gold medal award ceremony. Finally, he argues that immigrants have much to offer, citing the contributions of such children of diaspora as Edward Said, Frantz Fanon, and Bob Marley, as well as African American singer Nina Simone and Iraqi British architect Zaha Hadid. At the same time, the song takes on an extra political charge from Khalil's background chorus, which defiantly repeats such lines as "We never bow to the Queen," while declaring, in good internationalist fashion, that we "pledge no allegiance to the flag."

The first song released as part of Lowkey's comeback deals with many of the same topics as "Children of Diaspora," though "Ahmed" is delivered in a less strident and more emotional tone.[60] Building on such events as the 2015 drowning death of young Alan Kurdi, the Kurdish boy who was famously photographed lying dead on a Turkish beach after attempting to escape from war-torn Syria to Greece, Lowkey employs the name "Ahmed" as a general indicator for young refugees who die in the attempt to flee to safety—or who suffer from prejudice and abuse even if they make it to presumably safe havens such as Britain. In this very powerful song (accompanied by an equally powerful video clip) Lowkey effectively indicates the human tragedy of the fact that so many children have died in the way Alan Kurdi died, often anonymously, without any acknowledgment whatsoever. And he also notes the ignorance that informs the Western fear of refugees from the Middle East, when people from the Middle East have historically brought with them so much of value to the West.[61]

Rappers such as Lowkey, Shadia Mansour, Tamer Nafar/DAM, Omar Offendum, Narcy, and Qusai indicate the extent and diversity of the rap phenomenon in the Arab world and the Arab diaspora. This fact, of course, should come as no surprise given the way in which hip-hop culture in general

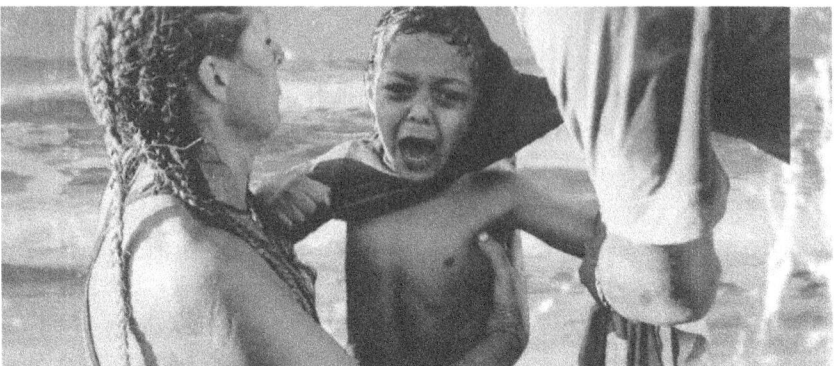

Figure 4.4 Lowkey's video clip for "Ahmed" (2016) contains a number of powerful images.

has become such an international phenomenon in recent years, with numerous mutual flows of influence traveling about the globe. Indeed, the political power of most of the artists just named must also be gauged in conjunction with phenomena such as the Rhythm Road Tours, in which, beginning in 2005, American musical performers were sent abroad as goodwill ambassadors for the American way. In particular, Muslim American rappers were sent to the Middle East to convey pro-American messages to Arab youth. Thus, if rappers such as Nafar have attempted to align their plight with that of oppressed African Americans, official programs such as this one have attempted to perform a similar alignment, but with assurances that African Americans are in fact now fully assimilated and as American as anyone, so that Arabs who seek to identify with African American culture are really just identifying with American culture in general, which now suddenly appears familiar and benevolent.

Hisham Aidi has discussed this phenomenon, which he refers to as the "blackwashing" of American culture (252), a strategy that has involved not only the appropriation of hip-hop culture as an emblem of Americanness, but that has even sought to inscribe such radical figures as Malcolm X within the confines of the American, thus attempting to "rebrand America's image" (221). As Rayya El Zein notes, this double figuration of Arab hip-hop can be understood within a Western imaginative construct that separates the culture into opposed notions of the "good" rapper and the "bad" rapper, in which figures such as El Général are envisioned as liberal, Western-style freedom fighters (who defy the Oriental despotism of oppressive Eastern regimes), while more thuggish rappers are associated with visions of terrorists who hate Western freedom ("From"). Citing conservative Israeli Likud Party political advertisements that have attempted to associate terrorism with hip-hop thuggery, El Zein then notes how this equation of "bad" Arabs with a caricatured version of American gangsta rap is designed to make them seem more dangerous and implacable—more street criminals than political operatives.[62]

Elsewhere, focusing on analyses of live performances by Lowkey, Mansour, and Offendum, El Zein notes that hip-hop can contribute to radical forms of identity- and community-building, but that the same culture can be co-opted in support of a neoliberal agenda ("Call and Response"). Of course, neoliberalism (whether in its political or in its commercial manifestation) is very good at this sort of co-optation. In this sense, it is important to note that Lowkey, in particular, has shown a distinct concern with avoiding such appropriation of the energies of his music by the powers-that-be. Thus, in a sort of companion piece to "Too Much" entitled "My Soul," Lowkey returns to a Latin American context (including a video clip shot in Cuba,[63] 2011) with further criticisms of US foreign policy, in this case with regard to the US embargo of Cuba. However, in this song he focuses his most effective lyrics on global capitalism itself—and on the commodification of the music industry within that system:

> They can't use my music to advertise for Coca Cola
> They can't use my music to advertise for Motorola
> They can't use my music to advertise for anything but truth.
> I guess that's the reason the industry won't let me in
> Refuse to be a product or a brand; I'm a human.
> Refuse to contribute to the gangster illusion.

Here Lowkey criticizes both the "gangster" mentality of much recent hip-hop culture and the tendency of other rappers to allow themselves to become mere commercial products (producing not genuine hip-hop but "McDonald's music"), something that he has avowedly refused to do. He also notes later in the song that his critics complain that his songs sound like lectures, recalling DeGhett's discussion of "hip-hop academia," though DeGhett does not mention Lowkey in that article.

Lowkey also makes his opposition to capitalism clear in a 2010 interview[64] in which he notes, "Before you even consider eradicating poverty, you need to eradicate capitalism, because it's capitalism that is causing the poverty in the world today." Indeed, YouTube is replete with Lowkey's speeches and interviews, as he seeks to get his message across in a variety of forums. His rap music is certainly the most popular and probably the most effective of these forums, but it is also clear that Lowkey draws no line between his music and his political activism, even as he pays considerable attention to the artistry of the former, in addition to the message.[65]

Among other things, the work of Lowkey and other politically engaged diasporic rappers indicates the ongoing vitality of hip-hop culture as an oppositional political form, even as so much that passes for hip-hop in America has now been co-opted by the capitalist system, becoming just another commercial product. The fact that hip-hop has become such an important cultural form for Arab and Arab diasporic performers is also a key indication of the kind of transnational cultural flow that now forms such a crucial part of world culture. There is, after all, nothing more transnational than the idea of an Iraqi British rapper, initially inspired by American rap music, engaging in a powerful critique of American policies in Cuba and Israeli policies in Palestine. This phenomenon importantly indicates that such flows are not always thoroughly dominated by the global spread of capitalism but that they can also include oppositional forms as well. Still, the most powerful transnational cultural flows probably are the most commercial ones, with the transnational flow of culture following the flow of capital itself. The following chapters concentrate on Arab commercial television and on the ways in which cultural energies from outside the Arab world have exercised a powerful influence on the recent evolution of the programming that is available to Arab television viewers.

5

As the World Turns from the East to the West: Tradition, Modernity, and Gender in the Arabic-dubbed Turkish Soap Opera *Noor*

The Turkish soap opera *Gümüş* (which originally aired from 2005 to 2007) became one of the great sensations of early-twenty-first-century Arab television when it was dubbed into Arabic and broadcast across the Arab world via satellite as *Noor* (light) in 2008. The series tells the romantic story of a young married couple as they struggle with the tribulations of life in the modern world—with the emphasis on modern. In particular, the strikingly handsome husband (Muhannad, played by Kivanç Tatlituğ) is a paragon of modern sensitivity and open-mindedness, while the beautiful wife (Noor, played by Songül Öden) is an independent-minded career woman, a stance that her enlightened husband fully supports. This depiction of marriage as a relationship between equals took the Arab world by storm (both positively and negatively), reportedly destabilizing marriages and causing many Arab women to question the conventional gender roles that had been assigned to them.

That they reacted so strongly to the program might, at first glance, merely make Arab women seem so naïve as to be unable to understand the difference between fiction and reality. We would argue, however, that the ability to envision the relationship between Noor and Muhannad as a possible prototype for their own relationships was not a failure of interpretation but a successful feat of the utopian imagination. Arab women did not confuse the story of *Noor* with reality but were simply able to make the imaginative leap that enabled them to conceive of a reality that was more like the world of *Noor* than was their own. That so many Arab women were apparently able to perform this leap suggests that they were not nearly as oppressed or as firmly held in the grip of traditional Islamic ideology as many in the West might think.

Figure 5.1 Muhannad (Kivanç Tatlıtuğ) and Noor (Songül Öden) in a quiet moment of marital communication in *Noor* (2008), the Arabic-dubbed version of the Turkish soap opera *Gümüş* (2005–7).

Sarsar and Stephan discuss the ways in which the process of modernization presents special challenges in the Middle East, where many want to enjoy the material benefits of modernization, but also want to preserve their traditional cultures and values. Further, they note that this situation is particularly complex where women are concerned, given that traditions in the region have so often worked to the detriment of women. Modernization offers many opportunities for women to improve their position in Middle Eastern societies, but the fact that this improvement is associated by many with Americanization and the destruction of traditional Arab societies threatens to increase resistance to change with regard to the status of women, perhaps even among women themselves. Modernization, Sarsar and Stephan conclude (citing numerous actual statistics), has thus far proceeded more in terms of superficial measures such as the appearance of skyscrapers and chain stores selling Western brands than in terms of improving the social status of women. But true modernization, they argue, should be measured "in relationship to the required social, political, economic, and cultural change designed to enhance the overall welfare of the populations in the Arab countries regardless of their gender, ethnicity, social status, religion, and place of residency" (349).

From this point of view, it is important to recognize that the Arab women who reacted so enthusiastically to *Noor* were reacting partly to its vision of a world in which modernization had proceeded more in terms of its benefit to women.

They were not simple-minded primitives who had never before been exposed to modern narratives. The effect of *Noor* on the Arab world was unprecedented, but programs that might be described as "soap operas" had been quite popular in the Arab world for some time when *Noor* was first broadcast, with a huge following made up mostly of Arab women. Subsequently, *Noor*'s broadcaster, the Saudi-owned (but Dubai-based) MBC,[1] has since 2010 operated an entire channel ("MBC Drama") devoted primarily to soap operas—and to associated promotional programming, such as entertainment news and talk shows related to the main programs, though other MBC channels broadcast soaps as well. The soaps on this channel feature a mix of original Arabic-language programs, or *musalsalat* (produced primarily in Syria or Egypt), and Arabic-dubbed programs from Turkey, Latin America, and India. Turkish soap operas (with Arabic dubbing) have been particularly popular in recent years, beginning in 2007 with *Çemberimde Gül Oya* (first broadcast in Turkey in 2004–05), broadcast in Arabic as *Ikleel Al Ward* (2007). MBC then scored their first major success with such programs as *Noor* the following year. However, programs that might be described as soap operas were at this time already an established part of Arabic-language television programming, with telenovelas from Latin America being a particularly popular form. For example, the Venezuelan telenovela *Kassandra* (originally broadcast in Spanish in 1992–93) was broadcast with Arabic dubbing beginning in the summer of 1996, becoming a pan-Arab sensation, accompanied by an extensive co-marketing campaign.[2] Such telenovelas (and, subsequently, Turkish soap operas) have also exerted a strong influence on Arab-language television dramas, especially on the Syrian-produced programs that have been particularly popular through much of the Middle East in recent years.[3]

The popularity of such programming—estimates are that, even in the ultra-conservative Saudi Arabia, roughly 10 to 15 percent of the population watched *Noor* on a regular basis—already poses a powerful challenge to some of the most Orientalist and ill-informed Western stereotypes about life in the Arab world (Ambah). Indeed, the very existence of high-tech satellite-based broadcasting systems, beaming dozens of channels of programming (much of it American) into modern Arab homes, provides an image that stands in stark contrast to visions of veiled women insulated from the world and primitive, bearded men battling sandstorms on their trusty camels. At the same time, the impact of such programs, especially *Noor*, demonstrates that there are genuine and important differences between the Arab world and the American-dominated West. These differences, however, are complex and need to be unpacked dialectically.

Musalsalat, telenovelas, and soap operas

Before exploring these larger social differences, though, it should be pointed out that telenovelas and *musalsalat* are different from American soap operas in structure and format. Most obviously, American soaps are typically open-ended, with successful ones sometimes running for decades. Telenovelas and *musalsalat*, however, are typically closed-form narratives, often designed to run only a single season and come to a reasonably coherent conclusion.[4] In the Arab world, a particularly popular form involves *musalsalat Ramadan*, programs that are designed to be broadcast daily during the month of Ramadan, concluding their entire run during a single month-long season. *Musalsalat*, including *musalsalat Ramadan*, typically place a great premium on entertainment, often employing soap opera–like material, though the programs can address more serious issues as well. For example, the MBC-produced Syrian soap opera *Bab Al-Hara* ("The Neighborhood Gate") has been a staple of Ramadan programming since 2006. A period piece set in the interwar period of French rule in Syria, it deals with a number of historical issues in addition to its central soap opera–like plots. More recently, the *musalsal Shawq* (originally broadcast on the pay channel OSN, in March–April 2017, but rerun on free-to-air television during Ramadan of 2017) centrally deals with the topic of the Syrian Revolution. The series deals with the tribulations of daily life during the war in Syria, also including scenes that depict the plight of Syrian refugees in Beirut. Here, Palestinian-Syrian actress Nesreen Tafesh plays the title character, a woman whose parents die in a car bomb attack in Damascus. Shawq works for a publisher that specializes in works about Syrian history and culture; she is also suffering from early-onset Alzheimer's, which makes it difficult for her to recognize anyone or remember anything. Her profession and her condition thus serve as an allegorical commentary on the destruction of Syrian cultural identity during the recent conflict. Meanwhile, she is the cousin of Wael (Bassem Yakhour) a lawyer, whose fiancée Rose (Suzan Najm Aldeen) is an activist blogger (loosely based on the story of real-world blogger Rezan Zaytoun) and an opponent of the Bashar regime. Much of the plot of the series involves the story of Rose's kidnapping by DAESH as part of a program to supply women to DAESH warriors as sex slaves, thus depicting DAESH in an extremely negative light.[5] *Shawq*, meanwhile, was quickly followed by the MBC *musalsal Ramadan Gharabeeb Soud* ("Black Crows") in May and June of 2017. Here, the focus is even more on the experience of women who become involved with DAESH in various ways, using real historical events and personages as background. The show is uncompromising in its depiction of

DAESH atrocities—so much so that DAESH threatened to seek revenge, leading MBC to increase security at its facilities ("ISIS Threatens").

For our purposes, the Lebanese-Syrian series *Al Hayba*, broadcast on MBC in 2017 and 2018 and set for a third series in 2019, is particularly notable among recent *musalsalat Ramadan*. Dealing with the machinations of a family of Lebanese arms dealers who operate in a remote region near the border with Syria, *Al Hayba* is overtly modeled on the American Netflix series *Narcos* (2015–), which deals with the career of Columbian drug lord Pablo Escobar and its aftermath. Indeed, Escobar is overtly presented as the hero of the series' chief crime-lord figure, Jabal (Tayem Hasan), while the series also overtly deals with East-West cultural confrontation in that the plot of the first season involves the return to Lebanon of Alia (Nadine Njeim), the widow of Jabal's brother; Alia has long lived in Canada and now finds certain aspects of the traditional Arab culture espoused by Jabal and his family to be decidedly problematic. Meanwhile (in an extremely unusual move for the genre), the second season is a prequel that provides the background to the events of the first season. *Al Hayba* has also already become an example of transnational flow in the other direction as well via its marketing to Eastern Europe, while the globally popular *Narcos* has been identified by Middle Eastern television executives as the kind of series that Arab television producers should be seeking to emulate in general as they themselves try to enter the global television marketplace ("Middle East Content Creators").

Figure 5.2 Collection of photos in the family home of Jabal (Tayem Hasan) in *Al Hayba* (2017). Note the central place accorded to Jabal's hero, Columbian drug lord Pablo Escobar (screen capture).

Of course, the international success of *Narcos* is largely due to the globalization of Netflix itself, which expanded in dramatic fashion by suddenly expanding to a list of more than 130 countries (including almost all Arab countries) in 2016. This move (accompanied by the addition of subtitling in numerous languages, including Arabic), meanwhile, was a key moment in the globalization of television in general, though it is not at all surprising given that one of the key sources of Netflix's American programming has long been television series that were initially produced in Europe and elsewhere. Still, the move of Netflix to become the first global television "network" indicates just how international popular culture is becoming in the age of late capitalism.

It should also be noted that Arab-produced television dramas have typically been made in a local vernacular (such as Syrian, as in the case of *Shawq*, or Lebanese, as in the case of *Al Hayba*), even though telenovelas have typically been dubbed in standard Arabic, a choice that perhaps made them seem more exotic and romantic, but that also might have made it more difficult for Arab viewers to relate the content of the programs (already taking place in a rather foreign cultural context) to their own lives. The producers of *Noor* opted to dub their Arabic version in a Syrian dialect (as had also been done with *Ikleel Al Ward*), which had the effect of making *Noor* seem more realistic and authentic to Arab viewers than had previous dubbed soap operas, just as the Turkish cultural context of the programs is more familiar than the Latin American context of the telenovelas.[6] Many of the names of characters (including Muhannad and Noor themselves—Mehmet and Gümüş in the original) were also Arabicized, while Turkish songs included in the original series were sometimes completely replaced with well-known Arabic songs, rather than simply translated and re-recorded. Such modifications no doubt helped Arab audiences to identify with the series and its characters, though no attempt was made to change the names of places or to indicate that the action takes place anywhere but in Turkey, thus providing a setting that was just foreign enough to boost the fantasy effect of the series without making it so foreign as to undermine the identification of Arab viewers with the series and its characters.

Utopia and entertainment

Designed to produce entertainment for viewers (and profits for the producers and broadcasters), *Noor* touched a nerve in the Arab world, revealing basic contradictions in and raising fundamental questions about gender relations in that world. The series thus became a key example of the complex—and sometimes confused—relationship between Western-style modernity and Islamic-style tradition that informs Arab life in the twenty-first century, allegorizing that relationship with an additional component suggesting that history is on the side of a movement beyond tradition and into modernity.

Noor, in short, went beyond its modest intentions to produce an effect that might be described as *excessive*, thus aligning it with some of the great works of art in world history, despite its own meager aesthetic aspirations. Of course, the very concept of the aesthetic as a distinct phenomenon is a fundamentally modern and Western one. Terry Eagleton has noted the extent to which the modern notion of aesthetics in general is inseparable from the rise of capitalism and from the construction of a new sort of (bourgeois) subject that is designed to function well with the new sorts of power and control that are at work in the emergent bourgeois society. This new subject is relatively flexible, autonomous, and fluid, as it must be to operate within the confines of capitalism, with its need for individuals with sufficient agency to compete on the open market. On the other hand, subjects with this kind of agency are hard to control completely, leaving open the possibility that they might evade the confines of bourgeois power. Meanwhile, Eagleton argues that the aesthetic as a category, which serves as a sort of pattern or model for the bourgeois subject, is inseparable from passion and the yearnings of the physical body. As a result, the aesthetic is also difficult to control, always in danger of getting out of hand and providing models for behavior that are difficult for bourgeois power to contain. Thus,

> the aesthetic as custom, sentiment, spontaneous impulse may consort well enough with political domination; but these phenomena border embarrassingly on passion, imagination, sensuality, which are not always so easily incorporable. (*Ideology* 28)

The soap opera as a genre has typically been held in low regard as an aesthetic category, though the genre generally derives its energies from precisely the sort of "passion, imagination, sensuality" that Eagleton here invokes with regard to the aesthetic. Moreover, the soap opera is also precisely the sort of "entertainment" genre that Richard Dyer has seen as similarly threatening to escape the domination of bourgeois power. In particular, Dyer argues that entertainment genres (he focuses specifically on movie musicals) function primarily through "escapism" and "wish-fulfillment," which might seem like lowly goals, but which are fundamentally utopian, in that they provide an image of something better than what is available in the status quo of current reality. However, this kind of utopianism is focused not on the conventional utopian motif of the imagination of alternative ideal worlds, but on the production of certain feelings, or affects. Thus, the utopianism of entertainment "is contained in the feelings it embodies. It presents, head-on as it were, what utopia would feel like rather than how it would be organized" (20).

Entertainment, for Dyer, contains a sort of utopian energy that provides only a temporary remedy for the perceived inadequacies of society, rather than full-scale political solutions to those inadequacies. Indeed, this sort of utopianism is (like the aesthetic for Eagleton) fundamentally oriented toward perpetuating, rather than challenging the status quo in the way that one might conventionally expect from utopian imagery. However (also as in Eagleton's vision of the aesthetic), these utopian energies are difficult to manage entirely and might potentially point toward more genuine (even revolutionary) forms of social change than was originally intended. Once the shortcomings in present-day society have been revealed and the need for alternatives declared, it is difficult merely to smile and go on as before. Once the genie is out of the bottle, as it were, it is hard to get it back in.

Dyer's analysis of the utopianism of entertainment involves the identification of five categories of social inadequacies, along with the corresponding categories of utopian solutions. These include scarcity (abundance), exhaustion (energy), dreariness (intensity), manipulation (transparency), and fragmentation (community). But these solutions, Dyer argues, are fundamentally of a kind already purportedly offered by capitalism itself, making it difficult for them to challenge the capitalist system directly. Thus, Dyer notes, capitalism provides abundance in the form of consumerism, energy and intensity are provided by personal freedom and individualism, and transparency appears in the form of freedom of speech. Community, always difficult to produce in a convincing way within the competitive ethos of capitalism, remains the sole possible exception in most Western entertainment genres.

Christine Geraghty has shown that Dyer's categories of utopianism can be usefully applied to American and British soap operas. We would argue that they also apply equally well (perhaps, in many ways, better) to the soap opera–like forms that have become so popular in the Middle East since the mid-1990s. The very fact that such forms have become so popular among Arab (especially Arab women) viewers since that time constitutes still another example of the continual cultural crossover that renders absurd any attempt to see Arab culture as the exotic and mysterious polar opposite of Western culture. At the same time, there are still distinctive differences between Western and Eastern soap operas that impact the application of Dyer's categories, often giving the Eastern versions even more powerful and difficult-to-contain utopian energies. For example, the soaps that have been popular in the Middle East typically contain an additional historical/utopian dimension that is almost entirely lacking in Western soap operas—a dimension involving the transformation of traditional Islamic society under the impact of its encounter with capitalist modernization.

Gümüş/Noor addresses this transformation in a number of ways, including at the basic level of the plot. As the series begins, young Muhannad Oğlu suffers tragedy when his pregnant fiancée, the actress Nihal (Hilal Uysun), is ostensibly struck down and killed by a speeding truck before his very eyes. Muhannad descends into despair, drinking heavily and behaving erratically, until his kindly and relatively traditional grandfather (who had disapproved of his relationship with the actress) decides to try to set Muhannad straight by arranging a new bride for him. The wealthy grandfather, Fikri (Ekrem Bora), who now lives in a palatial villa in Istanbul, had arisen through his own hard work from humble origins in the town of Afyon.[7] He chooses Noor—a poor, but virtuous young woman from the town—as Muhannad's bride, having known Noor and her family for many years. The rest of the series focuses on the evolving relationship between Muhannad and Noor, who wed despite initial mutual doubts and eventually build a strong relationship.

This quick summary should be sufficient to indicate that many elements of *Noor* would not seem all that foreign to Western viewers. *Noor* is composed, in fact, of a virtually nonstop stream of romantic crises, family crises, business crises, medical crises, legal crises, and other crises of a sort that could be found in any American soap. The very texture of life, as presented in the series, seems quite Western. Alcohol is consumed routinely, without any sense that there might be anything problematic about this practice. Many scenes are set in modern-looking restaurants, with ambience provided by American or British popular music playing in the background. The characters (as is common in modern Turkey) generally wear entirely Western dress, and the series features many scenes of kissing and even scenes of Muhannad and Noor side by side in bed. These scenes are demure by Western standards, just as all of these aspects of the series would seem ordinary to American (or most Turkish) viewers. But these Western scenes were considered shocking and disturbing by many in the Middle East—a response that might well have ultimately increased *Noor*'s popularity there.

This shock effect also greatly enhances the utopian dimension of the series, creating a powerful cognitive estrangement that potentially causes Arab viewers, especially Arab *women* viewers, to think about the differences between their world and the world of *Noor* and to wonder why their lives can't be more like the lives of the characters in the series. This estrangement effect is itself enhanced by the fact that the series contains just enough traditional Islamic attitudes and dilemmas to make its situations and crises seem recognizable, even familiar, to Arab audiences; at the same time, its characters (who are generally granted much more individual freedom of choice than might be dictated in a more traditional Muslim society) are offered opportunities that might not be available in the more conservative Arab world. Characters in the series observe and acknowledge the holy month of Ramadan, for example, but seem to regard the fasting normally associated with this observance as entirely optional, with no particular stigma associated with the decision not to fast. In addition, women in the series (especially the title character) have a wide range of personal and professional freedom, sometimes with the enlightened support of the men who love them. According to this dynamic, viewers are shown a world in which it is possible to be both modern and Muslim, to be liberated without the abandonment of morality that many associate with life in the West. The series suggests to Arab viewers (especially Arab *women*) that they can, in a society not all that different from their own, have their cake and eat it, too.

A quick look at the application of Dyer's categories to *Noor* shows that they generally apply well, suggesting that the series has a great deal in common with Western entertainment. For example, in the category of scarcity/abundance, it should be noted that Muhannad and his family live an elaborate lifestyle far beyond the means of ordinary people anywhere in the world. There is clearly a strong fantasy element in this lifestyle, which allows viewers to dream of living in similar luxury—though it is also important to recognize that the wealth of the family has been acquired through modern capitalist enterprise and not through some exotic system of inherited wealth. Moreover, capitalism being what it is, this wealth is sometimes put in considerable jeopardy due to the travails of the market (and the machinations of unscrupulous competitors or foes, including Western-style gangsters), a situation that in fact provides significant plot material for the series.

Such nefarious figures as the gangsters who almost cause the demise of the family business in *Noor* also provide a sharp contrast to the central figures of the series (especially Noor and Muhannad), who are (by and large) resolutely honest and virtuous, providing the images of transparency that constitute one of Dyer's key utopian categories. Muhannad and Noor each suspect the other of dishonesty (and Muhannad, in particular, is genuinely less than truthful at times, though he learns his lesson and goes straight by the end of the series), but theirs is generally a relationship marked by free and open communication and exchange of ideas. Ultimately, neither has any reason to doubt the love or sincerity of the other.

Similarly, *Noor* certainly overcomes the exhaustion and boredom of day-to-day life in the modern routinized world with its constant sense of crisis—and with its presentation of characters who, despite all that befalls them, are consistently up to the challenge of meeting these crises. Rich though they may be, the characters of *Noor* are anything but *idle* rich. They are constantly involved in a variety of projects to better themselves and to help those they care about. This is perhaps especially the case with Noor, who is able to transform herself from a simple, relatively traditional girl into a talented artist and dynamic career woman. At one point, when the family business is on the brink of collapse, their now-mortgaged palatial home on the verge of being repossessed by the bank, she even sells her own independent business in order to save the day.

Much of the energy of both Noor and Muhannad, of course, is driven by the growing intensity of the passion between them. Indeed, despite the range of materials that the series includes, the central love story between these two characters consistently remains at the heart of the series and was clearly the force that drove its popularity in the Arab world. Soap operas in general are driven by romantic relationships, of course, and it is not for nothing that much of Geraghty's analysis of the soap opera form focuses on the genre as a kind of romance. Moreover, Geraghty's analysis, while focusing on British and American soaps, describes the romance elements of *Noor* just as well. Noting the element of fantasy—especially fantasy involving relationships—that virtually all analysts of romance literature for women have seen as crucial to the genre, Geraghty concludes that "the story of the romance is indeed an escape to another world where the ideal relationship can be explored and enjoyed. At the heart of the romance is the development of the relationship between the hero and the heroine" (109).

Geraghty draws particularly upon the important work of Janice Radway, who surveyed the reactions of a group of actual readers of romance novels in an attempt to understand the genre and its impact on such readers. Among other things, *Noor* exemplifies what Radway calls the "ideal romance," the "most striking characteristic" of which is "its resolute focus on a single, developing relationship between heroine and hero"—though she also notes that "interim relationships" with "rival individuals" typically complicate this development along the way (122).[8] Further, and in a mode that also applies well to *Noor*,

Radway concludes that the "ideal romance" typically focuses on "the *inevitability* of the deepening of 'true love' into an intense conjugal commitment" (162).

What is especially relevant with regard to *Noor* is Geraghty's emphasis on the role of the male partner in romance, with romances succeeding because *both* partners have concluded that "the emotional sphere is to be taken seriously and that both men and women must commit themselves to doing so" (110). There is no place for domineering patriarchs or emotionally stunted macho men in Geraghty's vision of the successful romance, which depends upon the hero's ability to compromise and change in order to make the relationship work. Here, she again draws upon Radway, who has argued that the romance enacts women's basic need to connect emotionally with a member of the opposite sex and to form "an intense emotional bond with someone who is reciprocally nurturant and protective in a maternal way" (140). For Radway, "Although the ideal romance initially admits the difficulty of relying on men for gentleness and affective intensity, thus confirming the reader's own likely experience, it also reassures her that such satisfaction is possible because men really do know how to attend to a woman's needs" (140). Men, in the ideal romance, need to display a soft, feminine side in addition to their strong, masculine one, producing an ideal hybrid of gender stereotypes.

Geraghty also notes, incidentally, Tania Modleski's less rosy view of the transformation of the romantic hero. Viewing relationships as essentially agonistic, Modleski concludes that the successful consummation of the romance requires the submission of the male to the will of the female, concluding that the genre derives the characteristics of its ideal ending from revenge fantasy, women readers gaining satisfaction from the sense that the woman in the story has tamed the man and that she is "bringing the man to his knees and that all the while he is being so hateful he is internally grovelling, grovelling, grovelling" (Modleski 37).

There are numerous elements of *Noor* that in fact correspond to Modleski's analysis—including the fact that Muhannad spends much of the second half of the series practically begging a now-estranged Noor to return to him, while she rejects one strategy after another before finally agreeing to rejoin the marriage. In any case, while Modleski's vision of what is going on here is far less utopian than is Radway's, what is key to both visions is that the successful resolution of the romance plot involves a one-on-one relationship between a man and a woman, who exist as a sort of island apart from the rest of the world. The successful resolution of the plot involves the successful negotiation of various personal, individual hurdles in the path of the perfect relationship, typically involving the man's turning away from the public world of work and politics and toward the domestic sphere of intimacy and home. Indeed, one goal of the romance as a genre might be to provide its audiences with a fantasy of escape from day-to-day social reality and a retreat into the idealized private space of love and family, a world in which man and woman can be equals on the basis of their mutual love and respect, without having to change the attitudes, practices, and institutional structures of the rest of the world—which might be a much more difficult goal to achieve. As Geraghty puts it, "Imagining one man fulfilling a woman's needs is clearly hard enough work for any romance; extending the utopian possibilities further into the organization of social relationships is too hard a task" (112).

What sets *Noor* apart from American soap operas, however, is the fact that an idealized relationship between two loving equals is a far more radical vision—presenting far more powerful challenges to existing social structures—in an Arab context than in an American one. That the series had the power to present such challenges can be seen both in the fact that it was so popular in the Arab world and in the fact that it caused so much controversy.[9] Reaction was particularly strong in the ultra-conservative Saudi Arabia, where, for example, Grand Mufti Sheikh Abdul Aziz Al-Sheikh, head of the kingdom's highest religious authority, issued a fatwa against *Noor* during its initial run and declared that any channel broadcasting the series is acting as "an enemy of God and his Messenger." Accordingly, he declared that Muslims were forbidden to watch such shows, lest their morals be destroyed ("Mokhtar").[10]

Audiences generally ignored such warnings, however, and *Noor* remained wildly popular among viewers across the Arab world (including Saudi Arabia), becoming a sensation that spread beyond the television screen into the stalls in Arab street markets, where items such as T-shirts bearing photos of Muhannad and Noor (or just the photos themselves) became hot sellers. Nevertheless, perceptions that the show posed a threat to existing social structures were not confined to extremist Saudi clerics. In an article published in the *New York Times*, Robert F. Worth quotes Ramez Maluf, an associate professor of communications at Lebanese American University, to the effect that shows such as *Noor*, which test the limits on the treatment of sex and gender roles, are clearly "exposing people who are culturally isolated to modernity at a pace that is faster than they would like." Meanwhile, Worth notes that *Noor* is not an isolated phenomenon but merely an especially spectacular example of tensions arising in the Arab world from the growing power of television in general as a modernizing force that is difficult to contain within traditional Islamic values.

However general this phenomenon, though, *Noor* does seem to have struck a particular nerve among Arab women; during its initial run in 2008, the Arab media were replete with reports of smitten Arab wives who complained that their husbands were not as romantic or as understanding or as considerate as Muhannad—and of threatened Arab husbands who responded to their wives' Muhannad-mania by filing for divorce ("Turkish Soap Star"). In the Al Jazeera documentary *Kismet: How Turkish Soap Operas Changed the World*,[11] Jasam Al Maki, a government marriage counselor in the UAE, provides a warning against the potential negative impact of *Noor* on Arab marriages:

> We had a divorce case in which the woman wanted to organize her time according to the broadcast times of the series, so she wouldn't miss a single episode. [In such cases] we tell the husband not to let his wife pant over these romantic, animalistic stories. Where does your wife watch these shows? She watches them at your house and on the TV that you bought. This husband on the screen is a stranger; his wife is just playing the role of his wife. But their acting purports to reflect the kind of interaction that occurs between a husband and wife in real life. Thus, these shows, which are considered by some people as modern and civilized, have nothing but disastrous consequences. Whoever watches them will deeply regret it.

The media (including the Arab media) generally treated reports of the baleful consequences of watching *Noor* with considerable amusement, recounting such seemingly comic anecdotes as the story of a Saudi woman sheep farmer who sold off her entire herd of sheep so that she could devote her time to watching the series. In Jordan, a locally prominent singer, Mitab Sagar, wrote a song complaining of Muhannad's seductive and subversive effect on Jordanian women. In the song, Sagar claims to have traveled to Turkey to try to find out just who this "Muhannad" really is, only to discover that no one there knew him, despite his popularity among Arab women.[12] Attributing Muhannad's appeal to a lack of intelligence and religion among Arab women, Sagar concludes with a warning that yearning for Muhannad is causing considerable trouble in Arab homes and is akin to worshipping Satan:

> Enough is enough! What's happening is haram!
> We're always in courts, haram!
> Divorce and broken homes, haram!
> And the director of this game is Satan!

Sagar's lyrics seem satirical and comically extreme until a comparison with the pronouncements of the Saudi clerics cited above reveals that many in the

Arab world genuinely saw *Noor* as a sort of Satanic force interfering with the workings of traditional Arab families. The song also captures some of the sense that the series touched on fundamental tensions in Arab society. Indeed, while numerous stories of the impact of *Noor* in the Arab world seem humorous, the fact is that the stories are real and the lives of many individuals were genuinely affected.

No doubt *Noor* appealed to Arab women viewers for much the same reason that Radway's subjects were attracted to reading romance novels—because it provided a relaxing escape from the boredom and banality of their daily lives, providing glimpses of a better world in which many of the shortcomings of reality were overcome in emotionally fulfilling ways. And yet, women in the Arab world seemed to be carried away by *Noor* in ways that go well beyond the reactions of Radway's American women to reading romances—or of American women viewers to watching soap operas. The relevant questions, then, are why would Arab women react so strongly to the fantasy images projected by *Noor*, and why would Arab men feel so threatened by these reactions?

The answer to these questions surely lies in the Turkish context of the series, which presents an image of men and women standing side by side as equals in a Muslim society. Turkey, riding on the modernizing reforms instigated by Kemal Atatürk beginning in the 1920s, had long enjoyed a unique position as the most modern (and Western) country in the Muslim world. Nevertheless, it does remain a *part* of the Muslim world, and a number of traditional religious and social attitudes and practices still hold sway. Thus, physically situated on the boundary between Asia and Europe, Turkey has long been situated in a more symbolic (social and ideological) sense on the boundary between tradition and modernity.

Among other things, this particular placement makes Turkey a quintessential example of the East-West cultural hybridity that we discuss at many points in this volume, though the Arab world would seem to be moving rapidly toward a similarly complex combination of Western-modern-capitalist tendencies with Eastern-traditional-Islamic ones. This confrontation between tradition and modernity is one that is almost entirely lacking in American soap operas, cast as they are in a society in which the modern has already achieved an almost total triumph, consigning tradition to the dustbin of history. Meanwhile, the ongoing presence of certain traditional social bonds in *Noor* suggests that the typically personal dilemmas that drive soap opera plots in the West here have a sociopolitical dimension as well. One is reminded here of Fredric Jameson's controversial, problematic, and extremely useful argument, made back in the mid-1980s, that it is useful for Western readers to consider "Third-World" literature precisely because this literature is still informed by a strong sense of connection between the personal and the political, between private life and public life, that has now been lost to Western literature, after centuries of withering and unremitting pressure beneath the fragmenting tendencies of bourgeois ideology:

> One of the determinants of capitalist culture, that is the culture of the Western realist and modernist novel, is a radical split between the private and the public, between the poetic and the political, between what we have come to think of as the domain of sexuality and the unconscious and that of the public world of classes, of the economic, and of secular political power: in other words, Freud vs. Marx. ("Third-World" 86)

Jameson goes on to argue that, in Third-World texts, the public and the private remain connected, because these realms remain connected in Third-World societies. Thus, the experience of the individual character in a Third-World narrative is inevitably connected to larger social experience, even to the experience of his or her nation as a whole. "All third-world texts are necessarily," Jameson wants to argue, "allegorical, and in a very specific way: they are to be read as what I will call *national allegories*, even when, or perhaps I should say, particularly when their forms develop out of predominantly western machineries of representation, such as the novel" (86). In short, Third-World texts, Jameson concludes, "necessarily project a political dimension in the form of national allegory: *the story of a private individual destiny is always an allegory of the embattled situation of the public third-world culture and society*" (86, Jameson's emphasis).

Jameson makes it clear that he is perfectly aware of the pitfalls of this kind of sweeping analysis, and he himself pauses after initially delineating what he believes to be the most fundamental difference between First-World and Third-World texts by acknowledging that this emphasis on differentiation is in peril of falling into the habit of thinking that Said has described as "orientalism." Indeed, Jameson here comes perilously close to the old Orientalist view of turning to the East for invigoration of an enervated West—or at least to the well-intentioned 1931 call by eminent Orientalist H. A. R. Gibb to study the literature of the Orient to "liberate ourselves from the narrow and oppressive conceptions which would limit all that is significant in literature, thought, and history, to our segment of the globe" (209).

Jameson, however, concludes that the seemingly Orientalist points he is making are worth the risk and at least have the virtue of avoiding the opposite pitfall of

> falling back into some general liberal and humanistic universalism: it seems to me that one of our basic political tasks lies precisely in the ceaseless effort to remind the American public of the radical difference of other national situations. (94)

We ourselves, of course, are very much aware that our own approach in this volume, emphasizing the similarities between the popular culture of the Middle East and of the United States, might seem to trend toward this sort of universalism. We are not, however, claiming that the popular culture of the Middle East is interesting merely because it resembles that of the United States. We simply contend that this convergence of cultures is an important phenomenon worthy of close and critical analysis.

If nothing else, Jameson's argument implies that, because of differing social, political, and historical contexts, the same narrative situations that might pertain strictly to personal, private experience in a First-World text necessarily take on a different meaning and acquire different dimensions in a Third-World text. In particular, Jameson argues that, in Third-World texts, however seemingly private the story being narrated, the story is never fully private, as it would be in a First-World narrative. Instead, in the Third-World context "psychology, or more specifically, libidinal investment is to be read in primarily social and political terms" (89).

It is surely appropriate, in the case of *Noor*, to note that the specific cultural context of the series necessarily renders its meaning different (and more political) than the meaning of any similar story that might be conceived in an American context. But Jameson's broad (and almost polar) opposition between First World and Third World clearly does not encompass this difference, and not simply because those numerical "world" designations are growing increasingly irrelevant as the Cold War fades into the more and more distant past. Indeed, Jameson emphasizes that the national narratives allegorized in "Third-World" literature tend to focus on the historical experience of colonization and decolonization, so that the term "postcolonial" might have been more descriptive than "Third-World," anyway. *Noor*, of course, is in a unique position with regard to Jameson's model in this sense: as the seat of the former Ottoman Empire, Turkey was more in the position of colonizer than colonized, while most of the Middle East in which *Noor* was so popular (and controversial) was dominated by Turkey (and, with the collapse of the Ottoman Empire, Great Britain, and France). *Noor* thus demonstrates the inadequacy of any attempt to divide the world into a modern, First-World West and a more traditional Third-World East. Not only is *Noor* a different narrative because it emanates from Turkey than it could possibly be had it come from America, but the series, we would argue, is necessarily received differently by Arabs than it is in Turkey.

At the same time, *Noor* also helps to bring into focus that the real issue in Jameson's model is neither "First World vs. Third World" nor "colonizer vs. colonized," but the extent to which traditional social structures remain in force in the face of the looming power of capitalist modernization. Among other things, *Noor*, with its central emphasis on an extended family—many of whom live under one roof through most of the series—has a much stronger sense of community than the typical American soap opera, thus strengthening what Dyer has seen as the weakest utopian element in Western entertainment genres. This weakness, of course, comes largely from capitalism's inherent tendency toward individualism and fragmentation. Capitalism certainly plays a role in *Noor* as well, but the central capitalist enterprise in the series is very much a *family* business, and family connections within the company (which might strike many Westerners as pure nepotism) are of crucial importance. At the same time, the elements of community that are central to *Noor* are typically related to older forms of social organization that are very much under siege in the series and very much on the verge of being swept away into the past, creating some of the strongest political tensions in the series.

In one typical scene of community, Fikri, who maintains throughout the series a strong, nostalgic connection to his roots in Afyon, has dinner with his gardener Osman (also from Afyon) in Osman's humble quarters, despite the fact that a fancy dinner has been made for the family in the villa. Fikri is joined in Osman's room by his son (Muhannad's father) and by Noor's grandmother—then eventually by Muhannad and Noor, as they all end up sitting on the floor in a scene of down-to-earth communion that eschews the luxurious trappings of the nearby villa. Three generations thus momentarily join together, but it is also clear in the series that such scenes really belong to the past in Afyon and are becoming increasingly rare in modern Istanbul. The scene is a happy one, but the older times it represents are generally treated in the series in a surprisingly non-nostalgic way.

Such scenes might, however, remain more common in much of the Arab world, where the tensions between tradition and modernity that are central to *Noor* have much more urgency because tradition retains a stronger force. Indeed, despite the Turkish origins of the show, *Noor* probably has stronger political resonances in general within the context of the Arab world than it does in Turkey itself—which might explain the fact that the show was far more popular in its Arabic-dubbed version than it had been in its original run in Turkey.[13] For one thing, that the major characters of the series have strong allegorical resonances is far more clear in an Arab context than in a Turkish one. In addition, the way in which the stories of the characters participate in an overall narrative of transition from tradition to modernity is far more effective in an Arab context than in a Turkish one, because the forces of tradition remain far stronger in the former, making this confrontation between tradition and modernity a much more contested one, though it is also the case that forces of Islamic tradition have for some time been experiencing a resurgence in Turkey.

This kind of allegorical characterization that is so clear in *Noor* is central to Jameson's model of Third-World literature, though it is to an extent typical of the soap opera as a genre, even in the West. Thus, focusing primarily on British soap operas, Dorothy Hobson notes that "characters in soap operas have to be individuals who represent character types that we recognize. Some are destined to become icons. They are manifestations of what we know about our times and ourselves" (82). In Western soap operas, however, the key characters function primarily as icons of specific kinds of *personal* experience, while in *Noor*—as in the "Third-World" narratives discussed by Jameson—their experience is representative of larger, more public phenomena.

Muhannad, for example, is an allegorical figure of modern manhood who transcends traditional sexist biases, though he functions in this sense much more strikingly in an Arab context than in the original Turkish one. Even his famed good looks (Tatlıtuğ was a sort of male supermodel even before his casting in the series), marked by his blue eyes and blondish hair, appear much more striking in the Arab world, where such coloring is far more unusual—and where such coloring (however seemingly Western) is highly valued among both men and women. Even more important than his looks, though, is Muhannad's romantic style: his sensitivity and emotional transparency and his enlightened attitude toward women are all modern characteristics that many Arab wives who viewed the show apparently found lacking in their husbands. Muhannad, though, is not presented as a remarkable, unique individual, but as a *type*, or perhaps a prototype, of the new Muslim man.

Muhannad is frequently seen crying and otherwise showing emotion in the series, but these moments of vulnerability are clearly meant not as signs of weakness, but of strength. Unlike the Arab man who cannot afford such displays because his machismo perhaps disguises an insecure masculinity, Muhannad's masculinity is never in question, even in his weakest moments. He is physically strong, if tender, as when he gently lifts a sleeping Noor from a couch and carries her into their bedroom to put her to bed. He also takes it as no threat to his masculine pride if other men look admiringly at Noor, however revealingly (by Arab standards) she might sometimes dress. And yet, when a man in a bar goes too far and insults Noor, Muhannad does not hesitate to give the man a thrashing. That Muhannad would be perceived by Arab women as a paragon and by Arab men as a threat is thus not at all surprising, especially when he is read allegorically as an image of a new kind of husband and lover that any man could strive to be and any woman could hope for her own man to become. Importantly, this new kind of figure is a fundamentally modern, Western one, and the virtues that Muhannad displays are ones that would easily be recognizable (and nominally endorsed) in a Western context. At the same time, the Turkish setting of the series means that this modern figure does not seem impossibly foreign, but actually attainable in a Muslim context.

That Muhannad's characterization is specifically meant to suggest an historical step forward can perhaps best be seen in the contrast between him and his grandfather, an essentially positive figure who nevertheless retains a number of characteristics of the traditional patriarch—characteristics that are ultimately identified as backward and wrong-headed in the series. While he has succeeded in the modern city of Istanbul and in the modern world of business, Fikri retains

Figure 5.3 Muhannad, on the verge of tears, shows his sensitive side in *Noor* (screen capture).

a nostalgic vision of the more traditional life of his hometown. He also feels perfectly justified in manipulating the lives of his children and grandchildren, including arranging the marriages of both his son (Muhannad's father) and his grandson. It is also clear that he feels especially empowered to manage the lives of the younger *female* members of his family. Thus, when Muhannad's sister Dana returns from America early in the series, their grandfather is downright abusive (within the modern terms of the series) in his attempts to force her to remain in Turkey, rather than return to America, where she has lived, unwed, for years and in fact has a child awaiting her return there. Muhannad, of course, supports his sister's position, which ultimately prevails when she is reunited with the (Turkish) father of the child and they all come to live together in Istanbul in the family villa. Moreover, the grandfather blesses this new extension of the family and becomes a loving great-grandfather to Dana's daughter, providing a successful and community-building resolution to a situation that in a conservative Arab context might have ended much more tragically, perhaps in the killing of Dana to preserve the family's "honor."

The confrontation between tradition and modernity is also allegorized in the series in the contrast between the relatively traditional town of Afyon and the relatively modern city of Istanbul. Time seems almost to stand still in Afyon, where traditional practices reign supreme; those who come to Istanbul from the town in the course of the series are typically depicted as bewildered rustics unable to fathom the fast pace of life in the modern city.[14] In Mikhail Bakhtin's terms, then, the series takes considerable energy from the contrasting chronotopes that hold sway in the different geographic locales of the fast-moving Istanbul (where it is assumed that time brings change) and the slow-moving Afyon (where it is assumed that things stay pretty much the same over time, or at least change very gradually and slowly).[15] This contrast in chronotopes comes very close to the one that exists between the capitalist West in general and the traditional Muslim world, and the simultaneous presence of both chronotopes in *Noor* suggests that both still have considerable power in modern Turkey. On the other hand, it is fairly clear that *Noor* ultimately valorizes the modern world of Istanbul, where all of the interesting action takes place, as opposed to the traditional world of Afyon, which one must leave in order to fulfill one's potential. Then again, it could hardly have been otherwise, given that the very format of the television serial depends for its success on peripatetic sequential movement and continual frenetic plot development, while the high-tech world of satellite television would seem to provide a natural home for modern ideas, but not so much for traditional ones.

What is striking about *Noor*, however, is that (despite its reliance on the crisis-based plot structure of the soap opera) there is relatively little sense of crisis in its depicted movement from the organic community of traditional society to the imagined community of modern society, in the social transformation from *Gemeinschaft* to *Gesellschaft*. Indeed, this transformation (which has provided material for literature all over the world throughout the modern era) is presented in *Noor* as a battle that has largely been won in Turkey—even if some recent events in the Erdogan era might suggest that old ways retain more power in the country than might be obvious from the series.

This battle, in any case, has not been won in the Arab world, although the reaction (both positive and negative) to *Noor* there suggests that the anti-traditional chronotope of capitalism, in which all that is solid melts into air and which assumes that all ideas and practices are up for grabs and will change with time, has growing power among Arabs. Meanwhile, though much of the public attention paid to the series, especially in the Middle Age, has focused on Muhannad and his disruptive effect on Arab women, the central figure of *Noor* (as the title indicates) is actually Noor herself, whose impact might ultimately be even more powerful in the way she provides a positive modern role model for Arab women. Strong, independent, and talented, Noor not only pursues a successful career as a fashion designer (admittedly, with the initial help of her husband and his family), but at one point (after an altercation with Muhannad) returns to Afyon to restart her life and career on her own terms, without any help from her wealthy spouse. Class is a key issue here as well, as she feels that the wealthy family has never accepted her as an equal, despite the humble origins of their own patriarch. She then returns to Istanbul and goes to work for a rival firm, refusing to respond to Muhannad's entreaties to return to him until she has demonstrated that she can succeed without him. At one point, Noor even becomes a sort of feminist activist. Furious when she learns that many of the female children of the workers in the family factory are not being sent to school (because education would be wasted on girls, who will then merely get married and become housewives), Noor demands that the girls be allowed to go to school and even offers to pay for their education out of her own funds.

Such motifs again represent a movement away from tradition and toward modernity, and *Noor* as a series is, in fact, self-consciously aware that its principal conflict is one between tradition and modernity, which gives all of its various crises and resolutions a social dimension that is typically lacking in Western soap operas. The contrast between Muhannad and his grandfather, for example, is clearly one between modernity and tradition—and one that informs virtually every element of the series. It is clear in the series that this is a society in transition and that a modern man like Muhannad would have had no place in the world of his grandfather's youth. Attitudes toward women are crucial to this generational shift, with Noor's insistence on being treated as an equal serving as a key exemplification of modernity and Muhannad's acquiescence to her demands doing likewise. At one point, during the long arc in the second half of the series in which Noor is maintaining her distance from Muhannad (because of what she sees as his excessive chumminess with his old fiancée, the mother of his son), he attempts to win her back by playing the tradition/family card, bringing the entire family together as he comes to Noor to plead with her to return to him—and to the family. Noor again declines his effort at romantic reconciliation, leaving the new wife of Muhannad's grandfather baffled by her resistance. In her own younger days, the older woman tells Fikri, a woman wouldn't dare to stand up to her husband at all, much less rebuff his sincere apologies. Young women today, she concludes, are spoiled and demanding, and Noor should be grateful to have such a caring husband.

Noor does eventually return, of course, but only after a melodramatic moment in which she and Muhannad re-establish their bond when they are nearly killed together in a car crash. Their bond then becomes even stronger later when she donates a kidney to save his life after his kidneys are destroyed in a knife attack by thugs working in the interest of a business rival. Once again, then, Noor saves Muhannad, rather than the conventional narrative route, in which the man would be expected to save the distressed damsel. The series ends with a final episode that includes a thirteen-year leap into the future, by which time Noor and Muhannad have established a stable and lasting relationship—and are expecting their second child. Noor, meanwhile, is writing a memoir about all their experiences, and the content of her writing allows us to see what has become of many of the characters in the intervening years, including the fact that Muhannad has retired from the world of business so that he can devote his time to staying home and being a dedicated husband and father. Meanwhile, he has handed over the reins of the business to his cousin Bana, keeping the management of the company in the family—but in the hands of a *female* member of the family, and one who has succeeded spectacularly in the role, winning multiple businesswoman of the year awards.

The action depicted in the main narrative of *Noor* takes place over a period of several years, so that the gap in time during the final episode means that the entire series covers a period of close to twenty years (even though most of the action seems roughly contemporaneous with the original broadcast of the

Figure 5.4 Noor writes her memoirs in the last episode of *Noor* (screen capture).

series), which would place the final episode around the year 2020, or even later. *Noor* is not science fiction, however, and the producers of the program opted to remain fairly vague about the time period of the various events in the series. The series thus does not engage in the sort of dialogue with contemporary events that might place its action in historical time, nor does it show much interest in depicting specific changes in Turkish society between, say, 2000 and 2020. Cars, cell phones, and other technological markers of passing time stay the same throughout the series as well—presumably for budgetary reasons, given that the series was filmed during a single year. Nevertheless, *Noor* does depict Turkey as a society in transition, while the extended time frame of the series allows for the depiction of changes in specific *characters*, especially Noor and Muhannad, whose allegorical functions provide an indirect account of historical change in Turkey.

In short, though the series might lack specifics in terms of its depiction of historical change in Turkey, it does ultimately accept historical change as a given, thus adopting a perspective on history that is fundamentally modern and anti-traditional. From an Arab point of view, meanwhile, the depiction in the series of Muhannad as a tender and caring mate for his independent and talented wife could surely not help being seen as closely involved with this endorsement of historical change. This combination thus makes characters such as Muhannad and Noor seem not like impossible ideals but like logical results of the historical process. And, if that process can produce individuals like these (with relationships like theirs) in Turkey, then perhaps such people and such relationships can eventually emerge in the Arab world as well. Of course, even to suggest that such fundamental and dramatic changes might occur in certain parts of the Middle East represents either a thrilling utopian possibility or a terrifying (even Satanic) threat, depending upon one's point of view. Meanwhile, the very fact that such differences in opinion and perspective exist in the Arab world suggests that modernizing changes are already underway and that this world bears little relation to the timeless, unchanging, and homogeneous Middle East of classic Orientalist fantasy.

6

Arabs Got TV: The "Americanization" of Arab Televisual Culture

Arab television and global music competition franchises

As the beat-driven music builds, a matched group of twelve dancers wearing jazzy outfits—the six men in black pants and white T-shirts with cool suspenders, the six women in black pants and white tank tops with colorful cut-off jackets—launch into a carefully choreographed routine in support of a singer who stands at center stage. The singer, a young black man, is dressed somewhat similarly to the male dancers, except with a leather vest in place of the suspenders. The song is Michael Jackson's "Billie Jean," and the singer delivers it with aplomb and confidence. The delivery might be a touch less soulful than the original, and the slightly heavy singer certainly lacks the gravity-defying dance moves that made the reed-thin King of Pop such a special performer on stage, but the performance is as good as anyone other than Jackson himself might ever be expected to deliver. The singer has clearly studied his predecessor, and he does Jackson with the ease of a seasoned professional. Indeed, it might come as a surprise to some seeing this performance out of context (on YouTube, say) that the performer is not really an experienced pro but merely a budding pro competing for recognition on *The X Factor*, one of the numerous music competition shows that, emanating from Great Britain and the United States, became popular throughout the world in the early years of the twenty-first century.

This particular performer, of course, was no run-of-the-mill competitor. He would go on to take the top prize in the 2015 season of *The X Factor*, along the way showing the audacity to perform songs not just by Jackson, but by other rhythm-and-blues greats, including Stevie Wonder ("Signed, Sealed, Delivered") and even the Godfather of Soul, James Brown ("I Feel Good"). He might have lacked the emotional intensity of Wonder or the raw energy of Brown, but his smoothly accomplished performances measured up well to these mighty forerunners.

And, as if to show his versatility, he also performed well-known songs by such legendary British pop-rock predecessors as David Bowie ("Heroes") and the Police ("Every Breath You Take"). He performed more contemporary numbers as well, including a particularly effective rendition of Pharrell Williams's 2014 megahit "Happy" and finishing in his final performance with a rousing delivery of American John Legend's 2013 romantic pop ballad "All of Me."

With such performances under his belt, it might come as no surprise that this young singer would come out the overall winner in his season of *The X Factor*. What might be a bit more surprising is that this string of impressive covers of American and British rock, pop, and R&B classics—performed in a flawless African American–inflected English—was delivered not by a young man from Detroit or Chicago, but by Hamza Hawsawi (aka AyZee), an Arab from Jeddah, Saudi Arabia. The show on which Hawsawi won was the Arab-world version of *The X Factor*, broadcast during this season on the satellite channel MBC 4, though his performances might have looked perfectly at home on the American (or, for that matter, the British) version of the show or its various cousins in the genre.[1]

The slickly produced *X Factor* is typical of the sophisticated fare that now appears on Arab television, especially on the channels of the big players in the field, such as MBC. MBC, Rotana, and other such media companies broadcast multiple channels of extremely modern, Western-style programming, mixed in with an occasional example of more traditional Arab fare.[2] MBC in particular

Figure 6.1 Hamza Hawsawi performs "Billie Jean" on *The X Factor Arabia* (screen capture).

broadcasts a number of popular American shows (and movies) directly (generally with Arabic subtitles). Arab audiences thus have extensive familiarity with the American programs, and it is not insignificant that when Arab versions of American shows are remade in Arabic the producers usually take pains to make them look and feel as much like the American originals as possible, rather than trying to hide their sources in the sinful West.[3]

Hawsawi, in short, is not a one-of-a-kind phenomenon. For example, his "International Singing" team on *The X Factor Arabia* also featured a lanky, big-voiced brunette from Lebanon who performed (in flawless English) a series of American songs under the rather unArabic single name of "Latoya." Though perhaps less accomplished than Hawsawi, Latoya acquitted herself well in belting out such well-known hits as "Holding Out for a Hero" (originally recorded by Bonnie Tyler for the 1984 film *Footloose*, then re-recorded by Jennifer Saunders for the 2004 film *Shrek 2*), "What's Up" (by the California-based one-hit wonders Four Non-Blondes), and "I Will Always Love You" (originally recorded in 1974 by country superstar Dolly Parton, but probably best known for the version recorded by Whitney Houston for the 1992 film *The Bodyguard*).

Neither the English-language singing nor the elaborate, high-tech, American-style staging of the performances of Latoya and Hawsawi seemed particularly unusual amid the general tenor of the show, in which Hawsawi's most serious competition for the title probably came from a manufactured pan-Arabic boy band with the English name of "The Five," even though they, in fact, performed primarily in Arabic. This group, which included members from Algeria (two), Lebanon, Morocco, and Egypt, was obviously modeled on Western groups such as the Backstreet Boys, whom Hawsawi has listed as an important influence on the development of his own interest in music. Meanwhile, the members of The Five named numerous Western performers among their own influences, including Eminem, Bruno Mars, and Justin Bieber.

Hawsawi, Latoya, and The Five would have fit in perfectly well on any number of the music competition shows that have become a major phenomenon in twenty-first-century Arab television. The most popular of these shows are part of the international franchising that has directly translated the formats of Western programs such as *The X Factor, Pop Idol/American Idol, The Voice*, and *Got Talent* into global phenomena, with only slight modifications to meet the requirements of the dozens of local markets for which versions of the programs have been made.

Arab musical competition shows may be closely modeled on their Western progenitors, but they do sometimes produce results that one would never see in the Western world. For example, Jordan's Nedaa Sharara, the winner of the Arab version of *The Voice* in 2015, stirred considerable controversy when she performed throughout the competition wearing a hijab and traditional dress, thus breaking the longtime unwritten rule that singers in the Arab world have greater freedom of expression than ordinary Muslim women but must pay for that freedom by giving up the ability to claim to be a conventional Muslim woman.[4] Sharara won on the basis of her strong voice and of her impressive delivery of traditional Arab classics (mostly Egyptian and mostly associated with legendary singers such as Umm Kulthum). During the competition, in fact, Sharara's own father ceased speaking to her because of her appearance on the show, though she certainly had her supporters as well. After all, she won (becoming the show's first female winner) by a vote of the show's viewership—which MBC claimed reached 150 million (Khalaf, "Nedaa"). And, after winning, she received a congratulatory tweet from Queen Rania. Sherine, the judge who served as Sharara's mentor on the show, expressed pride in her protégée and in the show, arguing that it serves as a valuable platform by which Arabs can announce to the world that they are talented, capable, and modern. "When I come here every week," she said, "I feel like I'm attending a show in Las Vegas. We have an incredible set, we look great, the audience is always so excited and our contestants are stars" (Khalaf, "The Judges").

If Sharara stirred considerable controversy by mixing traditional Muslim feminine attire with modern show business performances, the Kuwaiti comedy group Sheyaab ("Old Men") had considerable success on *Arabs Got Talent,* making it all the way to the final round in 2013. The group features three young performers who come out on stage disguised as old men wearing Khaliji headdresses and flowing Khaliji robs. They thus appear to be the very personification of tradition in the Gulf region—but then proceed to boogie and get down while performing extremely Western-style music (one of their key performances on *Arabs Got Talent* can be found on YouTube[5]). The mismatch between their appearance and their performance thus becomes a perfect example of comic incongruity. On the other hand, the fact that this mismatch was perceived as amusing (and caused no controversy) when enacted by male performers (as opposed to the uproar over Sharara's performance in a hijab) can also be taken as an example of the double standards that still rule in the Arab world where gender is concerned.

A hijab was also central to the performance of Egyptian Mayam Mahmoud in 2013 when, at the age of eighteen, she became the first hijabi rapper to compete on *Arabs Got Talent.*[6] Employing politically charged lyrics that call for women's rights and protest the harassment of women on the streets of Egypt, Mahmoud

Figure 6.2 The Kuwaiti group Sheyaab performs on *Arabs Got Talent*.

gained considerable attention, winning the 2014 Freedom of Expression Award from the Index on Censorship in the area of the arts.[7] Especially from a conventional Western point of view, a hijabi rapper might seem an incongruous figure. Indeed, an *Arab* rapper might seem surprising.[8] However, as we noted in Chapter 4 of this study, rap/hip-hop has become an increasingly prominent part of the Arab music scene in recent years, and Mahmoud is only one of a number of Arab artists who have drawn upon what they see as the inherent oppositional political energies of hip-hop to address important contemporary issues with their music.[9]

The utopian potential of game shows

The direct franchising of such music competition shows is a special case, of course, but it is also the case that virtually every Western television genre has (amid the general explosion in Arab television broadcasting that has marked the early years of the twenty-first century) produced Arab equivalents. While the businesses behind Arab television remain less modern in their operation than their American counterparts (with an inordinate amount of ownership and control lying in the hands of a relatively small number of Arabs), Arab television programming is coming more and more to resemble American programming.[10] For example, the high-tension game show *Who Wants to Be a Millionaire?*, which became such a major phenomenon on American television in 1999, after itself being imported from Great Britain, was exported to the Arab world in 2000, in a perfect example of today's transnational flow of culture. The Arab version of

Millionaire (entitled *Man Sayarbah el Million?*—literally "Who Wants to Win the Million?") was hosted (for MBC) by Lebanon's George Kordahi, who had worked in Arab radio in Great Britain for a number of years. Adopting its format, music, sets, and so on almost directly from the British and American originals, the show was initially produced in London, where MBC was then headquartered, with Arab contestants flown in from the Middle East. The show was a huge success, becoming at one point the highest rated show in the history of Arab television, running for years and ultimately moving its production to Egypt (and its top prize from one million to two million Saudi riyal). Kordahi became a major star, ultimately hosting several other shows and having a lucrative career in television commercials, as well as launching his own line ("GK") of perfume and cologne.[11]

Such money-oriented game shows would seem to be little more than thinly veiled allegorizations of capitalist competition, a sort of reality TV version of the American get-rich-quick adventure story that Ernst Bloch dismissed as a locus of false utopian hope, as the "rot-gut epic of the jackpot, run off in millions" (351). The international proliferation of this particular game show might be taken as a key entertainment-world marker of the proliferation of capitalism itself, the global spread of such game shows announcing the globalization of greed. Indeed, a major element of the *Millionaire* show is greed itself, as contestants must continually choose between risking their current winnings to go for more or playing it safe and going home with what they have already won.

This situation adds irony to the fact that the Arab version of *Millionaire* debuted on the first day of the holy month of Ramadan in 2000—but then, however much about asceticism this month might ostensibly be, it is a jubilee period in Arab television, something along the lines of sweeps periods in the American television industry. Indeed, much like the commercialization of Christmas in the West, Ramadan is both the most spiritual time for Muslims and the period of peak consumption for many individuals and peak income for many businesses. Most ironically of all, even restaurants often achieve their peak sales during this month of self-denial, when each day's fasting is followed by an evening of feasting. Ramadan weight-gaining is a real problem in the Middle East.

In short, whatever their reputation (in the West) for religious fanaticism, many Muslims in the Middle East would appear to be susceptible to the same secular/consumerist lures as are their counterparts in the West. The region's true fanatics, the ISIS, have declared that television itself is a key source of this kind of secular "contamination." Thus, before Ramadan in 2016, ISIS announced a campaign to rid the Middle East of satellite dishes and the morally impure programming that they deliver to Arab homes, warning Muslims that this programming was "destroying their beliefs and polluting their ethics." Further, in a more detailed infographic explaining their reasons for banning the purchase or sale of satellite dishes in the areas under their control, ISIS declared that television programming was "spreading immorality, corruption and obscenity by showing women, music videos and so forth" (Webb).

In terms of the appeal of the *Millionaire* show, one could argue that the quest for wealth is much older and more fundamental to human life than television or even capitalism. After all, Bloch also noted how fundamental this motif is to fairytales and folk tales—even if he distinguishes between the active seeking of fortune in these forms and the later, more debased waiting of the modern American adventure-story hero "for happiness to fall into his lap" (367). And one could argue that the *Millionaire* format, despite the high-tech trappings of the stage settings, does have elements of the fairy tale and of the story in which the hero must actively struggle to overcome obstacles in order to succeed.

The Arab adaptation of the talk show format

However, one might argue that it is not the high-stakes game show that is the quintessentially American television form. Instead, it might very well be that the mainstream ideology of America is most directly reflected in the television talk show. For one thing, the classic talk show format was pioneered in America with the advent of NBC's *The Tonight Show*, which premiered in 1954 and has aired continuously ever since. The show was hosted by cocreator Steve Allen from 1954 to 1957, followed by Jack Paar from 1957 to 1962. Paar is usually credited with perfecting the format of the show, though his successor, Johnny Carson, who hosted the show from 1962 to 1992, is widely regarded as the greatest of all talk show hosts, perhaps challenged only by David Letterman, who never became the regular host of *The Tonight Show* but hosted similarly formatted programs from 1982 to 2015 (and even returning on Netflix in 2018 in a reduced-frequency format), thus topping Carson, at least for longevity.[12]

Among other things, the Nebraskan Carson and the Indianan Letterman are among the most quintessentially American of all major US television personalities, so it seems appropriate that they would be the two most prominent hosts of what is perhaps the quintessential American television format. This format has been widely copied, and most talk shows have followed a very similar structure, with only minor variations. Such shows generally begin as the host presents a brief "monologue" before launching into the heart of the program, in which the host sits behind a desk and chats about various topics in a rather lighthearted manner with guests (generally show business personalities, though they can come from other fields as well) who sit in chairs or on a couch nearby. This interview format, meanwhile, is punctuated by a variety of skits and stunts, sometimes including performances by the guests, especially if they are singers or musicians. This auxiliary material also includes segments in which the host interacts with a live audience or even goes out into the streets to encounter "regular" people. A live band provides music in the studio, while the bandleader (such as Carson's Doc Severinsen or Letterman's Paul Shaffer) occasionally banters with the host.

This tried and true format provides a comfort zone in which viewers can relax into a familiar setting almost as if visiting with the host as a friend (or even family member)—a friend who has particularly interesting or attractive guests with whom the viewer can also visit. Talk shows thus form a sort of simulated community that might be seen as substituting for the lack of genuine community in the modern societies of late capitalism. Talk show audiences are thus treated to an experience analogous to that of Mildred, the wife of the protagonist of Ray Bradbury's 1953 dystopian classic *Fahrenheit 451*, who considers the characters she watches on television to be her "family."

It is in this sense that talk shows are a paradigmatic American cultural form, providing some sense of human contact for their alienated viewers, enhanced by the fact that this contact is generally with well-known celebrities. More traditional and communal societies of the world would presumably have less need for this sort of substitute for genuine conversation, but then societies such as those in the Middle East are becoming less traditional and communal every day. Perhaps it is not surprising, then, that the talk show format has spread across the globe, including to the Middle East, where various forms of talk shows have been popular for a number of years.

Such shows have proliferated throughout Arab television in the early years of the twenty-first century. For example, MBC's highly successful *Kalam Nawaem* ("Soft Talk"), a panel discussion program modeled on America's hugely popular *The View*, has aired since 2002, attracting such guests as then US secretary of state Hillary Clinton (in 2011)—or even Jordan's Queen Rania, who appeared in 2010 to hawk her new English-language children's book. Devoted to the discussion of issues of special relevance to Arab women, *Kalam Nawaem* has become one of MBC's staple programs. A number of talk-oriented shows have, in fact, been specifically aimed at Arab women viewers. Meanwhile, the Beruit-based

MTV Lebanon has, since 2009, broadcast *Talk of the Town*, a show whose most distinctive feature might be that its principal host is a woman, the striking Mona Abou Hamza. This show perhaps announces its Western roots by keeping its title in English throughout; it also features a range of guests, including political and other "serious" figures. The show is still primarily designed for entertainment, but it does tend to operate with a bit more decorum than most talk shows. It also features its own distinctive set that does not appear to be modeled on any particular American talk show. The set, in fact, is even more modern and futuristic than one might expect to find on an American show. It looks almost as if the show might be set inside a giant spaceship.

Science fictional sets and striking female television presenters are a key phenomenon on Arab television. Egypt's Wafaa El Kilani has appeared on a number of venues since 1997, specializing in talk shows since 2012. One of her recent efforts is *Al Mataha* ("The Maze"), which began broadcasting on MBC MASR in 2015. Here, an impeccably dressed and immaculately coiffed El Kilani interviews a variety of guests amid what looks for all the world like a blasted postapocalyptic cityscape. Sometimes El Kilani wanders about the mazelike set, interviewing her guests as she goes. Sometimes she sits across from them at an industrial metal table that might have been at home aboard the *Nostromo* from *Alien* (1979). Over the years, El Kilani has interviewed such distinguished figures as Nawal El Saadawi, though the bread and butter of *El Mataha* is singers, actors, and other entertainment figures. In one episode she interviewed fellow talk show host (and former heart surgeon) Bassem Youssef, who himself generated considerable controversy with his own television news satire program *Al-Bernameg* ("The Show"), which began running on Egypt's Capital Broadcast Center (CBC) and ONTV in 2011, ending with a brief run on MBC MASR before its cancellation in June of 2014. Engaging with events following the 2011 Egyptian Revolution, *Al-Bernameg* was widely compared with America's *The Daily Show*, while Youssef himself has frequently been compared with *Daily Show* host Jon Stewart. In fact, Stewart and Youssef exchanged visits, each appearing on the other's show. The two hit it off like old pals, exchanging well-coordinated quips that showed little sign of a gap between their cultures. Youssef's biting wit, however, touched a chord that revealed important differences between the political climates in Egypt and the United States. Political pressure drove *Al-Bernameg* off the air and Youssef was at one point arrested, eventually moving to the United States to continue his career on American television, after a stint teaching at Harvard. In July of 2016, the first ten (brief, roughly six-minute) episodes of his new web series,

The Democracy Handbook, were released on the website of the Fusion cable and digital platform, as well as on YouTube. The project of this program—like the project of the current volume—is to deconstruct seeming differences between American and Arab culture, as Youssef focuses mostly on satirically deflating American pretensions to superiority over the Arab world (without making any claims that the Arab world is all that great, either.) Meanwhile, *Al-Bernameg* itself remains wildly popular on YouTube as well.[13]

Among other things, El Kilani, when Youssef appeared on her show, discussed with him the charges by one of his critics (posted on Facebook) that Youssef was a Satan worshipper who had been possessed by evil spirits and djinn, much like his counterpart Jon Stewart. When asked if these charges were true, Youssef simply answered no, then he and El Kilani had a good laugh. He declined, however, to respond to the critic, saying that, in this age of the internet, rumors can proliferate freely and rapidly; anyone can say anything about anyone, and it really isn't worth trying to respond. It's a chummy interview: like Youssef and Stewart, El Kilani and Youssef are colleagues; in this case they are also compatriots. As sophisticated and educated Egyptians, they are amused by Middle Eastern superstitions, even if those superstitions still run rampant in certain less knowing segments of the Arab population.

Even when El Kilani's guests come from the world of relatively light pop culture, her interviews can sometimes be a bit more confrontational than the light banter of many other hosts. When Lebanese pop star Myriam Fares appeared on the talk show *Bidoon Rakabah* ("Uncensored") in 2012, host El Kilani asked her about the controversy concerning her sexy dancing in "Moukanoh Wein"; she then showed the clip of Feghali's parody (see Chapter 3) while a noticeably irritated Fares looked on. Following the clip, Fares claimed that she had not been upset about Feghali's parody, but that some members of her family had felt it was excessive. In response, El Kilani argued that Feghali had not made up the parody out of thin air. She then showed a mixture of the clips from both "Moukanoh Wein" and "Moush Ananeya" to indicate the sources of Feghali's inspiration. "Your clips," El Kilani tells Fares straight out, "seem to feature an exaggerated focus on your buttocks." Then she points out that critics have argued that the buttocks in question might be artificially enhanced just for the video clips. When El Kilani asks if this charge is true, Fares anticipates Youssef's answer to the same interviewer about demonic possession, laughingly responding with a simple "no." El Kilani then points out the characterization by Emirati singer Ahlam of the video for "Moukanoh Wein" as pornographic, to which an uncomfortable Fares responds that her performance might have been sexy, but it was a perfectly normal Khaliji dancing style known as "Ma'alya." El Kilani responds that this dance is performed by men in the Gulf to announce their gayness and by women there to announce their availability for sex. Maybe now (in an altered form), Fares claims, but the version she performed was actually an old, traditional, and respectable dance. El Kilani, fighting a smile, then continues on the same course, playing a clip of an Egyptian critic who charges that Fares's main talent lies in her pornographic, silicon-enhanced appearance and that she has little real talent as a singer. She might not be the greatest singer, Fares responds, but at least her music entertains people and makes them dance.

Arab talk shows employ a variety of gimmicks to produce situations in which hosts and guests can interact in interesting ways. In the first season of the Egyptian live talk show *Ana wel Assal* ("The Honey and I"), broadcast during Ramadan of 2012, Lebanese host Nishan greets a string of female guests, each of whom enters the stage by descending an elaborate winding staircase wearing formal gowns of a type that might have been worn by a Disney princess. Then, to add a modern touch, Nishan begins the interview by taking a selfie with his guest, which he later posts on Twitter. The princess motif is maintained throughout the season, with a special emphasis on the Cinderella story as a sort of presiding theme. Nishan's questions probe into controversies or bad times in his guests' lives—with an emphasis on the way they ultimately emerged from hardship into triumph, Cinderella-style. The rather low-budget set itself is like a weird postmodern reinscription of a Disney castle, while a screen in the background displays projected images, including one of a Ferris wheel that gives the whole set a Disneyworld-like feel. Fares even wore a specially designed dress bearing prints of various Disney characters when she appeared on the show.

Ana wel Assal was a relatively minor show that lasted only two Ramadan seasons, but the roster of guests in this first season reads like a who's who of Arab female stars, including Egyptian singing star Sherine (in a two-episode sequence, the second episode of which was a sort of corrective to her angry and tearful first appearance). Nishan also interviewed Lebanese actresses/singers Cyrine Abdelnour and Haifa Wehbe, ending in the last two episodes with Lebanese singing superstars Nancy Ajram and Elissa. The second (and last) season of the show continued the fairy-tale motif but added some cross-cultural dialogue by switching the theme from Cinderella to Scheherazade. Still, the presentation of the show with *One Thousand and One Nights* as a backdrop still had a rather Disneyfied feel to it. The coverage was also broadened to include some male guests, but the show had clearly run out of ideas and did not appear for a third season.

One talk show that has attempted to project a more traditional Middle Eastern feel is *Ghanili Ta Ghanilak* ("Sing to Me and I'll Sing to You"), hosted by Syrian singing star Ali el Deek and Lebanese presenter Grace Al Rayess, though the latter is really more of a sidekick, along the lines of Carson's Ed McMahon or Conan O'Brien's Andy Richter. The show is broadcast on Lebanon's Al Jadeed TV, which reaches the entire Arab world and has recently expanded its operations to the United States, Canada, Latin America, and Australia. The opening sequence of this show announces its old-fashioned rural feel, beginning with a shot of a crowing rooster, then of a bleating sheep, and then of a line of traditional male dabkeh dancers—a form that implies community and collective action. El Deek is then shown firing a shotgun into the air, followed by a shot of Rayess and then one of an old woman making bread and pastries in the traditional fashion. The whole sequence is clearly designed to create an atmosphere that suggests an old-time village. Guests come onto the large, crowded set, which is teeming with what seem to be locals in traditional dress, going about their business. There are even farm animals on the set, to enhance the villagey feel, and the dabkeh dancers form an important part of the show. El Deek and Al Rayess wear modern, but informal dress as they chat with their guests in a living-room-like area of the large set, while munching on traditional regional foods. Interviews are light and superficial, while the main entertainment is provided by live, exuberantly cheerful (but informal and seemingly impromptu) performances of traditional-sounding songs by el Deek and the guests. The very fact that these performances are live enhances the traditional feel of the show, though it also limits the range of guests to those who are comfortable singing on live television.

Ghanili Ta Ghanilak is more *Lawrence Welk* than *The Tonight Show*, but, if American talk shows seem designed as a sort of compensation for the loss of community under late capitalism, the Lebanese show can be seen as an almost desperate attempt to recover a Levantine sense of community that is fast being swept away as well. Indeed, the prevailing mood of the show is nostalgia, as if in acknowledgment that the kind of community it celebrates is a thing of the past. In one particularly telling episode, the guests are Hussein, Ammar, and Hassan, the younger brothers of el Deek, thus further enhancing the attempt to create an atmosphere of traditional community. The brothers heap praise on their fraternal host and his show and the way the show and its set celebrate "our folklore." It's a real love-fest among the brothers, but then *Ghanili Ta Ghanilak* is all about getting along, and everyone seems to be having a great time, even if they sometimes seem to be trying a bit too hard and even if the village atmosphere at times seems a bit contrived.[14]

Perhaps the most Americanized of all Arab talk shows is MTV Lebanon's *Hayda Haki* ("Now You're Talking"), which began broadcasting in 2013. Hosted by Lebanese actor/comedian Adel Karam, *Hayda Haki* derives its format from American talk shows with essentially no modification, though it does air only once a week (in ninety-minute episodes) as opposed to the usual nightly broadcasts of the major American evening talk shows. Karam appears to have studied such American predecessors as Letterman and O'Brien, hosting the show with a familiar silliness that is augmented by his interactions with guitarist/bandleader Chady Nashef, who also provides American-style jazz and blues music for the show.

Karam's guests come from a variety of backgrounds, though the show clearly specializes in the sexy female pop singers for which Lebanon is so well known. Perhaps the sexiest of all of these is Haifa Wehbe, so it was no surprise that the program booked Haifa as the main guest for the opening episode of their third season in October of 2015. As if in acknowledgment of her fame (and reputation for sexiness), Karam introduces her merely as "Haifa," knowing that the audience will go wild at the mention of her name. The buxom actress/singer struts out in ultra-high spike heels and a tight black mini-dress that leaves her long legs (one of which sports a large tattoo) on full display. Haifa is probably past forty,[15] but she looks good and she knows it. She is charming and flirty throughout the interview. Her plump pouty lips, short straight nose, and prominent cheekbones are almost doll-like, perhaps partly with the aid of the famed Lebanese plastic surgery industry. Her nails are long, painted, and immaculately manicured; the brilliant blue of her eyes is probably the product of colored contact lenses. Though a Shia Muslim, she is perfectly packaged and displayed, a spectacle of feminine allure, the virtual opposite of the covered-up modesty that many in the West associate with Muslim women.

In the course of the interview, she pauses to perform a couple of sexy, lip-synced musical numbers (no live singing required here), undulating tantalizingly for Karam and the band. Karam himself teases and flirts and feigns an uncontrolled adolescent anticipation when she pretends to invite him to her house for an assignation. By his standards, though, he treats Haifa with relative respect, perhaps because she is such a big star, even if she is known mostly for her sexiness. Indeed, Karam tends in general to show relative respect for major established stars such as Wehbe or Elissa or Ajram, though his most representative shtick is the leering wolfishness with which he greets younger, lesser-known (and generally more scantily clad) female singers who come on the show. Each new pair of partly exposed breasts that comes on the show appears to be the first that Karam has ever seen, and his principal act seems to consist

Figure 6.3 Haifa Wehbe sings to host Adel Karam on the Lebanese talk show *Hayda Haki*.

of calling sophomoric attention to those and other strategic body parts of his guests, who generally respond good-naturedly. After all, they are here to market their wares. They are generally slightly less exposed than their Hollywood counterparts who come on American talk shows, though more attention is called to their dishabille.

Another Arab talk show that illustrates a number of important phenomena is *Siwar Shuaib* ("Corralled by Shuaib"), hosted by Kuwait's Shuaib Rashed. Among other things, this show, which premiered in 2015 and appears only on YouTube (with a viewership of upward of forty million), highlights the importance of the internet and social media in the Arab world.[16] Much of the content of the show deals with online phenomena as well, and many of Rashed's celebrity guests are known primarily (or even exclusively) for their online activities. For example, *Siwar Shuaib* sometimes features guests who are famous primarily from their appearances on sites such as Instagram, and the show includes in their on-screen credentials the number of followers that they have on the site. The show addresses a number of topical issues, with an emphasis on satire, though the satire is typically lighthearted. On the other hand, Rashed also specializes in putting his guests on the spot, often overtly insulting or embarrassing them. For example, episodes of the show typically end with a segment called "Under the Table," in which Rashed confronts a guest with information that they had thought to be private, sometimes visibly upsetting them. Thus, when Rashed presented fellow

Kuwaiti television personality Halima Boland with some written information (never revealed on the show) involving some prominent personages, she stormed off the set, warning Rashed that revealing this information could be significantly dangerous for him.

On the other hand, Rashed's humor can also be self-deprecating, as when he interviewed American actress Lindsay Lohan in English, all the while mumbling asides in Arabic that mocked his own infelicity with English. Meanwhile, he ended the interview by serving Lohan a large platter of Machboos laham, the national dish of Kuwait, then helping her to eat it by hand, dipping his fingers into the food (and then licking them off) in a way that Lohan clearly found off-putting ("It seems a bit inappropriate," she commented), thus having fun with the stereotype that Arabs are unsophisticated primitives who tend to eat messily with their fingers. Meanwhile, as the interview with Lohan (much of which focused on her professed interest in Islam and in which she surprised Rashed with her knowledge of Arabic) demonstrates, one of Rashed's favorite topics in fact involves the issue of "co-existence," in which he emphasizes in various (usually comical) ways that people in the Eastern and Western worlds should be able to find ways to get along. In fact, his show—the first talk show in Kuwait to employ lively and irreverent comical methods reminiscent of many Western shows—is by its very nature already an example of transnational cultural flow between the East and the West.

Khawatir: Thoughtful television

Other elements of the Arab entertainment industry have also engaged in dialogue with contemporary issues, sometimes in more serious ways. One of the most interesting phenomena on Arab television of the early twenty-first century was the Ramadan educational/current affairs show *Khawatir* ("Thoughts"), which ran on MBC for eleven seasons from 2005 to 2015. The show was hosted by Ahmad Al Shugairi, a charismatic young Berkeley-educated Saudi. Addressed especially to younger Arabs, *Khawatir* was designed to call attention to social problems in the Arab world, while also offering practical advice for the solution to these problems. The show, while often pointing out grim realities (as when Shugairi visited the dismally poor in an otherwise wealthy Saudi Arabia, the grim slums of Cairo, or impoverished water-starved villages in the Sudan), was fundamentally optimistic, consistently arguing for the possibility of progress in the Arab world. At times, Shugairi offered examples from the West (and Japan, to which the entire fifth season was devoted) that he felt should be emulated by Arabs, a practice that drew considerable criticism in the Middle East. However, Shugairi also pointed out ills in the West and consistently argued that young Arabs could and should be responsible for their own futures. Sometimes, the advice given on *Khawatir* was on individual improvement, as when the show pointed out the disadvantages of smoking or the advantages of reading. One episode in the tenth season was devoted to the obsession with beauty worldwide, including the waste of resources on expensive plastic surgery or the distortion of individual lives (especially of girls) to try to force them into a particular socially prescribed notion of beauty. The emphasis of the show, however, was on the need for fundamental systemic change if the Arab world was to be successful in meeting the challenges of the twenty-first century.

Young Arabs responded well to the entertaining and upbeat approach taken by Shugairi, and the show was increasingly popular, despite opposition from conservative forces within the Arab world. The show also grew increasingly complex, with higher and higher production values, beginning with a first season of very short episodes in which young people gave their opinions on various topics, and expanding to find Shugairi traveling the globe in search of specific examples to illustrate his points. Many episodes of *Khawatir* were directed at the education of children. During his 2009 trip to Japan, for example, Shugairi visited the Tokyo franchise of the Mexican-based global children's entertainment center chain Kidzania. Here, children participate in a simulated city environment in which they work at dozens of different jobs (from firefighting to television production), serve as customers for the other kid workers, and perform "adult" tasks such as opening bank accounts, managing money (in Kidzania's own currency), or taking driving tests to receive drivers' licenses so they can drive about the city in small cars. As a result, the children are exposed in a hands-on manner to various aspects of adult life, having good make-believe fun, but also learning a great deal about how the world works.

One might, of course, argue that the Kidzania concept also teaches children simply to accept the way the modern world works, making the amusement park merely another Ideological State Apparatus as described by Louis Althusser. Still, Shugairi's endorsement of the concept as a possible educational entertainment has a special resonance for an Arab world in which modernity has often been viewed with suspicion. His advice was apparently well taken, and modern, sparkling Kidzania franchises began to spring up in the Arab world almost immediately, opening in Dubai in 2010, then spreading to Kuwait and

Cairo by 2013, and to Jeddah in 2015, with an additional (especially elaborate) franchise scheduled to open in Doha in 2018.

Some of *Khawatir*'s more socially oriented episodes occurred in the final season, for which the stated theme was "to encourage every individual in every society on earth not to take the planet for granted and to help build a better world for future generations." The episodes of this season undertook projects ranging from encouraging an entrepreneurial spirit among young Arabs, to urging religious tolerance, to railing against littering and calling for environmental responsibility. Occasionally, the episodes seem a bit simplistic from a Western point of view, as when Shugairi conducts a one-sided diatribe against the evils of alcohol that might have come from a pre-Prohibition American temperance campaigner. A single sip of alcohol, this episode seems to imply, threatens to ruin one's life forever. In general, however, the spirit of the show, despite frequent mentions of Allah and numerous appeals to the Quran, is very modern, very capitalist, and very liberal. From a Western perspective, in fact, the show is mostly filled with familiar wisdom; from a Middle Eastern perspective, it is forward-looking, even daring. Indeed, the very fact that Shugairi finds it necessary to argue such points as that tolerance of diversity and working hard are good, while littering and disrespect for others are bad, suggests his own belief that some of the Orientalist stereotypes identified by Said might actually derive from a grain of truth. On the other hand, the fact that Shugairi can deliver such advice on a popular Ramadan show suggests that the virtues he extols are not nearly as foreign to Arab culture as Said's Orientalists might believe.

Cross-promotion on Arab television

Shugairi seeks both to entertain and to educate, but, as in the West, the main emphasis of the Arab entertainment business is on the former. Meanwhile, given the range of Western-style entertainment produced in the Arab world—and given the prominence in that world of Western-style celebrity culture—it should come as no surprise that the Arab world also features entertainment "news" programs that combine entertainment with information. The long-running American show *ET* also exists in an Arab version (*ET bil Arabi*), for example, to help Arab fans keep up with their favorite performers—both East and West. (Of course, the texture of contemporary Arab television is such that, on any given day, one can watch, on, say MBC2, the American version of *ET*—with Arabic subtitles—but watch *ET bil Arabi* on MBC4.) The Arabic version of the show also includes a more specific marketing element, providing a venue for MBC, which broadcasts the show, to emphasize the activities of its own stars and to ensure that they stay in the public eye.

The Arab media are particularly good at this kind of cross-promotion. In addition to the use of video clips essentially as advertisements for musical performers and to the use of appearances on talk shows to promote films or albums—much as one might find in America—Arab performers also use the Ramadan television bonanza to promote their careers. The theme songs for *musalsalat Ramadan*, for example, are a phenomenon in themselves, and these shows can often attract top performers to record their songs, while recording these songs can provide major exposure and career boosts for the singers. In 2014, for example, Lebanese megastar Elissa scored a huge success with the eponymous theme song for the MBC Ramadan series *Law*—which was based on the 2002 American film *Unfaithful*, which was itself based on the 1968 French film *La Femme infidèle*. And "Law," not surprisingly, was itself promoted by a video clip featuring actors from the series.[17]

In the second season of the *musalsalat Al Hayba*, singer Nassif Zeytoun, who performs the title song that opens each episode of both seasons of the show, actually appears in one episode, seemingly encountering the series protagonist Jabal. It is a quintessentially postmodern moment that collapses the boundary between fiction and reality, as the real-world Zeytoun suddenly enters the fictional world of Jabal and the series. The two exchange knowing glances as the title song plays, despite the fact that one is a fictional character in a television series, and one is a real person from our world. The glances gain extra irony from the fact that this second season of *Al Hayba* is a prequel, so that Zeytoun knows things about what is coming that Jabal doesn't know. In fine postmodern fashion, it's a very clever moment but one with little in the way of real significance other than superficial entertainment. We enjoy it, but it really doesn't teach us anything.

Such examples illustrate the way in which television is as good as music at transcending national and cultural differences. Indeed, these examples suggest that music and television are especially intertwined in the Arab world, though the "television" here also needs to be broadened to include YouTube and other forms of online distribution. Television, of course, was the first major cultural form to be dominated by the American version almost from its very beginning, and so it perhaps comes as no surprise that the impact of American culture on Arab culture would show up most clearly in televisual formats. Indeed, the fact that the Arab television industry grew up explicitly modeling itself after its American predecessor is the clearest example of the self-conscious transculturation through which Arab popular culture came so closely to resemble American popular culture. As we discuss in the next chapter, it was, however, in the realm of film that this sort of phenomenon first occurred—and in which it still occurs in some of its more interesting forms.

7

Deconstructing the Myth of the Western Hero through Arab Film: *Theeb*, the Orientalist Logic of Good versus Evil, and the Birth of Jordan

Naji Abu Nowar's Jordanian film *Theeb* (2014) focuses on the experiences of a young boy in the deserts of what is now southern Jordan as he gets caught up in the efforts of his Bedouin tribe to provide aid to the British in their battle against the Turks during the Arab Revolt of the First World War. As such, the film deals with historical events that ultimately led to the birth of modern Jordan and, in particular, with the key role played by the Bedouins in the founding of the new nation. The film does not, however, romanticize the Bedouins, nor does it place much emphasis on the role of the Arab Revolt in the founding of Jordan. The film, in fact, is most striking (and has received the most critical praise) not for its treatment of important historical material, but for its highly modern technical artistry and for its deft use of motifs derived from the genre of the Western film, and particularly of the Spaghetti Western. It is not a provincial film, but a highly cosmopolitan one.

Of course, the Arab film industry has been heavily influenced by Western film from its very beginning. In the Cairo Trilogy, young Kamal Abd al-Jawad is described as a fan of the British/American film comedian Charlie Chaplin, while his more upper-class friend Hasan Salim is a fan of the French film comedian Max Linder (705). Western-produced film is thus presented as a prominent part of the culture of urban Egypt by the mid-1920s (when this comparison takes place). Meanwhile, when Egyptian-produced film itself began to rise to greater prominence in the 1930s, this new film industry was strongly influenced by Western (especially Hollywood) models. And this influence continues today, making film the realm of the most extensive and long-term exchange between Western and Arab popular culture.

Western-inflected films, so common in today's Middle East, are thus nothing new. For example, Youssef Chahine's *Bab el hadid* (*Cairo Station*, 1958), set in

Cairo's main train station, is one of the classics of Egyptian cinema. Among other things, this film is dominated by images of massive trains of a kind that have functioned as a symbol of modernity in Western culture since the nineteenth century. And this highly accomplished work of cinematic art, while showing the influence of a variety of Western models (especially Italian neorealism and American film noir), also reflects the distinctive vision of a talented director who is a legitimate *auteur*. It's also a highly secular film, with the considerable charms of lead actress Hind Rostom (variously nicknamed the "Queen of Seduction" and "the Marilyn Monroe of Arab Cinema") on full display. The only veiled woman who figures in the film is a comic character who becomes hysterical because a man looks at her; she is then abused by her husband for inviting the other man's stares by momentarily removing her veil. Otherwise, Islam is represented in the film primarily by two comic clerics who shake their heads in despair at the modern decadence of some young Egyptians they observe gleefully dancing and singing Western-style music. This film is concerned with the problems of this world (especially economic inequality), not with visions of the next.

Musicals were especially prominent in Egyptian film of the 1950s, though many Egyptian films of the era included elements of multiple genres. The 1955 film *Sigarah w kas* (*A Glass and a Cigarette*, directed by Niazi Mostafa), for example, is a virtual compendium of pastiches of Hollywood genres, including family melodrama, farcical romantic comedy, and musicals, though the highlights of the musical numbers have a distinctively Egyptian flavor in that they feature the dancing of female lead Samia Gamal, a famed belly dancer who had been declared the "National Dancer of Egypt" by King Farouk in 1949.[1] In general, though, *A Glass and a Cigarette* is a very Western-looking film filled with rather modern problems: the main plot, for example, revolves around the excessive drinking of Gamal's character, which threatens her marriage to a talented surgeon. Anyone watching this film, belly-dancing scenes notwithstanding, would be hard-pressed to recognize the mysterious, foreign, and exotic culture described by Said's Orientalists.

Even films with the most seemingly Egyptian subject matter defy Orientalist stereotyping and show an engagement with Western culture. The 1969 film *Al-Mummia* (literally The Mummy, but usually rendered into English as *The Night of Counting the Years*), for example, is based on an important event in Egyptian history, the 1881 discovery of a cache of forty mummies from the time of the pharaohs, hidden in a remote mountain tomb long ago to protect them from grave robbers. This haunting masterpiece features some of the eeriest cinematography in all of Arab film, but this unusual cinematography is less a matter of Oriental exoticism than of modern technical virtuosity. As Amany Ali Shawky puts it, *Al-Mummia* is "a sort of *Citizen Kane* of Egyptian cinema." Meanwhile, the central conflict of the film, a clash between tradition and modernity, between reverence for the past and belief in the future, reveals an Egypt whose troubled national identity derives from the fact that Egyptian culture at the time was both more ancient and more modern than that which was found in the rest of the Arab world.

While Egyptian film has in many ways become more conservative in recent years, it has often continued to feature topics, characters, and techniques that would be very much at home in Hollywood. Some films, for example, are direct remakes of American films. Meanwhile, the 2006 film adaptation of Alaa Al Aswany's best-selling novel *The Yacoubian Building* (at the time, the highest-budget film in the history of Egyptian cinema) features scenes of drinking, homosexuality, political corruption, and extramarital sex of a kind that might easily appear in a Hollywood film. The most important character (amid an extensive ensemble cast) is a cosmopolitan engineer, Zaki El Dessouki (played by iconic Egyptian actor Adel Imam), who seems to be a connoisseur of wine (and women) and who declares himself as much at home in Paris as in Cairo. The film does feature some distinctively Muslim motifs that would seem out of place in most Hollywood films, but these motifs in fact seem out of place in the Cairo of the film as well. For example, one character is recruited by Islamic fundamentalists who are engaged in terrorist activities, but they themselves are presented as marginal and exotic figures, conveyors of an extremism that is quite foreign to most of the citizens of Cairo.[2] It also features another seemingly devout Muslim character who engages in polygamy after he is assured by a Muslim cleric that the practice is endorsed by Allah. However, this character is presented as corrupt and vile (and turns out to be a drug dealer to boot), while the polygamy itself is problematic enough that he has to keep his second wife a secret from the world (and particularly from his first wife).

Such slickly produced, well-made films are helping the contemporary Arab film industry to gain more and more global attention, with the production of state-of-the-art films often following recognizable Western models. For example, Marwan Hamed's Egyptian box-office hit *El Feel el Azraq* ("The Blue Elephant," 2014) is a hi-tech psychological thriller with significant elements of fantasy and horror. It has also gained significant international attention, screening (and winning prizes) at film festivals worldwide. Further, the Arab film industry has now expanded beyond the domination of Egypt to include newly emergent national cinemas. Other North African Arab countries have been particularly visible on the stage of global cinema, as has Lebanon, while Palestinian film has been prominent as well, with films such as Hany Abu-Assad's *Paradise Now* (2005) and *Omar* (2013), both of which were nominated for Best Foreign Language Film Oscars, having a special political charge. Finally, the UAE has been particularly active in recent years in attempting to build a film industry. Among other things, the Dubai International Film Festival (initiated in 2004) provides an important venue for the introduction of works by new filmmakers from around the region—and is specifically designed as part of an effort to stimulate Arab filmmaking. Abu Dhabi also hosts an important annual film festival, though it is less specifically oriented toward encouraging new Arab films than to putting Abu Dhabi on the map as a venue for the introduction of international films. But filmmaking in the UAE itself is on the rise, and often in ways that are clearly designed on Western models and even to attract Western audiences—as when the 2013 horror film *Djinn*, filmed in Abu Dhabi, was made mostly in English with imported American Tobe Hooper as director, hoping to build upon his reputation as the director of such horror classics as *The Texas Chain Saw Massacre* (1974) and *Poltergeist* (1982).

Even Jordan, whose film industry has a very limited track record, gained visibility in 2016 when *Theeb* was nominated for the Academy Award for Best Foreign Language Film. Given that even Egypt has *never* received such a nomination, oddly enough, the nomination was something of a milestone for the Jordanian film industry, which had never before received such a nomination and which had previously submitted only one film (2008's *Captain Abu Raed*) for consideration for the nomination. On the other hand, *Theeb* is a very international film that received funding support from a number of different countries, including the UK, Qatar, and the UAE, as well as Jordan.[3] *Theeb* did not win the Oscar, but its nomination was no fluke: the film scored a number of awards at international film festivals leading up to the Oscar nomination, and it is a highly accomplished and professional piece of cinema. What is just as interesting as the nomination itself, however, is the enthusiasm with which that nomination was greeted in Jordan, including by the Bedouins whose history and traditions provide the principal material of the film, a very personal drama set against the public backdrop of the Arab Revolt. This enthusiasm is indicative of the complex cultural context in which the film was produced, while the film itself is equally complex, clearly undermining the simple binary logic of both Orientalism and Occidentalism.

American reviews of *Theeb* have generally been glowing, but in an inadvertently Orientalist way, expressing amazement and admiration that a Jordanian film could be so accomplished, making one wonder if the reviewers' attitudes toward Arab cinema might not be somewhat similar to Dr. Samuel Johnson's oft-quoted attitude toward women preachers. Then again, there are legitimate reasons why the technical and aesthetic accomplishment of *Theeb* might be surprising, given that it is a relatively low-budget film by a first-time director, featuring a cast made up almost entirely of Bedouins who had never acted before, including an amateur preadolescent who has the lead role (Jacir Eid Al-Hwietat). There is also the fact that the country of Jordan is a relative newcomer to the world of filmmaking, despite the fact that numerous outside productions have filmed there, including David Lean's *Lawrence of Arabia* (1962), the film to which *Theeb* has most often been compared by reviewers.

The connection to Lean's film is a natural one, given that *Lawrence of Arabia* deals with the same historical material and relies on some of the same visual iconography as *Theeb*. On the other hand, *Theeb* actually puts relatively little emphasis on the real-world historical events among which it is set but is instead a highly self-conscious work of cinematic art. However, this self-consciousness includes an ongoing dialogue with *Lawrence of Arabia*, as well as any number of other cinematic predecessors. That dialogue itself, meanwhile, can be read as part of *Theeb*'s self-conscious dialogue with the American-dominated tradition of the cinematic Western, on whose style and iconography *Theeb* draws extensively. But *Theeb* also challenges many of the ideological inclinations of the Western, which can often be colonialist and Orientalist, or at least logically consistent with colonialism and Orientalism. From this point of view, it is significant that Nowar has specifically identified his film as drawing upon the tradition of the *Spaghetti* Western, which also frequently challenges and disrupts the ideology of the classic American Western.

It might also be noted that the Spaghetti Western was a landmark in the globalization of the film industry. Designed for international distribution, these films also typically had international funding and were filmed in a variety of locations, including the United States and Spain, as well as Italy. They also usually featured mixed casts of American and European actors, while the greatest of the Spaghetti Western directors, Sergio Leone, was influenced not only by American Westerns but also by the great Japanese director Akira Kurasawa. When Spaghetti Westerns were filmed, actors typically spoke their own first language; later dubbing would then produce versions in a variety of languages, including Spanish, French, English, and Italian, keeping the original dialogue of actors who acted in that language.

Theeb clearly avoids the Orientalism of predecessors such as *Lawrence of Arabia*—even though many of its central images (gun-toting Arabs riding about the desert on camels) draw upon the very heart of Western stereotypes about Middle Eastern culture. *Theeb*, in fact, seems custom designed to shatter such stereotypes. Not only are its central characters all Arabs, but they are Bedouins—a group that has frequently been marginalized and treated as "Oriental" Others even by other Arabs, especially by modern, urban Arabs. Yet much of *Theeb*'s project involves the careful (and respectful) delineation of Bedouin culture as a genuine form of social organization that is neither primitive nor savage.[4]

In this, the film resembles the project of postcolonial cultural recovery undertaken by such texts as Chinua Achebe's *Things Fall Apart* (1958), which seeks to demonstrate that the Igbo of Nigeria had a well-developed and smoothly functioning culture long before their British colonizers arrived, bearing "civilization." But *Theeb* is even more closely related to the subgenre of the revisionary American Western that undertakes a similar demonstration for Native American culture, Native Americans having been pictured largely as bloodthirsty savages in earlier Westerns. Indeed, Hadani Ditmars has cited Nowar as saying that the portrayal of Bedouins in mainstream Arab cinema and television has not been unlike that of Native Americans in classic Westerns.

Theeb thus seeks to correct earlier negative depictions of Bedouin culture much in the way that a film such as *Dances with Wolves* (1990) sought to overcome earlier negative depictions of Native Americans. *Dances with Wolves* had significantly more success with the Oscars than did *Theeb*, winning seven Academy Awards, including Best Picture and Best Director. As a Western, it is notable for the extent to which it focuses on the representation of the everyday Native American culture of the Lakota Sioux, and the film has been lauded for its "sensitive exploration of a native culture" (Castillo 63). It was effective enough in presenting that culture that the Sioux made star and director Kevin Costner a full member of the tribe. On the other hand, despite its focus on the culture of the Sioux, it might be noted that *Dances with Wolves* still depends on the white protagonist to provide a central point of view with which mainstream audiences can identify, while *Theeb* presents its material from an entirely Bedouin point of view, making its lone British character an outsider who remains on the margins of Bedouin culture and of the film.

Still, it should be noted that *Theeb* is far from a piece of Bedouin esoterica and that the film seems to have been carefully constructed to be accessible to Western audiences, as well as Middle Eastern ones. Thus, despite the detailed depiction of Bedouin life, certain elements (such as religion or the role of women) that might distance the film from a Western audience are missing from the film almost entirely. Instead, the experiences, feelings, and cultural practices that are depicted (such as loyalty, brotherly love, struggles of humans against a harsh and inhospitable nature) are, in their essence, cross-cultural and virtually universal. The themes of the film are, in fact, virtually all common themes in Westerns, a fact of which the film itself is intensely aware. Though it has a great deal in common with the salvage ethnography of *Things Fall Apart* or of a film such as *Nanook of the North* (1922), *Theeb* is far from being a mere anthropological dramatization of life among the Bedouins. *Theeb*, in fact, is a complex film that is intensely aware of its status as a *film*; its representations of Bedouin culture are, however authentic, just *representations*, and ones that are often developed within (or in opposition to) specific *Western* cinematic traditions. Accordingly, the film needs to be read within the context of its cinematic predecessors, including *Lawrence of Arabia*, classic American Westerns, Spaghetti Westerns, and Arab and other postcolonial films.

Theeb, Lawrence of Arabia, and the classical Western hero

Lawrence of Arabia is essentially a biopic of British author, archaeologist, and diplomat T. E. Lawrence (played by Peter O'Toole in his first significant movie role). According to the film, Lawrence played a central role in galvanizing Arab resistance to Turkish rule during the First World War, thus significantly aiding the British cause in that war—though most historians have agreed that the film exaggerates Lawrence's importance in that conflict. War correspondent Scott Anderson, in an even-handed account of Lawrence's importance in the war, as well as of the importance of the war in the making of the modern Middle East, notes that Lean's film resurrected a romantic image of the role of the Arab Revolt in the war, an image of "berobed warriors and charging camels and flapping banners, a touch of medieval pageantry amid the inglorious slaughter." This image, Anderson argues, originally fed the hunger of the wartime and postwar British and American public "to find even a trace of grandeur in a war so utterly grotesque." It was, in particular, based on a simplistic polar opposition of oppressed Arabs rising up in romantic revolt against their Turkish oppressors, an image, in short, of freedom versus tyranny, one of the key linchpins of Orientalist thinking. This binary situation, however, was far from accurate: among other things, Anderson notes that there were different Arab clans fighting on both sides in the war, and that the Arab combatants were often fighting more for monetary gain than for ideals or principles (366).

Lawrence of Arabia begins with a four-minute overture, featuring sweeping and dramatic music that announces the epic intentions of the film. The first scene, however, involves Lawrence's 1935 death in a motorcycle accident, after which a reporter seeks information about the enigmatic figure. Following a structure roughly similar to that of *Citizen Kane* (one of the ways in which it announces its intention to be a "great" film), the film then loops back to reveal the key events of Lawrence's life. One of those the reporter interviews in this quest is American syndicated columnist Jackson Bentley (Arthur Kennedy). Bentley merely repeats the standard public image of Lawrence, noting that he was "a scholar, a poet, and a mighty warrior." However, after the other reporter leaves, Bentley adds in an aside that "he was also the most shameless exhibitionist since Barnum and Bailey," thus suggesting that Lawrence's heroic image might have been largely manufactured.[5] Indeed, Bentley goes on to suggest that it was his own promoting that was mostly responsible for Lawrence's public image—making it clear that Bentley is really a stand-in for American writer and broadcaster Lowell Thomas, whose book *With Lawrence in Arabia* (1924) supplemented his traveling roadshow touting Lawrence's achievements and did, in fact, contribute substantially to Lawrence's fame.[6]

The film thus begins with a certain skepticism regarding Lawrence's heroism—then proceeds mostly to romanticize its hero, passing up a chance to comment substantially on the nature of manufactured fame in the manner of, say, Robert Altman's anti-Western *Buffalo Bill and the Indians, or Sitting Bull's History Lesson* (1976). Indeed, while the film goes out of its way to emphasize Lawrence's unconventional nature, it ultimately makes him a fairly conventional hero whose ingenuity and courage help him to lead a rather confused and disorganized Arab Revolt to victory against Ottoman rule. Both the music and the cinematography (which is designed to make Jordan's Wadi Rum desert, where much of the film was shot, look far more expansive than it really is) are self-consciously *big* (including its nearly four-hour runtime and dialogue featuring rhetoric so inflated it might have been written for Norma Desmond, whose judgment on the size of modern "pictures" clearly would not apply to this film). This sense of magnitude helps give an epic quality not only to the film itself, but to Lawrence's exploits. It has also helped the film to gain a reputation for greatness. The most critically acclaimed film of 1962, it was nominated for a total of ten Academy Awards and won seven, including the coveted ones for Best Picture, Best Director, Best Cinematography (Freddie Young), Best Actor (O'Toole), and Best Supporting

Actor (Omar Sharif). Though *Lawrence* is really more a British film, in 1998 the American Film Institute named it the fifth greatest "American" film of all time, though it slipped to seventh in their 2007 update of the list.[7]

Lawrence is depicted in the film as being a great friend of the Arabs and as an admirer of their culture, especially as he gets to know them better. However, his first major encounter with that culture in the film occurs in an early scene in which his Bedouin guide Tafas (a member of the Hazimi branch of the Beni Salem tribe) is shot and killed by Sherif Ali (Sharif), a leader of the Harith Bedouin tribe, merely for drinking from a well belonging to the Harith (though Tafas is also attempting to take aim at Ali at the time he is shot). Ali (a composite of several different real Arab figures, though apparently named for the real Harith leader Sharif Ali bin Hussein) is himself a rather swashbuckling figure (though with a dash of stereotypical Arab cruelty and mercilessness tossed in). He and Lawrence will ultimately become close allies, though this first encounter does not get them off on a positive note. As Ali rides away (taking with him the British military pistol that Lawrence had earlier given to Tafas), Lawrence yells at him, angrily and condescendingly, "So long as the Arabs fight tribe against tribe, so long will they be a little people, a silly people. Greedy, barbarous, and cruel!"

Lawrence here not only sums up a series of key Orientalist stereotypes about Arabs, but he also sets the stage for much of the rest of the film, in which his efforts to bring the Arabs together to battle against the Turks help them to move beyond intertribal squabbles to become a formidable fighting force. He presumably learns greater respect for Arabs and their customs along the way (shown primarily in his tendency to wear Arab dress), but the film never really challenges the notion that the Arabs are too primitive and unsophisticated ever to be able to mount a successful campaign against the vile Turks without the help and guidance of the British—especially the heroic Lawrence.[8] When Lawrence finally reaches the camp of Prince Feisal (Alec Guiness), for example, it is almost immediately ravaged by an attack from Turkish planes, Feisal having understood too little about the capabilities of aircraft to take the advice of his own British adviser, Colonel Harry Brighton (Anthony Quayle), to move his camp south, out of range of the planes. After the attack, the stubborn Feisal (based on the real-world Arab leader Faisal bin Hussein bin Ali al-Hashimi, later to be king of Syria, then Iraq after he was expelled from Syria by the French) finally moves his camp, but the point has been made: Arabs simply do not understand modern warfare or modern weaponry and thus must rely on British expertise to conduct successful modern warfare.

But Lawrence is not simply superior to the Arabs in terms of his knowledge of modern machinery. He apparently knows more than they about crossing the desert on camels, which allows him to conceive a daring plan to attack the strategically crucial Turkish fort at the port city of Aqaba from the rear by crossing the desert—even though the Arabs tell him it can't be done. He's right and they're wrong, of course, though the crossing is extremely difficult—a fact that only makes the success all the more heroic. Expressing his admiration for Lawrence's courage and determination during the desert crossing, Ali tells Lawrence, "Truly, for some men nothing is written unless they write it." It doesn't help, of course, that as soon as they have neared the end of their journey, they encounter Auda Abu Tayi (Anthony Quinn) of the Howeitat clan, and friction immediately arises when they try to drink from his clan's well. Lawrence, of course, saves the day, and peace is restored. The Howeitat join with the Harith in Wadi Rum, and Aqaba is soon taken by their combined force (in a battle that is depicted as far more dramatic than it historically was)—after which the unruly Arabs immediately start looting and pillaging, while Lawrence heads back to Cairo to report the taking of Aqaba and to collect fresh supplies and weapons. In Cairo, the virtuous Lawrence stands up for Arab pride by marching into the British officers' bar in full Arab dress and with his Arab servant boy Farraj in tow. He also demands a room and a bed in Cairo's finest British hotel for the boy. Then the brilliant Lawrence explains proper military strategy to the British commander General Allenby (Jack Hawkins). Surprisingly, after all this, he is a big hit with Allenby, who gives him a promotion and a new assignment to continue rallying the Arabs to the cause, concentrating on disrupting the Turks via activities such as sabotaging their railways. He also gives him all the support he asks for—except artillery for the Arabs, because that, of course, is out of the question.

In the second half of the film (after an intermission that again emphasizes the sheer magnitude of the film), Lawrence returns to his Arab allies troubled by the realization that his British bosses might be planning to make the Middle East part of their empire after the war rather than leaving the Arabs to rule themselves, as Lawrence had earlier been led to believe would happen.[9] As the second-half action begins, Bentley comes to the Middle East seeking material for a story about Lawrence and the war there. Interviewing Feisal, he is shocked to learn that the Arabs kill their own badly wounded men so that they will not fall into the hands of the Turks. As he concludes his interview with Feisal, Bentley explains his mission, "I'm looking for a hero," and the prince quickly and insightfully deduces that Bentley hopes to romanticize the war for his

American readers and thus help drum up support for American entry into the conflict. Bentley's cynicism here (reminiscent of the way Charles Foster Kane's newspapers help to trigger the Spanish-American War just so they will have something sensational to report on) makes clear that *Lawrence of Arabia* is not a war movie, but an anti-war movie, as much as it heroizes the anticolonial efforts of Lawrence and the Arabs.[10]

In Lawrence's first appearance in the second part of the film, he is shown pushing the plunger that detonates a charge that derails a Turkish train. The Arabs then savagely attack the Turkish soldiers who are on board; Lawrence is a bit taken aback by the violence and the looting, but it's a great victory nevertheless. Bentley is pleased that he has found his hero. Lawrence hates violence and is tormented by the whole war, but he is nevertheless able to be an effective military leader—and even to kill Farraj after he is wounded in the course of planting charges to blow up another train track. The Turks place a large bounty on Lawrence's head, showing their recognition of his importance. But Lawrence apparently admires himself even more than do the Turks. And when Ali complains that Lawrence is asking too much of the men, Lawrence responds, "Do you think I'm just anybody, Ali? Do you?" He then goes to the men and asks them, "Who will walk on water with me?" clearly making himself a sort of Christ figure—at the head of a Muslim army. Such imagery is crucial to the heroic depiction of Lawrence in the film. Carl C. Curtis thus notes "the messianic and Christological images and symbols that dot the film almost from beginning to end," suggesting that for every historical inaccuracy historians have noted about the film, there is also "an image of Lawrence as savior, god, or prophet" (275). Lawrence, meanwhile, at one point compares himself to Moses, adding still another element to the film's biblical imagery. Granted, Lawrence proclaims several times in the film that he is just an ordinary man, but these protestations only serve to highlight how extraordinary he appears to be—especially given the number of times he gives in and admits, as he does to General Allenby late in the film, "All right. I'm extraordinary! What of it?"

There is, of course, a subtle Orientalism at work in this deification of Lawrence. A key Orientalist stereotype is that "Orientals"—perhaps especially when they are Muslims—tend to be religious fanatics. Thus, what better way to gain their loyalty and provide strong leadership for them than by being a godlike figure? Indeed, while *Lawrence of Arabia* tries to be quite politically correct in its sympathy for Arab self-rule and its condemnation of British imperialism, it can still be quite Orientalist, and the film's politics are mostly anti-war and anticolonial, rather than pro-Arab.[11] Indeed, the film's pro-Arab

Figure 7.1 T. E. Lawrence poses heroically atop a captured Ottoman train in *Lawrence of Arabia* (1962), while a crowd of his Arab followers cheer him from below.

sympathies are largely theoretical, based on an abstract vision of Arabs as colonial subjects, rather than on any real appreciation of or support for Arabs and their culture. Meanwhile, in striving to make anti-war points, the film even seems inadvertently to suggest that anticolonial resistance is futile. In the end, the final climactic taking of Damascus from the Turks by the Arabs is rendered as somewhat beside the point. Wild desert tribesmen, they are unable to run the city properly and most of them soon abandon it to return to the desert. The British and French move in, and the Arabs, despite having won a great military victory, simply exchange one set of colonial masters for another, and the sound and fury of the war have signified little.

The war is de-heroicized in the end, presented as a dirty affair unworthy of the true individual heroism of its protagonist. Ultimately, then, in keeping with his Christlike image, Lawrence is more victim than hero in the traditional sense, but he is a victim in a way that glorifies his victimization and that fails to escape the ideology of heroism in the end. He returns to England seemingly an outcast, though of course fame (partly from Thomas's promotions and partly from the success of his 1922 book *Seven Pillars of Wisdom*, his own account of his role in the Arab Revolt) still awaits him.[12]

No such fame appears to await the boy protagonist of *Theeb*, an ordinary Bedouin child who understands nothing about the geopolitical situation in which he has become embroiled. Indeed, *Theeb* can usefully be read as a careful deconstruction of the various myths of individual heroism upon which *Lawrence* is built. But this project can also be read as a deconstruction of the Orientalism of *Lawrence* itself, whose vision of a lone Christlike hero is built on the kind of polar self versus other oppositions that lie at the very heart of Orientalist thinking. Lawrence is very much a lone man against the world, sometimes presented as both British and Arab, but able to have this dual identity because he is really neither. Theeb, on the other hand, is thoroughly Arab, and firmly situated within his community in a way that undermines the kind of individualist self versus other thinking that lies at the heart of *Lawrence*. At the same time, by presenting events from a Bedouin point of view, *Theeb* is able to produce an authentic-seeming representation of Arab culture, free of the tendency of *Lawrence* to show the Arabs as both savage and romantic.[13]

Theeb begins with a segment in which the on-screen text of a poem relates the advice that had been given to his sons by the recently deceased Sheikh Abu Hmoud, read in a haunting voice that almost makes it seem as if the sheikh is speaking from beyond the grave. Poetry is extremely important in Bedouin culture, so that presenting this advice as a poem (commissioned for the film from a local Bedouin poet) immediately begins a sequence in which the first minutes of the film provide a subtle and succinct introduction to numerous elements of Bedouin culture, which the filmmakers studied intensively before making the film, living for a year in the Bedouin village of Shakriyeh to learn as much as possible about the culture. For example, that the advice in this opening poem comes from a father (and that it is largely heeded by his sons, the eldest of whom succeeds him as sheikh of the clan) suggests the patriarchal nature of this culture. Meanwhile, the nature of the advice (which basically urges solidarity with one's own people and wariness of outsiders) is also telling, suggesting not only the strength of communal bonds in this society, but also a clannishness that makes it difficult to relate to outsiders. This Arab clannishness is also a theme of *Lawrence of Arabia*. However, whereas *Lawrence* emphasizes the negative aspects of this clannishness (opposition to other tribes), *Theeb* emphasizes the positive aspects (solidarity within one's own tribe).

In *Theeb*'s first actual scene we are introduced to other important elements of Bedouin culture. Here, the boy Theeb draws up water from a well to give to his camel, aided by his big brother Hussein. Wells and water are, of course, crucial to any desert culture, so this scene comes as no surprise as an element of Bedouin life. Water and wells are crucial elements of *Lawrence of Arabia* as well. Then again, water is scarce in many parts of the American West as well, and the quest for water is a central focus of many Westerns, including such diverse examples as Sam Peckinpah's *The Ballad of Cable Hogue* (1970) and the children's animated Western *Rango* (2011).

Figure 7.2 Theeb's brother Hussein with camels at one of the wells that are crucial to the survival of the Bedouins in *Theeb* (2014) (screen capture).

Hussein next gives Theeb a lesson in shooting, again no doubt an authentic representation of an important element of Bedouin culture, but also again a scene that might be found in any number of Westerns. In the classic *Shane* (1953), for example, the eponymous gunslinger teaches a young boy to shoot, though (for safety reasons) he has the boy use a toy gun. Shane also explains to the boy's concerned mother that a gun is a useful tool in the West if used properly, a description that might well apply to the Bedouin attitude as well—as opposed to the glorification of guns in NRA weapons culture. After all, Hussein similarly refuses to allow Theeb to have bullets in his rifle until he has mastered the weapon.

This quick introduction to Bedouin culture then continues with a scene in which several Bedouin men (women are essentially absent from this film) play a game of Tâb in their camp as someone is heard approaching from the dark desert. Hussein disappears ominously into the dark toward the sounds, but then re-emerges with friendly visitors in tow—a British officer named Edward (Jack Fox) and his Bedouin guide/interpreter, Marji (Marji Audeh). The Bedouins greet the newcomers with great, if somewhat formal, hospitality.

Hussein and Theeb slaughter a goat in honor of their guests, though Theeb shows his youth when he is unable to bring himself to wield the killing knife, leaving Hussein to perform the actual slaughter. That night, though, when the men share the meal around their campfire, Edward is shown furtively disposing of the food offered him rather than eating it, subtly suggesting that the Englishman is perhaps less gracious than his hosts—and differing sharply from Lawrence's attempts to participate in Arab culture. The Bedouins also agree to let Hussein serve as a guide for the visitors on their mission to reach the Turkish railway that runs through the desert, though they do not ask questions about the purpose of the mission, especially after they learn that it has been endorsed by the "sharif."

Though not mentioned by name in the film, that sharif would be Hussein bin Ali, the Sharif and Emir of Mecca and the key leader of the Arab Revolt. Neither he nor any other major historical figures appear in the film, which is much more interested in depicting the everyday culture of the Bedouins within the context of the revolt than in tracing the constellations of alliances and betrayals that underwrote the actual revolt and its aftermath. This emphasis, however, does not mean that *Theeb* is disengaged from history, and one of the things of which it is most cognizant is the way in which the process of modernization transformed—and essentially eliminated—the traditional nomadic life of the Bedouins of the Hejaz. Edward, echoing Lawrence, has been sent to deliver a detonator and other key supplies that are to be used in an attack on the railway recently built through the Hejaz by the Ottomans. The railway itself, meanwhile, is a key image of modernization in the film, as is the detonator, suggesting the way in which modernization is a complex phenomenon with many internal conflicts. One of the central plot points of the film involves the way in which the formerly honorable profession of guiding pilgrims across the desert to Mecca has essentially been eliminated by this Hejaz Railway, which (opening in 1908) linked Damascus with Medina (though the planned extension of the railway to Mecca itself was never completed).[14]

When the group sets out on camels the next day, Theeb secretly tags along on his donkey, though he soon joins the group on their mission. This mission then sets in motion the rest of the film, in which the travelers move across the desert in a sequence that introduces us to Bedouin modes of travel, aided by a network of wells in the desert. Theeb, meanwhile, shows a growing fascination with the Englishman and the mysterious devices he carries, such as a pocket watch and the initially mysterious detonator for use in dynamiting the Turkish train tracks. Patented (by Alfred Nobel) only in 1867, dynamite provided a crucial boost to the weapons technology that was used to tame the American West; it is, accordingly, one of the iconic images of the Western film, featuring especially prominently in films such as Sergio Leone's *Duck, You Sucker!* (1971) and the John Wayne vehicle *Rooster Cogburn* (1975).

On the way, though, the group encounters bandits. Worried about the safety of their two young guides, for which he feels personally responsible, Marji wants the whole group to turn back, but Edward refuses, arguing that there are bigger things at stake than the fate of two boys. Clearly frustrated at what he sees as the narrow thinking of his guide, Edward asks, in a strongly Orientalist mode,

Figure 7.3 Theeb sits on the cracked earth of his arid homeland in *Theeb* (2014) (screen capture).

"Do you even know what a country is? Do you know what a king is?" "These," he declares, "are things people fight for." In a clear clash of priorities, Marji clearly feels that personal loyalties are more important than the abstract, big-picture items cited by Edward. "Brotherhood," he says, "is more important than your railway." Still, with the sharif behind him, Edward ultimately convinces Marji to go on with him and to send the boys back home alone. At Hussein's insistence, however, the boys stay with the mission after all, fearing that the newcomers will be lost in the desert. The bandits soon attack, and Edward, Marji, and Hussein are all killed.

Thus, the English outsider is removed from the film fairly early on, rather than becoming the central character in the action, in the mode of Lawrence of Arabia (or of Lt. John Dunbar, the white protagonist of *Dances with Wolves*). Hussein poignantly dies before Theeb's very eyes, and the young boy then improvises a grave for his brother in the desert, echoing such burial scenes in many Westerns. Eventually, Theeb continues the journey in the company of a wounded bandit (credited simply as "The Stranger," played by Hassan Mutlag), neither trusting the other, but each needing the other to survive in the harsh desert: The Stranger is too weak to make it on his own, and The Stranger's camel refuses to obey Theeb's commands.[15] Meanwhile, we will learn late in the film that The Stranger (along with generations of his forebears) had formerly served as a guide for pilgrims to Mecca until the construction of the railway, which made such guides unnecessary, driving him into banditry.[16]

Theeb and The Stranger remain wary of each other, but also establish an uneasy sort of bond—with The Stranger particularly showing increased respect for the boy once he realizes that he is the son of Sheikh Abu Hmoud, apparently a much-respected figure in the region. Shortly after reaching the train tracks, they encounter a band of Arab revolutionaries, mounted on horseback and looking not all that different from the Mexican revolutionaries who are found in so many Spaghetti Westerns. The Stranger explains that he is a pilgrim guide, the last one; Theeb (scared and not really understanding the situation) goes along with his story. They are told to go in peace and to avoid the railway, where there might be trouble. Later, they find dead revolutionaries scattered about the train tracks, having apparently attempted to attack the train without the aid of the technology that was being brought to them by the Englishman.

Theeb and The Stranger eventually make their way to an Ottoman outpost, where The Stranger confers with a Turkish lieutenant (Baha Othman), to whom he sells the Englishman's watch and detonator for a few gold coins. The lieutenant offers an additional coin to Theeb, but the boy, shocked by the transaction he has just witnessed, refuses to take the money and rushes outside in confusion. Clearly, Theeb, having already recently lost two father figures, has made The Stranger a sort of surrogate father, but one who has now deeply disappointed and disillusioned him. When The Stranger emerges from his meeting with the lieutenant, Theeb shoots the bandit dead on the spot (with the Englishman's pistol, stolen by The Stranger, echoing the fate of Lawrence's pistol in *Lawrence of Arabia*), then explains to the lieutenant that the man had killed his brother. The lieutenant simply nods and tells Theeb to go home. The boy rides The Stranger's camel away into the desert, presumably following this advice.

This departure is clearly reminiscent of the endings of any number of American Westerns, in which a lone hero rides away westward into the sunset. On the other hand, Theeb is presumably riding eastward on his way home (given that we know they were moving westward toward the railway), though there are no direct cues in the film to make this clear. In any case, it is important to note that Theeb is riding homeward, while the heroes of American Westerns ride westward to indicate that they are moving farther *away* from home. These heroes are loners who belong to no community and owe allegiance only to their own personal codes of conduct, suggesting the individualist emphasis of American culture. In contrast, that Theeb's concluding ride is oriented *toward* home can be taken to indicate a greater emphasis on community in Bedouin culture. On the other hand, before taking this reading too far, we should probably also note that Theeb is still a child (though he has seen much and learned much in the course of the film), but even this aspect can be taken as a movement away from individualism, the use of a child protagonist suggesting the need for support from a community rather than reliance on individual capability.

Figure 7.4 Theeb heads for home at the end of *Theeb* (2014). Note the Ottoman train in the distance (screen capture).

In this sense, one might again compare *Theeb* with *Shane,* perhaps the single most famous instance of a Western that ends with its protagonist riding away into the distance. This ending is particularly interesting in comparison with *Theeb*, because Shane famously leaves behind a young boy who begs him to stay. But Shane must go, because, having saved the day and restored order to the community, he finds that there is now no longer a place in it for someone with his particular skillset. The boy, meanwhile, must stay behind with his family, because that is what boys must do. Richard Slotkin calls attention to the particularly American connotations of the fact that Shane and similar gunfighter figures are professionals, responding to the American respect for professional expertise and showing a "hard-boiled" (one might simply say "capitalist") worldview that is indicative of certain assumptions about "the role of power and force in American political and social life" (402). On the other hand, Theeb, as a child, embodies a relatively innocent worldview of a kind that might be associated with the simpler, precapitalist social organization of the Bedouin world, in which individuals might have a great deal of skill and specialized knowledge, but skill and knowledge that are put to use in the interest of their own survival, not used simply to generate income. The Bedouins' skills, one might say, still reside in the kingdom of use value, whereas the gunfighters of American Westerns have already entered the realm of exchange value, the term "hired gun" capturing well this status.

Perhaps the most important (and least obvious) way in which *Theeb* resembles *Lawrence of Arabia* is that the latter, too, bears many similarities to the Western genre.[17] The dangerous-but-beautiful desert setting, the sweeping waves of yelping warriors on horseback (or camelback), and the sense of a wild land on the verge of encroaching modernization all mark *Lawrence* as a close relative of the Western. This is also the case with the depiction of *Lawrence*'s protagonist as a sort of loner who stands apart from the crowd. Of course, the somewhat effeminate and Christlike Lawrence differs substantially from the ruggedly masculine heroes normally associated with the Western, but his status as a unique individual nevertheless partakes of many of the same ideological inclinations as do the more conventional Western heroes played by John Wayne or Gary Cooper.[18]

Such figures, of course, represent an idealized norm of American masculinity. The effeminate Lawrence represents a deviation from this norm, and there is clearly an Orientalist energy at work in the way his deviant masculinity vaguely rhymes with the exotic setting in which he finds himself, including the way in which he is aligned *with* rather than *against* the film's "Indians," that is, the Arabs. As Slotkin and others have argued, "normal" Americanness has often involved certain visions of activity and virility, with the strong, silent frontiersman who goes forth conquering whatever obstacles nature thrusts in his path serving as a key prototype. For Slotkin, "nature" in this case has also often included "savage" humans such as Native Americans, with the American national identity being forged in "savage wars" against such foes, the United States thus emerging as that nation which defeats such foes and thus makes the world safe for decent, civilized, God-fearing Americans. Such figures have loomed particularly large (often literally) in American film (and in American culture in general), with towering, hypermasculine stars such as Wayne and Cooper functioning as veritable national allegories of American manliness, strength, resourcefulness, independence, and overall capability.

The savage war motif, as detailed by Slotkin, has served as justification for a variety of imperial and quasi-imperial adventures, most centrally involving the wresting of control of the North American continent from its previous inhabitants, but also including more recent otherwise unjustifiable events such as the 2003 invasion and subsequent occupation of Iraq. Indeed, the self versus other structure of the savage war motif is clearly a colonial one that partakes of much of the same logic as Orientalism. The violence that informs this savage war motif, according to Slotkin, is central to the American national mythology, which pictures the United States as a nation defined by success in conflict. In particular, Slotkin concludes, "since the Western offers itself as a myth of American origins, it implies that its violence is an essential and necessary part of the process through which American society was established and through which its democratic values are defended and enforced" (352). As an anti-war film, *Lawrence of Arabia* certainly does not support this dynamic. The principal binary opposition in the film is not between the "good" British and the "bad" Turks (both are depicted as corrupt and self-serving), but between the goodness of the individual Lawrence (who abhors violence, despite leading an army to war) and the badness of nations in general.

The Arab world is certainly not without its own versions of macho masculinity (and Arab men in *Lawrence of Arabia*, such as Ali and Auda, clearly seem much more macho than Lawrence). *Theeb*, however, seems unconcerned with exploring different versions of masculine heroism. This film, in fact, seems directly designed to undermine such myths of heroism altogether, rather than presenting alternative versions of them. *Theeb* refuses to demonize or deify any of its characters. Its protagonist is just a boy trying to survive as best he can amid events he neither controls nor understands. The Turks he encounters, presumably the most likely candidates to serve as evil and savage Others in the film, actually seem relatively decent, while even the bandits (or at least The Stranger, the one bandit we actually get to know) have stories of their own and good reasons for becoming bandits. The British officer of *Theeb*, meanwhile, is quickly dispatched and has no opportunity, Lawrence-like, to do anything heroic at all. As a result, the good versus evil dynamic of the classic Western has little strength in this film, which therefore tends to undermine the kind of polar oppositional thinking on which Orientalism and the classic Western both thrive. It is clear, then, that Nowar's choice of the Spaghetti Western, rather than the classic Western, as his primary generic model, was a good one, given that the Spaghetti Western also often undermines this kind of thinking.

Theeb, Bedouin culture, and the Mansaf Western

This is not to say that *Theeb* does not bear many resemblances to classic American Westerns, all of which are, as Slotkin repeatedly emphasizes, ultimately stories about the birth of a nation, as is *Theeb*. *Theeb*, however, refuses to glorify that birth. As opposed to the romanticization of the Arab Revolt in *Lawrence of Arabia* (or in much of Jordan's official culture) or the romanticization of the taming of the West in so many classic Westerns, *Theeb* presents the revolt as an event the Arab characters of the film are only vaguely aware of and in which they participate only because they have received orders to do so from their emir; it is this emir, not the Turks, who is to them the ultimate locus of political authority. The Arabs are thus not rebelling against authority in the romantic way envisioned in *Lawrence of Arabia*. They are, in fact, working simply to substitute one authority for another.

As a whole, *Theeb* is a highly original, even unprecedented film. However, virtually every individual scene in the entire film is a variant of a similar scene that has appeared in any number of Westerns. In one scene, for example, Theeb and his older brother take refuge among the rocks on a hillside, engaging in a gun battle with the bandits, who attempt to attack them from below. Such scenes appear in any number of American Westerns and related films, perhaps most famously in the scene in which Mexican bandits with no stinkin' badges lay siege to a group of gold miners in *The Treasure of the Sierra Madre* (1948). Similarly, the status of *Theeb* as a sort of road movie places it in the company of any number of American Westerns, a staple of which, from John Ford's *Stagecoach* (1939) onward, is travel across the difficult terrain of the harsh but beautiful frontier West. Ford, in fact, was the great master of such "cross-country" Westerns, becoming particularly successful at making the landscape through which his characters traveled a major element of his films. Ford made especially prominent use of Utah's Monument Valley and Castle Valley, which physically resemble Wadi Rum in a number of ways. Indeed, Wadi Rum, with its expanses of desert sand complemented by weird and colorful rock formations, looks very much like the setting of any number of American Westerns, which is one reason why Wadi Rum does not look all that unfamiliar to American audiences. In fact, though, Wadi Rum *isn't* unfamiliar to American audiences, who have seen it in numerous films, beginning with *Lawrence of Arabia* itself. The landscape of Wadi Rum is so otherworldly, for example, that the Mars scenes in films such as *Red Planet* (2000) and *The Martian* (2015) were shot there, as were scenes from the alien planet in Ridley Scott's *Prometheus* (2012)[19] and the sacred desert moon Jedha in *Rogue One: A Star Wars Story* (2016). Wadi Rum also stood in for the Iraqi desert in Kathryn Bigelow's *The Hurt Locker* (2008). It is, one might say, a highly cinematic location, and *Theeb* takes full advantage of that fact, enhancing its story with impressive visuals that seem very much like something from a movie.[20]

"Cross-country" Westerns such as *Stagecoach* place great emphasis both on the beauty of the landscape and on its harshness. Survival is often difficult in this terrain, and one of the staples of the Western is the crucial role played by horses in the survival of those who travel across the American West, especially in its more arid regions. In fact, horses are so crucial to the Western that films of the genre are sometimes referred to as "horse operas," while animals such as the Lone Ranger's Silver and Roy Rodgers's Trigger became icons of the genre in their own right. In a similar way, *Theeb* puts a great deal of emphasis on the obvious importance of camels to the survival of humans in the Arabian desert.[21] Thus, at one point, the bandits offer to let Hussein and Theeb go free if they will just hand over their camels. "We lose the camels, we die," Hussein tells Theeb, then opens fire on the thieves, initiating the exchange of fire that will eventually end his own life.

In terms of the landscape across which the camels of *Theeb* travel, the film can also sometimes be visually reminiscent of the stunning cinematography of *Lawrence of Arabia*, with its emphasis on sweeping panoramic desert vistas on which whole armies move like fleets of ships on a sea of sand. In general, however, *Theeb* is a much more intimate film, focusing on the personal stories of a small number of characters. Even the cinematography, despite the desert setting, can be almost claustrophobic, as the characters spend much of their time not on the open desert but winding their ways through narrow passages between looming outcrops of rock. Such scenes, of course, are ideal for ambushes, and as such they figure extensively in American Westerns, as when the principals of *The Professionals* (1966) make their way through such passages on the way to the remote stronghold of a Mexican rebel leader.

The Professionals also brings to mind another key similarity between *Theeb* and any number of American (and Spaghetti) Westerns—the use of large-scale historical events as a background for localized personal dramas. For example, the American Civil War (and its immediate aftermath) provides crucial background for films such as *The Searchers* (1956) or *Dances with Wolves*, in which Civil War veterans move West to try to put the war behind them and seek a better life. Meanwhile, films such as the Spaghetti Western classic *The Good, the Bad, and the Ugly* (1966) or *The Outlaw Josey Wales* (1976) are set during the war itself and use the war as crucial plot material. However, the historical context that perhaps provides the closest analogy to the First World War/Arab Revolt context of *Theeb* is that of the Mexican Revolution, which provides the setting for numerous Spaghetti Westerns.

For one thing, though the Mexican Revolution was a nebulous and complex event with no clearly defined end, it is generally considered to have spanned the period from roughly 1910 to 1920, making it contemporaneous with the 1916 setting of *Theeb*. In addition, much of the terrain of Mexico is desert-like, providing an excellent setting for Westerns, but also providing landscapes similar to those of *Theeb*—though it should also be pointed out that most Westerns set in the Mexican Revolution were not actually filmed in Mexico. Most importantly, though, the Mexican Revolution and the Arab Revolt were both times of great political instability in which the existing order—whether it be the regime of Porfirio Díaz and his successors in Mexico or the Ottoman Empire in the Middle East—was challenged, but in which a new emergent order was still ill-defined.

Spaghetti Westerns set in the Mexican Revolution are so prominent that they have acquired their own label—the "Zapata Western"—though, in point of fact, many American Westerns (including *The Professionals*) might be called Zapata Westerns as well. Indeed, an important forerunner of all Zapata Westerns is Elia Kazan's *Viva Zapata!* (1952), a highly fictionalized biopic starring a young Marlon Brando as Mexican revolutionary leader Emiliano Zapata. Among the leading examples of the Zapata Western are Damiano Damiani's *A Bullet for the General* (1967 and Sergio Corbucci's *Compañeros* (1970), both of which employ the Mexican Revolution to comment (generally from a leftist perspective that endorses revolution against oppressive regimes) on more contemporary political themes, such as the US interventions in Vietnam, Latin America, or the Third World in general. *Duck, You Sucker!* treats such issues as well, but from a less unequivocally leftist point of view that questions the romanticization of revolution in most other Zapata Westerns, an attitude that it has in common with *Theeb*'s treatment of the Arab Revolt, in which the only real revolutionaries wind up scattered dead around the train tracks.[22]

Where these films differ from *Theeb* is in the way they foreground the political events with which they deal, generally featuring characters who are heavily involved in these events, up to and including major figures in the Mexican Revolution, such as Zapata or Pancho Villa. At first glance, *Theeb* minimizes its engagement with such issues and in fact never makes clear even what the issues are—presumably because the entire film is essentially related from the point of view of its Bedouin boy protagonist, who does not himself understand the issues. The film is more concerned with presenting the personal story of that protagonist and his people than with telling the story of the Arab Revolt. Indeed, the film only includes two characters of any consequence who are not Bedouins. The first is the British officer, who is aligned with the Arab side in the revolt, and the second is the Turkish lieutenant at the end of the film, who is aligned with the Ottoman forces against whom the revolt is directed. But both of these figures are treated in an essentially neutral fashion. Granted, the Turk does rather callously discard the body of The Stranger at the end of the film, suggesting a possible disregard for Arabs as people, though he treats Theeb kindly, and he has also been told that the bandit had been a killer. Meanwhile, it is not clear that the Bedouins of Theeb's clan even regard the Turks as enemies or the British as allies; they simply aid the British officer in his mission against the Turks out of allegiance to their emir, who may well have his own agenda.

Theeb here directly recalls *Lawrence of Arabia*, which features an attack on the railway (led by its protagonist) as a major plot point—just as the real Lawrence was involved in the extensive (but largely unsuccessful) attempts to undermine the railway during the First World War, when it became a key military asset to the Ottomans. Of course, trains and railways were also central to the modernization of the American West, and they accordingly function as central plot elements in any number of Westerns, including Leone's *Once Upon a Time in the West* (1968), perhaps the greatest of all Spaghetti Westerns. In that particular film, perhaps the most villainous of all the characters is a rich man who lives on a train and drives the building of the railroad, but railway technology in general (as a bringer of modernization and civilization) is treated as having at least some positive effects, even as it destroys older ways of life in the West.

This destruction is a major element of an entire subgenre of Westerns, known generally as "waning of the West" films, in which the encroachment of capitalist modernization brings increasing urbanization and routinization, removing the relatively free and nomadic existence of former Western frontier heroes such as cowboys and gunslingers. Both *The Professionals* and *Once Upon a Time in the West* are key examples of such films, as are *Butch Cassidy and the Sundance Kid* (1969) and Peckinpah's *The Wild Bunch* (1969), both of which also feature railroads as key images of modernization, focusing on outlaws who are hounded to their dooms after committing the anti-modernization sin of robbing a railroad. The protagonists of such Westerns, of course, are representatives of an essentially modern culture that has already displaced the traditional culture of Native Americans, so the details are slightly different, but the Ottoman railway in *Theeb* nevertheless functions precisely as a sign that older ways of life are coming to an end thanks to the incursion of modernity.

Theeb is reminiscent of *Once Upon a Time in the West* in other ways as well, such as the fact that the Leone film also ends as the major character shoots and kills the man who had earlier killed the protagonist's brother. But *Theeb* is perhaps most similar to the mesmerizingly gorgeous Spaghetti Western in the beauty of its cinematography, both in the presentation of their striking arid landscapes and in their more intimate shots, especially in the close-ups of the characters' faces, which the camera seems to probe, examine, and caress. Where the two films differ in this respect, however, is in the representation of *things*. Especially in the interior shots, the mise-en-scène of *Once Upon a Time* is especially rich and extremely busy, the profusion of *things* that underwrites virtually every shot serving as a sort of advance announcement of the coming days of American consumerism. Such shots in *Theeb*, however, are quite impoverished in terms of things: the Bedouins have few possessions, and the one major interior scene, inside a modest tent, is dominated not by things, but by people, who value each other more than they value material objects.

Such differences again point to the way in which, while *Theeb* resembles both American Westerns and Spaghetti Westerns in any number of ways, the Bedouin culture that is so central to the film is much more similar to the culture of Native Americans than to that of the cowboys and soldiers of the typical Western. As a result, the emphasis on Bedouin culture in *Theeb* calls attention to the fact that the cultural perspective of the film is very different from that of the typical Western. Because of its Arab/Jordanian source, *Theeb* is very usefully

Figure 7.5 The title character pokes his head into a Bedouin tent in *Theeb* (2014) (screen capture).

Figure 7.6 Henry Fonda is ready for his close-up in the Spaghetti Western *Once Upon a Time in the West* (1968). Even very big American stars sometimes appeared in these Italian films.

read as a work of postcolonial culture, rather than as simply another take on the ordinary Western. Not simply a Western, or even a Spaghetti Western, it might be considered a Mansaf Western.

Postcolonial cinema: *Theeb* as national allegory

Theeb's Oscar nomination seems to have been greeted by Jordan's Bedouins as a sort of validation of their culture, just as many in Jordan also took it as a validation of Jordan's fledgling film industry. Of course, the very idea of producing films in the Arab world contains complications, complexities, and potential controversies that do not occur in the production of Western cinema. One might compare here the situation of early postcolonial novelists such as Achebe, who had to grapple with the fact that the novel is a fundamentally Western genre, deeply embedded in the same bourgeois ideology that fueled the colonial conquest of Africa and much of the rest of the world, so that writing postcolonial novels—ostensibly meant to contribute to the development of viable cultural identities for emerging postcolonial nations—might potentially do the opposite, contributing to the perpetuation of cultural domination of these nations by their former colonial masters. "The master's tools," as Audre Lorde famously stated "will never dismantle the master's house."

In the same way, Arab filmmakers must come to grips with the fact that, as Viola Shafik puts it in her important study of Arab cinema, "film as a medium was invented in the West and is connected to a quasi-industrial form of production that mainly relies on the division of labor and on mass production and distribution" (4). That is, film has origins not only in Western culture, but is also the first major cultural form to have its origins specifically in the capitalist system that powered the Western domination of the Middle East after the shattering of the Ottoman Empire in the First World War. Arab film production is thus a double-edged sword. While many might see it as a foreign incursion that threatens the purity of Arab culture (especially Arab *Muslim* culture), others might see it as a step toward putting the Arab world in a position to compete with the West in global cultural and economic influence and power. As Shafik puts it, as Arab cinema evolved in the latter part of the twentieth and early part of the twenty-first century,

> getting into industrial film production was considered a national achievement in the former Arab colonies and protectorates. The acquisition of cinematic techniques was a sign of progress and offered a real opportunity to expand

economically. On the political level, cinema was believed to create a political platform for counter-representations, giving the formerly colonized a chance to challenge Western dominance, at least on the screen. (209)

Theeb is not an overtly political film. At the same time, the avowed hybridity of *Theeb* (which confounds any attempt to see it simply as an Eastern response to Western cinema) has complex political implications of its own, particularly in the way it addresses the complicated cultural hybridity of modern Jordan itself. Of course, director and cowriter Nowar is himself a hybrid figure, a Jordanian national who was born in Great Britain to a Jordanian father and a British mother and who has lived most of his life in Britain. And it is clear from interviews (and from *Theeb* itself) that he learned his craft largely from watching Western movies.[23] And yet *Theeb* is clearly significant partly because of its specific cultural context and its special status in a Jordanian film industry that is still struggling to get off the ground.

Despite the numerous obvious Western influences on the film, *Theeb* has been popular in the Middle East and was greeted with particular enthusiasm by Jordanian audiences, who treated its Oscar nomination as a matter of national pride. According to Nowar (cited by Nabih Bulos in *The Los Angeles Times*) the Bedouins of Wadi Rum celebrated news of the Oscar nomination in their traditional manner: by firing their rifles into the air. As the Oscar ceremony itself approached, the website *The New Arab* reported considerable anticipation in Jordan's capital of Amman, where "parties are being held in honour of the Oscars. If *Theeb* returns home with an Oscar, it would be a first for the country and celebrations would likely continue throughout the night." Further, noted the site, "Special costumes inspired by the kingdom's tribal traditions were worn by cast and crew on the red carpet. A promotion campaign has even given the Oscar statue a makeover with the traditional Bedouin headdress." The film has drawn recognition from more official Jordanian sources as well. After the news that the film had lost the Oscar to Hungary's *Son of Saul*, Her Majesty Queen Rania tweeted, "An epic film, a brilliant team, and a beautiful adventure! @TheebFilm proud of you for taking #Jordan to the #Oscars" (cited by Freij). HRH Prince Ali, chairman of the Royal Film Commission's board of commissioners, similarly took to Twitter to express his pride in the film's achievement: "Congratulations to all who worked on Theeb; You didn't come home with the Oscar but you are our Jordanian stars! You make us all so proud" (cited by Freij).

The Jordanian royal family is, of course, notably Westernized, and Rania is the queen not only of Jordan, but of modern social media, so it is not surprising that the royal family would use a modern, Western forum such as Twitter to voice their support for *Theeb* in its quest for an Oscar. In addition, Twitter and other such media are popular throughout the Arab world, as their important role in the Arab Spring uprisings (beginning in December 2010) made clear. What might be more telling is that the Oscars, possibly the single most prominent symbol of the international power of American popular culture, would be held in such high esteem in an Arab nation where so many still rail against the contaminating influence of that culture. It is one thing for the film itself to employ techniques and technologies derived from Western cinema. It is another thing entirely for the film to be embraced as a symbol of Jordanian national cultural achievement—and for that achievement to be marked most visibly by an American Oscar nomination.

As an example of Jordanian film, *Theeb* is virtually without precedent. For example, it has virtually nothing in common with its only major predecessor in that sense, *Captain Abu Raed*, a small-scale film set in modern Amman that deals with very contemporary issues, especially patriarchy-fueled spouse and child abuse. In the larger sense of Arab cinema as a whole, the counter-representations mentioned by Shafik take on a different flavor as *Theeb* in many ways seems to want to establish itself (and Jordanian film in general) not in opposition to American or European films, but in opposition to Egyptian or Lebanese films, which are now part of extensively developed histories. But these histories are themselves inseparable from the history of Western cinema, so that, while *Theeb* seems more directly related to Western cinema than to, say, Egyptian cinema, the latter two cannot be separated in a simple and binary way.

Theeb is not particularly unusual among Arab films in drawing upon Western cinema in constructing its own artistic vision, though in point of fact it bears little resemblance to films that might, based on their subject matter, seem to be obvious predecessors. One might consider here the 1981 Libyan-produced desert epic *Lion of the Desert* (1980). Focusing on the battle of Libya's Bedouins against their Italian fascist colonial rulers at the end of the 1920s and beginning of the 1930s, *Lion of the Desert* is much more of a war film (and anticolonial film) than is *Theeb*, featuring scenes of spectacular violence that perhaps reveal the background of director Moustapha Akkad as a protégé of Peckinpah, famed impresario of cinematic violence. Nowar has also acknowledged Peckinpah as an important predecessor, though the most important way in which *Lion of the Desert* resembles American Westerns is in its heroic presentation of its protagonist, a figure of almost superhuman courage and piety. At the same time, the film also heroizes the Arab anticolonial struggle against fascism in general, while *Theeb* refuses to glorify the Arab Revolt or its protagonist.

Akkad, incidentally, was also the director of *The Message* (1976), which narrates the beginnings of Islam. Treading dangerous ground, the film is careful not to show the Prophet Muhammad or otherwise to offend the faithful, though it nevertheless did cause considerable controversy. It also relies heavily on binary logic, with Muhammad predictably representing the forces of good, and his foes representing the forces of evil. As a film per se, *The Message* often veers into the territory of the desert epic, inevitably recalling *Lawrence of Arabia*. It also shows some Peckinpahesque violence, but what it is more reminiscent of than anything are the American Biblical epics of the 1950s, of which Cecil B. DeMille's *The Ten Commandments* (1956) is the greatest example. This parallel has little to do with *Theeb* directly, but it does show that Arab film maintains constant dialogue with Western film, even when it deals with the most non-Western of material—and that Arab film often falls into the habit of constructing binary oppositions of the kind on which colonialism thrived.

Meanwhile, Shafik notes that, though Egyptian cinema has a particularly long and rich tradition, beginning especially in the 1930s, Arab nations during the colonial period "had almost no opportunity to represent themselves or their cultures by means of cinema until national independence" (18). *Theeb*, by locating itself at the beginning of what would become the British colonial period in Jordan, can be seen as attempting a partial corrective to this lack of Arab cinema during that period. In this sense, the film can again usefully be read through Jameson's discussion of national allegory within the context of "third-world" culture. In particular, Jameson argues that the form taken by the national allegories he finds in third-world texts typically traces the narrative of anticolonial struggle, independence, and subsequent cultural and economic domination by the West. These third-world cultures, he argues, cannot be understood apart from their relationship with first-world culture, because they are "locked in a life-and-death struggle with first-world cultural imperialism—a cultural struggle that is itself a reflexion of the economic situation of such areas in their penetration by various stages of capital, or as it is sometimes euphemistically termed, of modernization" (85). In the formerly colonized nations of Asia and Africa, he argues, "nominal conquests of independence open them at once to a kind of indirect economic penetration and control" (86).

Aijaz Ahmad has usefully detailed the ways in which this model fails to comprehend the narrative richness and variety of third-world texts (and third-world lived experience), especially in the case of India, but then Jameson himself describes his model as Orientalist and as a gross simplification designed to highlight certain basic differences between first-world and third-world literatures. His focus on national allegory as a narrative of struggle for postcolonial national identity is particularly relevant to *Theeb*, the events of which are so central to the birth of the Jordanian nation, but which are so complicated by the particularly complex nature of this birth in Jordan and in most of the Arab world. The Arab Revolt that forms the historical background to *Theeb* did in fact lead to independence from Ottoman rule, only to plunge much of the former Ottoman-ruled Arab world into colonial domination by France or Britain. Meanwhile, *Theeb*'s thorough entanglement in the culture of Western cinema further reflects the postcolonial "penetration" of which Jameson speaks, while reminding us that this phenomenon is not one of one-sided, passive submission on the part of Jordan to Western cultural and economic influences, but is instead one of dynamic two-way exchange, however uneven the mechanisms of power might be in this exchange.

The character of Theeb himself is a classic case of what Jameson means by national allegory. His clear fascination with the technological devices of the English officer indicates the seductive power of Western material culture, a power that is being exerted more and more in the Arab world today, even amid the rise of ISIS and other fundamentalist groups, but which certainly was beginning to show itself even at the end of the Ottoman period. Similarly, Theeb's rejection of the coin offered by the Turkish officer suggests Jordan's refusal of further participation in the Ottoman Empire—but also a resistance to the lure of the wealth that modernization potentially brings, whether it be Turkish or British (or American). But, a mere boy, he is not yet quite ready to assume full independence, which, in the case of Jordan, would take another generation. He does not understand the geopolitical situation in which he is embroiled. However, in the course, of the film, he takes important steps toward the kind of maturity that will enable him better to understand that situation. His youth thus mirrors the youth of the Jordanian "nation" at the time of the Arab Revolt, which led to a generation of British colonial domination before the arrival of true independence.[24]

If Theeb is thus in many ways a figure of the Jordanian nation, what he most certainly is not is a heroic figure, even if he does successfully avenge his brother's death. The film thus eschews nationalistic fervor in favor of an attempt to present the birth of the Jordanian nation as it must have appeared to most of the inhabitants of the region at the time—complex, confusing, and possibly a matter to be dealt with by distant others. They do not, in fact, have any idea that they are participating in this birth. But, by refusing to figure the Arab Revolt in heroic terms of self versus other or good versus evil, *Theeb* successfully evades both Orientalism and Occidentalism. And it does so in a particularly powerful way because it resides so clearly inside generic conventions that would have made it much easier to go the other way.

Theeb's "appropriation" of Western (in both senses of the word) cinematic techniques clearly does not represent a mere acknowledgment that Western models are superior and must be followed in order to produce sophisticated films. Instead, it represents a filmmaker's creative use of whatever resources happen to be available to him in a way that is much better understood in terms of transnational cultural flows than simple cultural imperialism.

Conclusion: Ideology, Utopia, and Arab Popular Culture

As the term "McDonaldization" indicates, American fast food is one of the most visible examples of capitalist globalization in the early twenty-first century. In cities (and often even in smaller towns) all over the world, one can walk into McDonald's (or KFC, or Taco Bell, or Starbucks) and order from pretty much the same menu as one would find in stores of the same franchises in America. The Middle East is no exception. However, one can sometimes find local variations on the menu as well. Taco Bells in Kuwait (perhaps the Middle Eastern country where American fast food is the *most* popular) feature not only the standard Tex-Mex fare of American Taco Bells but also serve local modifications, such as chicken or beef shawarma burritos. This kind of glocalization of food is, of course, precisely what we have been talking about with respect to popular culture throughout this book, as Middle Eastern culture producers add their own flavors to forms imported from the West.

We have demonstrated in the preceding pages that, while the kind of colonialist Orientalism described by Edward Said remains a part of the American ideological landscape, that landscape has also been informed (at least since the end of the nineteenth century) by other forms of Orientalism, including a second—and distinctly different—major form that arose in conjunction with the birth of American consumer capitalism at the beginning of the twentieth century. While Said's form of colonialist Orientalism thrives on maintaining a separation between the East and the West, the driving force behind consumerist Orientalism is a thoroughgoing globalist commodification that demands free flow of goods, services, people, and culture between the East and the West. This new system of transnational flow helps to explain the extent to which the popular culture of the Arab world—whether it be television, film, music, or the internet—has in recent years come more and more to resemble the popular culture of the United States and other Western countries. Of course, this convergence of popular cultures works both ways, though it is far from an equal and symmetrical exchange. While Arab culture has, in recent years, exerted an increasing influence in America, it is certainly the case that American culture has influenced Arab culture—especially in the realm of media-based popular culture—far more than the other way around.[1] Still, while one might be hard-pressed to find a shawarma burrito in an American Taco Bell, shawarma itself is becoming more and more popular and available throughout the United States.

Said didn't seem to have much interest in these sorts of pop cultural phenomena, but he does note increasing contact between the United States and the Middle East, complaining, late in *Orientalism*, that "the Arab world today is an intellectual, political, and cultural satellite of the United States" (322). Further, he sees this fact as contributing to the proliferation of Orientalist ideas even in the Middle East. Said, however, was writing in the 1970s and in a different world from the one we describe in this volume. He was also writing primarily about universities and businesses, not popular culture. Fifteen years later, in *Culture and Imperialism* (1993), Said (now writing in the wake of the first Gulf War, but still before the explosive growth in Arab popular culture to which we have attended in this volume) turns to more contemporary concerns. There, however, he still depicts the American dominance of the media and information industries (focusing on news organizations such as CNN) as a matter of sheer cultural imperialism. Thus, though Said scoffs at Arab conspiracy theories that would attribute virtually every event in the Middle East to behind-the-scenes American manipulation, he also notes that the American media presence now "insinuates itself, frequently at a level below conscious awareness, over a fantastically wide range," potentially giving the United States far more power in the Middle East than the British or French ever had with their more direct colonial control (291).

The impact of American popular culture on Arab popular culture cannot be fully separated from these kinds of power relations. However, the texts we have discussed at length clearly demonstrate that this is more than a case of mere colonial mimicry or slavish imitation of American culture by the Arab Culture Industry. As Homi Bhabha has argued, seeking (in a poststructuralist mode) to deconstruct Orientalist polar oppositions, even the phenomenon of colonial mimicry was a complex one with subversive and unsettling implications that went far beyond a desire of the colonized to imitate and attempt to be like the colonizer. For Bhabha, colonial mimicry "articulates those disturbances of cultural, racial, and historical difference that menace the narcissistic demand of colonial authority" (88). Mimicry, in short, challenges the binary oppositions upon which Orientalist (and colonialist) thinking so crucially depends, helping to create a situation in which the colonizing culture is unable to fully dominate the colonized one, producing instead hybrid cultures that include elements of both the original cultures.

Abdul JanMohamed has argued that Bhabha fails to give sufficient attention to the uneven distribution of power in the colonial situation, a distribution that makes it much harder to overcome the Manichean oppositions of the colonial situation than Bhabha suggests (78–79). Indeed, the kind of hybridity of which Bhabha speaks might more obviously apply to the current postcolonial situation, in which the Manicheanism of the colonial situation has already been deconstructed by the leveling effects of late capitalism, and in which the dynamics of cultural exchange are much more reciprocal. Indeed, it seems patently obvious that contemporary American popular culture is enhanced and enriched by exchanges with other cultures, including Arab culture. But that is, in a sense, the very nature of American culture, perhaps most especially in the era of late capitalism. If postmodernist culture is, as Jameson suggests, constructed largely in a mode of pastiche, then the larger the collection of sources from which images and styles can be borrowed the better.

But this postmodern culture is at home in America, where it resides quite comfortably amid the complete modernization that produces it. Meanwhile, even if global culture has now been thoroughly commodified, so that cultural artifacts and trends can circulate freely through the late capitalist system like capital itself, then surely postmodern culture is less naturally at home in the less thoroughly modernized Middle East. And if, as Margaret Mead suggests, we are now—amid the constant and rapid change that marks late capitalism—all immigrants in the cultures of our children, then surely this situation is more jarring to older Arabs than to older Americans. American culture of the 1950s might have now been swept away by the frantic scramble for change that marks postmodernity, but that culture was surely less foreign to the postmodern culture of the early twenty-first century than was 1950s traditionalist Arab culture, which has, entirely swept away even now.

Of course, this kind of, in fact, not been continual sweeping away has been central to the texture of the history of the United States since its own colonial beginnings, to the point that America sometimes seems to have no real substance at all. Thus, Arjun Appadurai has argued that the United States is not merely a land of immigrants who have joined a giant melting pot. Indeed, for him the United States has no real national identity in the traditional sense but is merely "one node in a postnational network of diasporas. In the postnational world that we see emerging, diaspora runs with, and not against, the grain of identity, movement and reproduction" (171). America has long been a nation of immigrants and nomads, a place where the new displaced the old, and where, beginning especially with the burgeoning of American capitalism in the late nineteenth century, the demands of capital triggered massive flows of populations both within the country and into it from abroad. But this diasporic texture is now the texture of the world and not just of America. It is only in this sense that the world has been "Americanized."

William Leach notes in his tellingly titled book *Country of Exiles* that, by the end of the twentieth century, America had become "a vast landscape of the temporary" (*Country* 6). This situation, he notes, is the culmination of the consumer capitalism the rise of which he details in his earlier *Land of Desire*. For Leach, the emerging consumer capitalism

> was not just about shopping. Intrinsic to it was the cult of the new, the need to overturn the past and begin again, and to disregard all kinds of attachments in the interest of getting the "new and improved," whether goods, jobs, entertainment, or places. (*Country* 13)

Given the globalization of this consumer capitalism in the century-plus since it first emerged in its American form, the globalization of the American diasporic condition that Appadurai describes could hardly have been otherwise.

The insubstantiality of life under modern American consumer capitalism described by Leach is, of course, really just the culmination of the all-that-is-solid-melts-into-air vision with which Marx and Engels described capitalism a half century before consumerism began to gain a solid footing in America. Moreover, given Leach's description, it is easy to see why many tradition-oriented inhabitants of the Middle East might find the United States to be a dangerous contaminating influence—just as it is easy to see why many Americans, battered by the shocks of continual renovation and rebooting, could see the appeal in Donald Trump's nostalgic call to make an imaginary America "great again." Still, this capitalism-driven lust for change has been a powerful force behind the modernization of the United States, just as it seems clear that the coming of late capitalist culture to the Middle East can be a powerful modernizing force in the region. One thinks here of Marx's complex, problematic, but nevertheless insightful writings on the British colonization of India, which have sometimes been reduced (by Said, most particularly) into a simplistic argument that Marx saw the British colonization of India as a good thing because it shook Indian society out of its Oriental changelessness, paving the way for Western-style progress. But, as Aijaz Ahmad has very effectively argued, Said's dismissive attitude toward Marx as just another nineteenth-century Orientalist is informed by both a fundamental lack of knowledge of Indian society and a fundamental misunderstanding of Marx's dialectical analysis of Indian history.

Marx, in fact, did see colonialism as a modernizing and progressive force in India, just as the same capitalism that drove colonialism had served as a similar force in sweeping away the feudal world of medieval Europe. Yet he also saw both capitalism in Europe and colonialism in India as terrible and destructive forces that brought great pain and suffering via the violence with which they ripped traditional societies from their roots. As Ahmad puts it, Marx's comments on the resistance to change in the traditional Indian village represent "a virtual paraphrase of his comments on the European peasantry as being mired in 'the idiocy of rural life'" (225). If anything, then, Marx depicted India as being too similar to England, not as being its Eastern polar opposite. "Marx's position," Ahmad goes on, "was in fact the exact opposite of what can accurately be called the *Orientalist* position in India" (235).

Ahmad also notes that, while Marx's comments on India were not always particularly well informed, they are quite consistent, in their overall vision of the confrontation between modernity and tradition in India, "with a whole range of reformist politics and writings in India" itself (225). Central here, of course, is simply the question of whether one believes that modern capitalist society, with all its sometimes dramatic negative consequences, is still an incremental improvement over what came before—whether it be medieval Europe, pre-colonial India, or traditional Islamic society. We, with Marx (and Ahmad), believe that it is. The greater material wealth and comfort, the advances in medicine and health, and the greater opportunities for individual material advancement and intellectual development (especially among members of formerly oppressed groups, including women) are for us positive features of modernity that outweigh the loss of the stability and sense of comfortable belonging that mark traditional societies. Moreover (and perhaps more importantly), the shattering of stability, however terrifying and psychically damaging, that comes with the maelstrom of change that marks life in the postmodern world also opens avenues for potential future change that takes society toward more positive and utopian directions in which human beings can be at home in the world without the terrible sacrifice of freedom and opportunity that traditional societies demand.

It might be instructive here to consider Thomas Hardy's *Jude the Obscure* (1895), conventionally viewed as one of the most depressing novels in world history thanks to its grueling exploration of the negative impact of modernity on its protagonist, Jude Fawley. By this reading, modernity creates desires for advancement in Jude that he would never have had in the traditional society of Wessex, only to ensure that those desires can never be fulfilled, thanks to the rigidity of the British class system and the lingering effects of traditional attitudes toward sexuality and marriage. He is thus displaced from what might have been a comfortable, if uneventful existence, and thrust into a world of frustration and torment. Said, in *Culture and Imperialism*, reads *Jude the Obscure* in just this way. Said sees Jude's story as one of loss and defeat, which he contrasts with the more optimistic story of Kipling's Kim O'Hara, who is able to have success because, as a white man in India, he is in a position of automatic privilege that Jude, a poor man in England, can never hope to attain (156–57). How different, Said claims, is the world of possibility that opens before Kim in colonial India as compared with the "lusterless world of the European bourgeoisie, whose ambience as every novelist of importance renders it reconfirms the debasement of contemporary life, the extinction of all dreams of passion, success, and exotic adventures" (157–58).

Said here is not that far from any number of Marxist commentaries on the bourgeois society of late-nineteenth-century Europe, as when Lukács argues that Flaubert exoticizes the (largely Oriental) past as a form of protest against "the ugliness and sordid triviality" of his contemporary capitalist world (183). What such readings fail to acknowledge, however, is the positive, utopian side of capitalist modernity. Jude Fawley, for example, is far from a total failure. He might fail to achieve his ambitious goals, but he continually strives to break free of imposed bonds and to explore an authentic, ever-evolving life. He also breaks free of many inherited modes of thought and continues to explore new territory almost to the very end. He is thus a perfect illustration of certain specifically Marxist (as exemplified in the work of Bloch and Jameson) modes of utopian thought that emphasize the quest for utopia as a positive good in itself, rather than requiring the actual achievement of utopia.

Terry Eagleton argues against the grain of conventional criticism of *Jude the Obscure* when he notes of Jude that "his will does not consent to be beaten" and that he "continues to struggle almost to the end." For Eagleton, "*Jude the Obscure*, like all of Hardy's novels, proclaims no inexorable determinism" ("Thomas Hardy" 44). The freedom detected by Eagleton is the result of self-awareness, knowledge, and the individual's responsibility toward his freedom. Granted, Hardy depicts the universe as an inhospitable one in *Jude the Obscure*, and it is certainly true that, everywhere Jude goes, he feels himself to be an alienated outcast. Never feeling at home anywhere certainly adds to his struggles, but it also facilitates those struggles by offering him greater flexibility to fashion his own identity, his Sartrean being-for-itself, apart from any preexisting suppositions that are thrust upon him by others.[2]

Arabs in the twenty-first century are certainly in a far different position than that occupied by Hardy's Jude Fawley, living as he did in a world in which modernity had arisen organically and was already far advanced, as opposed to the Middle East, which has experienced modernity as an incursion from the West and where premodern traditions remain strong, even as modernity is now proceeding at an increasing (and increasingly confusing) pace. The Middle East has also experienced modernity in fits and starts that make the sometimes-brutal process of modernization in the West seem smooth by comparison. As Tagharobi and Zarei succinctly describe, modernization in the Middle East began with liberal, largely intellectual, beginnings in the nineteenth century, inspired by contact with the West and marked among other things by the inchoate rise of the Arab novel and the birth of a struggle toward modernization in the failing Ottoman Empire. This period helped to lead to the Arab Revolt of the First World War and to the alignment of many Arabs with the West against the Ottoman Empire, only to see baleful betrayals such as the Sykes-Picot Agreement and the Balfour Declaration plunge most of the Arab world into colonial dependency on the West in the interwar period. These events ultimately led to a new post–Second World War phase in which modernizing forces in the Arab world were driven largely by anticolonial, if not specifically anti-capitalist inclinations and by an attempt to exert independence from the West, both politically and intellectually, while moving toward a more nativist form of modernity. The nominally socialist Nasser regime in Egypt can be taken as paradigmatic of this phase, which has now been supplanted, in the post–Cold War era, by a movement toward inclusion in the system of global capitalism. This movement has ominous neoliberal possibilities, but also promises greater success than earlier efforts at modernization by potentially situating the Middle East *within* the system of modernity rather than as a supplicant for entry into modernity (as in the nineteenth century) or as an antagonistic alternative modernity (as in the post–Second World War era). Of course, the complex political situation in the Middle East—in which modernity is sometimes equated with America or Israel or some other combination of outside enemies—continues to complicate this situation, making modernity appear to be an invading foreign force as it never had been in the West.

The works of Arab music, film, and television that we have discussed in the preceding chapters of this volume demonstrate the potential ability of Arab culture to participate in global culture as an equal partner with the United States,

Japan, and the other nations that are generally perceived as being at the forefront of this culture. Indeed, one could argue that the complex transculturation that occurs in the production of a film such as *Theeb*, or any number of Arab video clips or television series in many ways, places Arab culture in a particularly advantageous position relative to these global cultural powers. After all, the fact that Arab popular culture has been influenced by American popular culture far more than the reverse also means that Arab culture draws far more inspiration and energy from American culture than the reverse. Arab artists and the Arab Culture Industry in general are thus now able to produce complex and sophisticated works of the kind produced in the West, while the American Culture Industry is often reduced to trivial instances of Orientalist cultural appropriation as it attempts to draw upon the East for cultural energy.

Arabs and Americans are not, of course, the world's only producers of culture, and the increasingly free global flow of culture under late capitalism means that contemporary transculturation involves far more than an exchange between just these two cultures. Japanese animé, Korean pop music, and Bollywood films are just three examples of non-Western cultural phenomena that have gone increasingly global in recent years. In the American context, the free flow of artists and artifacts in the white, Anglophone world has created a situation in which the cultures of Great Britain, the United States, Canada, and Australia are virtually indistinguishable. Still, the discernible impact of animé or Hong Kong martial arts films on American culture notwithstanding, American culture has remained relatively resistant to foreign influences from outside the Anglophone world. Meanwhile, the emergent popular culture of the Arab world—perhaps partly because it is relatively new—has been more open to a variety of influences. Bollywood films (and soap operas), for example, have become increasingly prominent components of the Arab mediascape in recent years, no doubt partly because they come without certain negative resonances and fears of cultural imperialism that accompany American culture.[3] The important influence of Turkish, Indian, and even Latin American cultural products in the Arab world further enriches the process of transculturation there, while at the same time ensuring that Arab popular culture, by drawing upon such a diverse array of influences, is not simply colonized by American culture. The same might also be said of the important influence of French culture in the former French colonies of North Africa and Lebanon, except that French culture differs far less from American culture than does, say, Bollywood film.

Of course, all of these various cultures are themselves being gradually colonized by late capitalism. Meanwhile, there would seem to be a danger that the increasing cross-pollination among all of these different cultures will ultimately lead to a homogenization that significantly decreases cultural diversity, but it is also the case that cultural hybridization can actually *increase* diversity by producing new and unprecedented combinations.[4] Thus, if the convergence of global cultures in the early twenty-first century is centrally informed by the growing hegemony of postmodernist culture (as we, after Jameson, believe it is), and if postmodernism is merely the cultural logic of late capitalism, that does not mean that global culture is descending into a homogenous mass of sameness. We believe this convergence produces a new culture that is somewhat richer than what Tariq Ali has called "market realism," in which global commodification enables people all over the world to "eat the same junk food, watch the same junk on television and, increasingly, read the same junk novels" (140). Moreover, this convergence offers innovative visions that go beyond the shutting down of alternatives that Mark Fisher has described as "capitalist realism"—a virtual synonym for "postmodernism."

At the same time, mere diversity is not, in and of itself, much of a weapon against the onward march of late capitalism. After all, diversity and pluralism are hallmarks of capitalism itself. As Eagleton puts it, "Capitalism is the most pluralistic order history has ever known, restlessly transgressing boundaries and dismantling oppositions, pitching together diverse life-forms and continually overflowing the measure" (*Illusions* 133). Eagleton here is disputing the enthusiastic claims of apologists for postmodernism (Hassan, Lyotard) that would see its fragmentation and inherent pluralism as somehow mounting a challenge to capitalist authority. Jameson himself, decrying the thorough commodification that he associates with postmodernist art, has declared the "facile celebration" of postmodernism as subversively innovative to be "complacent and corrupt." But Jameson also insists on a dialectical approach to postmodernism that refuses a "facile repudiation" of postmodernist art as lacking all merit as well (*Postmodernism* 62). Jameson, in fact, finds much postmodernist art to be of great aesthetic interest, complex, and enjoyable. Capitalism is very, very good, if nothing else, at producing shiny and seductive objects. And, if Jameson finds that postmodernist art is almost entirely lacking in any power to break free of the grip of ideology and mount a genuine critique of late capitalism, he also insists that this does not mark the final, total, and permanent victory of the capitalist system. Instead, he has argued that the postmodern era might be "little more than a transitional period between two stages of capitalism, in which the earlier forms of the economic are in the process of being restructured on a global scale," a restructuring process that might yet yield up a new proletariat that will act as the gravediggers of capitalism in the mode Marx originally imagined (*Postmodernism* 417).

The "global scale" in this statement might, in fact, be crucial, because the globalization of capital also means that diverse cultural forces are brought into contact with one another, bearing reminders of the possibility of alternative forms of social organization. Such reminders might, in fact, be key to the restructuring that Jameson writes of. The current convergence of Arab and American popular cultures is, after all, also a dialogue. Whether or not this dialogue can contribute to positive and productive social change—to the birth of an as yet unimagined better future—remains to be seen. What is clear is that the recent emergence of a postmodern Arab popular culture has already had a powerful modernizing effect on the Arab world, an effect that we view as ultimately positive, however unsettling and troubling it might be to many Arabs. The very existence of this culture should also pose a challenge to the legacy of Orientalist stereotypes about the Middle East, and we hope that this volume, by bringing this culture to the attention of our Western readers, can make a contribution to that challenge by helping to demonstrate just how intermixed different cultures from around the globe are in this day and age. After all, it's a mongrel world.

Notes

Introduction

1 See Stiffler for a discussion of the ways in which Middle Eastern restaurateurs in the early twentieth century often attracted American customers by openly marketing their goods as exotic.

2 Gyan Prakash, for example, argues that *Orientalism* "opened the floodgate of postcolonial criticism" (199), while Martin Kramer claims that the book "crippled Middle Eastern studies" for decades (22).

3 Many of the debates over *Orientalism* are reviewed by Daniel Martin Varisco, who is fundamentally critical of Said's methodology and conclusions, but in a way that acknowledges the importance of Said's work. For a particularly sharp critique of Said that also constitutes a defense of Western culture itself, see Warraq. Of the well-known critics of Said's work, we might say that our own position is closest to that of Aijaz Ahmad.

4 Said does, however, mention Fanon frequently and approvingly in the later *Culture and Imperialism*, where among other things he conducts an extensive comparison between Fanon and Foucault in Fanon's favor. This move suggests that the rise of postcolonial studies, so heavily influenced by Said, had by this time also influenced him in turn.

5 For an overview of the current political situation in the Middle East that pays central attention to this conflict, see Cockburn.

6 The term "McDonaldization" is associated primarily with the work of sociologist George Ritzer, who originally used it in 1993 primarily to describe transformations in American society since the 1950s. The term, however, has also come to be almost synonymous with the notion of the "Americanization" of global society and culture.

7 One might note here the extensive chumminess between the supposedly anti-Islamic American Trump administration and the ruling powers in Saudi Arabia.

8 Roland Robertson, one of the thinkers most closely associated with the notion of "glocalization," insists that globalization already implies a combination of the global and the local, which are not polar opposites but are dialectically interrelated.

9 There has, in fact, been substantial recent work on the utopian potential of globalization. Hayden's essay, for example, is part of a collection—edited by himself and Chamsy el-Ojeili—of essays on this topic.

10 For a specific example of this disease metaphor, see Jalal Al-i-Ahmad's *Occidentosis* (1978), which essentially sees the West as a sort of disease that has affected his native Iran in nefarious and damaging ways. Though written and informally circulated in a sort of *samizdat* version in 1962, this tract was (ironically) officially published in the same year as Said's *Orientalism*. But it outlines anti-Western attitudes that in many ways have only spread in the ensuing decades.

11 On the other hand, some Muslim artists have produced entertainments—with a strong (but progressive) religious dimension—that fit well within the parameters of Western popular culture. This is especially the case with artists of the Arab diaspora, such as the Lebanese-born, Swedish-based global star Maher Zain, who records for the British-based Awakening Records, which specializes in progressive Islamic music for a global market.

12 As Rinnawi notes, there has been a recent trend toward the establishment of Islamic TV channels as an alternative to Westernized programming (157). However, these channels are almost entirely oriented toward religious programming and do not attempt to compete with Westernized programming on its own terms. On the other hand, as Sakr notes, the entertainment channels and the religious channels are often backed by the same investors, complicating the situation, but also suggesting that even the religious channels are ultimately commercial enterprises, more interested in the profit than in the Prophet (*Arab* 11). For more on Islamic programming, especially in Egypt, see Abou-Bakr.

13 For a fuller discussion of this topic, see Hazbun.

14 Crary's insight here is importantly influenced by a number of thinkers, including Giorgio Agamben's insistence that every moment of human life in the twenty-first century is controlled by some sort of "apparatus" and our relation to it.

15 Note that the scenes of a futuristic outer-space city in the 2016 film *Star Trek Beyond* were shot in Dubai.

16 As Waïl Hassan succinctly puts it, the *Nahda* sought to "rebuild Arab civilization after centuries of decay under the Ottoman Empire" via a combination of "Arab Islamic heritage" and "modern European civilization" (xi).

17 Muhammad Husain Haykal's *Zaynab* (1912) is conventionally considered the first true Arabic novel, though its rural emphasis makes it seem less than fully modern.

18 Even apart from Western literary forms such as the novel, Arabic literature since the *Nahda* period has often been driven by a modernizing impulse, with popular poets such as Syria's Nizar Qabbani and Adonis often chiding the Arab world for its excessive fascination with the past and urging Arabs to move aggressively into the future.

19 See, for example, Stefan Meyer.

20 See Brian Edwards for an extended discussion of *Being Abbas el Abd* as an example of the impact of globalization on Arab literature, especially via the book's complex

dialogue with the novel *Fight Club* (1996), by the American author Chuck Palahniuk. Edwards emphasizes, however, that this relationship goes beyond influence and is best understood as an example of cultural "circulation" (73). Among other things, Alaidy's novel is a linguistic and cultural hybrid that mixes standard and colloquial Arabic while drawing upon both Eastern and Western literary models.

Chapter 1

1. The "Garden of Allah" is the Muslim paradise, a significantly more sensual place than the Christian heaven. Orientalism, however, turns this sensuality into a sign of lustful Oriental wickedness. One might note, for example, that a Hollywood hotel called "The Garden of Allah," was a well-known locus of debauchery, especially among the elite of the film industry.
2. See Berman for a more extended account of the place of the Middle East in nineteenth-century American culture.
3. For an interesting contextualization of the Orientalist aspects of the Exposition, see Çelik.
4. That this song would appear in a version of the Cinderella story suggests the symbolic parallels between fairy tales and the Orientalist version of the exotic Middle East.
5. An early recorded performance of this song can be found at (https://youtu.be/cldWysIgRmk). URLs in parenthesis after the first mention of songs or music videos in this volume will point the reader to YouTube sites (all active as of September 2016) for the videos to facilitate direct viewing.
6. For an overview of the careers of Montgomery and Stone within the context of early-twentieth-century Broadway, see Mordden (59–62).
7. There is still, for example, a substantial traffic in Americans (many of them graduate students or even professional scholars studying the Middle East) visiting the region in a mode of exotic adventurism, posting pictures of themselves on Facebook or Instagram, backed by camels and desert landscapes (and perhaps dressed like Lawrence of Arabia), thus supposedly proving the authenticity of their engagement with the Middle East.
8. On the introduction of the Camel brand, see Brandt (54–55).
9. Indeed, the Egyptian tobacco industry arose specifically as a rival to the Ottoman industry—and as an attempt to avoid Ottoman regulation and taxation. On the Egyptian tobacco industry, see Shechter.
10. The 1966 film *Khartoum* features Charlton Heston in the role of a heavily heroized Gordon. This film, perhaps the most prominent Western cultural product about

Sudan, presents the Mahdist rebels essentially as bloodthirsty religious fanatics, though the Mahdi himself, played by distinguished British actor Sir Laurence Olivier in blackface, is presented as a rather dignified figure who becomes an admirer of Gordon.

11 As Holly Edwards notes, Americans around the turn of the century often saw a "consonance between the Wild West and the exotic East," as when famed Western artist Frederic Remington traveled to North Africa, where he found artistic inspiration in Arab horsemanship, but also concluded that the French colonial management of indigenous Arabs might have something to teach the American government about techniques for dealing with Native Americans (35).

12 "Princess Rajah" was actually a Coney Island Vaudevillian by the name of Rose Ferran. Another of her specialties was a dance known as the "Cleopatra Dance."

13 See May for a discussion of such phenomena within the context of the growth of mass culture in the United States in the early twentieth century (156).

14 Camels do, in fact, exist in China, though they are indelibly associated in the American popular mind with the Middle East.

15 There are also other films—most notably *The Exorcist* (1973)—in which the Middle East is treated as a locus of ancient horror. See Semmerling's chapter on *The Exorcist* for a detailed account of the film's Orientalism.

16 See Greene for a detailed account of the representation of China in American film, with Fu Manchu as a founding figure.

17 While most of the dancers are scantily clad (white) women, the best dancing of the sequence is provided by the African American Nicholas Brothers, here presented as even more scantily clad slaves, possibly meant to be eunuchs tending the sheikh's harem.

18 https://youtu.be/790b0ub8J9c

19 https://youtu.be/esfH-_1nhrs

20 https://youtu.be/kg9IVhaSxPE

21 https://youtu.be/41KMByxE6lo

22 https://youtu.be/VqElJnsUvtE

23 The opening lyrics to this song mentioned the capricious lopping off of ears in the original theatrical release, though this reference to amputation as punishment was removed in the subsequent home video version in response to protests from Arab American groups, replaced instead by a reference to the brutal heat of the Arabian desert.

24 https://youtu.be/b66NQbxGYV4

25 This scene was almost certainly an inspiration for Madonna's notorious entrance as an Egyptian queen in her elaborate Super Bowl halftime performance in 2012, (https://youtu.be/X3ik_8QjM3U).

26 The Sheik was successful enough that an Iranian-born wrestler performed as "The Iron Sheik" from 1972 to 2010.

27 https://youtu.be/5dNGU772_cI
28 https://youtu.be/1H2QvmWLT4s
29 https://youtu.be/7YyBtMxZgQs
30 Jack Shaheen, in *Reel Bad Arabs* and *The TV Arab*, has documented some of this conventional stereotyping. But see Evelyn Alsultany for a more nuanced view of the ways in which the representation of Arabs and Muslims in American popular culture has become more complex in recent years under the impulse of multiculturalism, without really solving the problem.
31 In flashbacks to Elliot's childhood, his mother is played by Indian American actress Vishnaivi Sharma, suggesting at least some sort of non-European heritage. Numerous Indian American and Arab American actors in fact appear in the series.
32 Available on YouTube at https://youtu.be/xk_67YsHG4A
33 In the second half of this interview (in Arabic), Arab Hollywood reporter Husam Asi enthusiastically proclaims to the show's hosts that it is important to have someone like Esmail doing this show, which he regards as a very positive step toward overcoming the stereotyping of Arabs on American television.
34 The E Corp logo, incidentally, seems based on the tilted E logo of Enron, the real-world company that now stands as the paragon of the evil, arrogant, and abusive corporation. Within the computer world, this tilted E also recalls the second letter in the logo of Dell Computer Corporation.

Chapter 2

1 In a television interview recorded in Dubai and available on YouTube at https://youtu.be/VTeZ8Rdkbu8
2 https://youtu.be/YykjpeuMNEk
3 One might compare here bell hooks's recent discussion of Beyoncé's *Lemonade* as pure capitalist money-making enterprise, aesthetically impressive, but ultimately a mere commodity that appropriates black women's bodies for financial gain, not a revolutionary expression of black feminine power.
4 https://youtu.be/mqFLXayD6e8
5 The reference here is presumably to the 1965 Elvis Presley vehicle *Harum Scarum*, which is partly a send-up of *The Sheik*. Here, Elvis sometimes wears Arab garb as he battles dastardly Arab assassins, then wins the heart of a beautiful Arab princess (who is even generous enough to bring along some of her dancing girls on their honeymoon—in Las Vegas). The movie is both awfully Orientalist and awfully awful.
6 https://youtu.be/tYn_6NjcopY
7 See Shay on the long history of the American fascination with "exotic" dance forms such as belly dancing.

8   https://youtu.be/Cv6tuzHUuuk
9   Compare Georg Lukács's description of Flaubert's *Salammbô* (also adduced by Said as a key instance of Orientalism in literature) as an example of the use of an exotic foreign culture to escape "the ugliness and sordid triviality" of life under modern capitalism (183).
10 To add to the comic effect, the video also uses (crude) animation to make such figures as Princess Diana, Muammar Gaddafi, and the Statue of Liberty do the Egyptian walk.
11 The Bangles were originally conceived as a group in which all four members were of equal importance. It was this video that propelled Hoffs to the forefront of the group in the public imagination.
12 Boone, noting that ancient Egyptian gods are often depicted with erections, is discussing the extent to which ancient Egyptian imagery has become iconic for the international gay male community.
13 https://youtu.be/0KSOMA3QBU0
14 Apparently not a lot of high-level thought went into the concept for the video. Mathew Cullen, the director of the video, has said in an interview that the Egyptian theme was Perry's idea because she was fascinated by the fact that "there's actually a place in Egypt called Memphis, and she thought it was so interesting that Juicy J is from Memphis, Tenn" (Rothman).
15 https://youtu.be/51hlBQq2POM
16 See Derr for a discussion of how inappropriate this common image of the geisha actually is.
17 https://youtu.be/LeiFF0gvqcc
18 In his interview with Rothman about the making of the "Dark Horse" video, Cullen calls ancient Egypt a part of our "shared collective mythology." It might be telling, of course, that he characterizes ancient Egypt as a myth, when in fact it was a historical reality.
19 See the collection edited by Lefkowitz and Rogers for a sampling of critiques of Bernal's methodology and conclusions.
20 Among other things, Bernal argues that the "Afroasiatic" roots of Greek civilization were widely accepted by Western scholars prior to the nineteenth century, but that revisionist versions were developed to deny this heritage in order to make Western civilization seem separate and superior. This project, of course, could be seen as a key part of the Orientalist project.
21 Said, incidentally, cites the work of Bernal quite approvingly in *Culture and Imperialism* (15–16).
22 For a skeptical discussion of attempts to promote belly dancing in the United States as a forum for feminism and/or fitness, see Jarmakani.
23 https://youtu.be/kIDWgqDBNXA

24 https://youtu.be/B9-B3XRCCN4
25 The widespread notion that Oriental women are able to move their bodies in particularly erotic ways no doubt owes a great deal to the centrality of belly dancing in the popular Western imagination concerning Oriental women. This same stereotype is the central image in the video to U2's 1991 song "[She Moves in] Mysterious Ways" (https://youtu.be/TxcDTUMLQJI). This video features both snakes and a belly dancer among its many Orientalist images.
26 This line was amended to "I love the way you work it"—with a noticeable discontinuity in the vocal track—in the "clean" version of the song that was used in the official music video.
27 https://youtu.be/v9w9mQx7MN4
28 https://youtu.be/RbtPXFlZlHg
29 https://youtu.be/6Px7XvOD6KA
30 Arab and American stars have also performed together live in the Middle East. For example, Haifa Wehbe's provocative dancing onstage with Jamaican-American performer Shaggy during a performance of his song "Hey Sexy Lady" in Cairo nearly a decade ago is still being talked about today in the Arab world (https://youtu.be/_cGxIseYzQg).
31 https://youtu.be/TWHNr0BrNgo
32 https://youtu.be/bcuAw77J8_Y
33 The original version includes a repeated hook that is apparently meant to sound as if it is in Arabic, but that is in fact merely nonsense syllables. The remix replaces this with a hook that is actually in Arabic and that in fact consists of the opening line that introduces each sura of the Quran, plus the first verse of the first sura. In Islamic culture, this same "hook" is commonly used as an opening to speeches or presentations. Still, one could argue that the latter is the more offensive of the two versions of the hook, even though Rhymes has characterized the entire song as a tribute to Arabic culture.
34 But see Iskandar for an argument that Shakira's performances represent less of a potentially empowering cultural fusion and more of a pure commodification in which "companies invest in the hybrid orientalized imagery of Shakira for financial gains that reiterate and ossify the underlying hegemonic system."
35 https://youtu.be/ey4Fc9DP5Rw
36 https://youtu.be/uLLsMzfIeWE
37 William Pietz argues that the mapping of certain traditional Orientalist stereotypes onto the Soviets not only helped to "justify the practical policy of containment, but it contributed to a new theory of the neurotic psychological basis of all 'ideology,' that is, of all left political argument." Further, such stereotyping was offered as an explanation for the "component of state-backed social terror so prominent in twentieth-century European history" (69). Meanwhile, Booker and Juraga argue

that, in Cold War America, "Sovietology was a well-elaborated discourse in the sense meant by Foucault and in the way associated by Said with Orientalism. That is, Sovietology tells us very little about what was actually going on in the Soviet Union but a great deal about the fears and fascinations of the West" (13). Finally, see the conclusion to Booker's *Colonial Power, Colonial Texts* for a discussion of the ways in which the anti-communist rhetoric of Cold War America drew directly upon the discourse of Orientalism.

38 The video also includes shots of the Toronto skyline, including the highly phallic CN Tower, further breaking down the distinction between the East and the West in the video.

39 See, for example, Theo d'Haen for an argument that modernist collage is meant to suggest an ultimate unity and simultaneity, while postmodernist collage shows an "obstinate refusal . . . to 'come together,'" thus defying any attempt at a single unifying interpretation (222).

40 https://youtu.be/PEGccV-NOm8

41 One might compare here Jameson's (Marxist) argument in *Postmodernism* that the fragmentation and rampant commodification characteristic of late capitalism/postmodernism collapse a number of cherished Marxist analytical structures, transforming "alienation" into psychic fragmentation and rendering hierarchical models such as the base-superstructure model of societies obsolete, as "the *cultural* and the *economic* . . . collapse back into one another" (xxi).

Chapter 3

1 There is some uncertainty about the date of Umm Kulthum's birth, which might have been as late as 1904.

2 Music channels specializing in the broadcast of video clips began to emerge in Arab television in the early 1990s. Kraidy and Kahlil estimate that, by 2009, there were roughly seventy such channels in the Arab world.

3 Some Arab pop stars are more Western than others, of course. The Egypt-based Syrian pop singer Assala Nasri, for example, displays a more traditional Arab singing style (supported by a strong, resonant voice) than, say, Ajram or Elissa—and is a bit more conservative both in her costuming and in the overall style of her video clips in general. But even Assala's video clips seem rather contemporary and could not really be called traditionalist or conservative.

4 On the historical evolution of Arab pop music, including the role played by Western influences, see Aziz.

5 LeVine attributes this withdrawal to EMI's sense that they were unable to compete with the mighty Rotana in the MENA region (143).

6   All translations from the Arabic in this volume—unless otherwise obvious or indicated (as in the titles of books that have been published in English translation)—are our own. Available at https://youtu.be/_Fwf45pIAtM
7   https://youtu.be/8zCwFCKOfJY
8   https://youtu.be/SyGI8TrrXx8
9   The Murex d'Or is an annual award given since 2000 to celebrate achievements in the arts in the Arab world.
10 https://youtu.be/ucNF2GHhk2k
11 "Gazelle" is commonly used as an affectionate term for females in Morocco. Available at https://youtu.be/lhnmVSB-Rxc
12 https://youtu.be/9UT9JOO9xN8
13 https://youtu.be/UBBxGHvjNFM
14 https://youtu.be/bghEyqhcWzA
15 This kind of pairing of opposed female characters is quite common in film noir, of course, so that the choice of the mode for this clip shows an excellent understanding of that distinctively American film phenomenon.
16 This overt combination of Eastern and Western elements has become more and more common in Arab culture. For example, mash-ups combining Eastern and Western music have become particularly popular in recent years. The Jordanian band Harget Kart has made a specialty of such musical combinations, as has Palestinian singer Noel Kharman, who gained considerable attention with her 2015 mash-up of Adele's "Hello" (in English) and Fairouz's "Kifak Enta" (in Arabic), which now has nearly twenty million views on YouTube (https://youtu.be/qqLtPbEmbJs). Kharman's 2017 mash-up of the international megahit "Despacito" and the Arabic song "Akhiran Galaha" (https://youtu.be/bHUh7aBBKU4) was even more popular on YouTube. Interestingly, Kharman's own original music has been much less popular than her mash-ups.
17 https://youtu.be/bytVUsDTqFI
18 https://youtu.be/lKg-cMrvzMM
19 https://youtu.be/XutYffQy4Ag
20 https://youtu.be/Jfm6kfbGHSo
21 For another (less interesting) take on this same mixture, see Nawal Al Zoghbi's "Tewallaa" ("On Fire," 2017, https://youtu.be/yePecMliSs4).
22 https://youtu.be/K8utLC4iUZU
23 https://youtu.be/_ZqEM_4dYWU
24 https://youtu.be/lKZp1Okkctw
25 https://youtu.be/fBVXozfR8pg
26 https://youtu.be/Zt3nLasF9ks
27 https://youtu.be/If0m6EYNUlU
28 https://youtu.be/GPJAcFFAht4

29 Fares's clip for "Moush Ananeya" can be found on YouTube at https://youtu.be/YimggIlkpqY. Feghali's parody performance can be found at https://youtu.be/Z-67nFdHRpU.
30 https://youtu.be/c8hVPjZLJlA
31 http://damasjewellery.com/about-us
32 https://youtu.be/D_hH-bn5dD0
33 https://youtu.be/kWKNP7nY8pc
34 https://youtu.be/ZZwdBV1SDIg
35 Meanwhile, both Ajram and Wehbe have promoted Sony Ericsson phones in their clips.
36 https://youtu.be/8YzabSdk7ZA
37 https://youtu.be/vwtaL-8IXO8
38 https://youtu.be/RjRp6xq3z4Y
39 In an instance of hyper-marketing, this particular Pepsi commercial features an embedded product placement for Motorola cell phones.
40 https://youtu.be/-_DLsR7fn8Y
41 See Louis and Yazijian for a discussion of the growing globalization of the battle between Coke and Pepsi for dominance in the "cola wars," beginning in the 1970s.
42 https://youtu.be/3ObVN3QQiZ8
43 https://youtu.be/f7-YyghdmzU
44 https://youtu.be/8be8zBJWDJw
45 https://youtu.be/RvK19xgAxSU
46 The internationalization of raï has received considerable critical attention. See, for example, Gross, McMurray, and Swedenburg.
47 See Shoup on the function of raï as an expression of working-class identities in North Africa.
48 https://youtu.be/H7rhMqTQ4WI
49 In 2013, the song went even more international when it was recorded in a Spanish salsa version by American Marc Anthony as "Vivir Mi Vida." This version was also highly successful and became the title song for Anthony's subsequent fifteen-nation tour.
50 https://youtu.be/V-GE78Vy6Lk
51 Omran is an artist with a growing international profile. For example, she is featured, alongside headliner Jason Derulo, in the Arab version of the Coke-sponsored official 2018 World Cup music video for the song "Colors" (https://youtu.be/v6FA4eZXvkE).
52 https://youtu.be/sPhhZg9v9NU
53 https://youtu.be/-Urjas5Nt0I
54 https://youtu.be/DUUCNS5dybc

55   Four-wheeling in the desert near Dubai is a popular tourist activity. Wiz Khalifa similarly four-wheels near Dubai in the video for "So Much" (2016, https://youtu.be/HqTNDJgvaj0).

56   In an example of East to West cultural flow, "habibi" is an Arabic term of endearment that is increasingly heard in Western pop culture. Thus, in addition to Wehbe's English-language "Habibi," in the song "Got This" (2017, https://youtu.be/_R9w6jWYMvo), American rapper Russ brags of his prowess with the ladies by declaring "You would think I got Middle Eastern blood / By the way the girls call me 'habibi.'" Russ also references Middle Eastern culture (amid a proud display of his wealth and fondness for champagne) by declaring that he is so successful at making his dreams come true that he feels like his own "genie."

57   Assaf has, in general, become more and more a part of the capitalist world since rising to fame. For example, in 2016, he became a spokesman for the Max Clothing Stores and was featured in their "Fashion for Real People" marketing campaign. In this role, Assaf starred in a series of television commercials (shot in both Arabic and English versions) that emphasize the down-to-earth, affordable nature of Max's clothing, an emphasis that is presumably furthered by Assaf's own humble image. See, for example, https://youtu.be/hEUtYOsBj7M.

58   This same image of Dubai is central to the video clip for "Brown Rang" (2012, https://youtu.be/ZbKaRZFnqn8), by Indian rapper Yo Yo Honey Singh. This clip was directed by American David Zennie, who also directed the clip for "Roll with It."

59   https://youtu.be/XZw9nxEk1GI

60   This sort of snake imagery (with obvious phallic implications) is a stock image of exotic sexuality. One might compare Britney Spears's notorious live performance at the 2001 MTV Video Music Awards, in which she wore a particularly skimpy version of a belly-dancer outfit with an albino python draped over her shoulders while she performed her song "Slave 4 U" (https://youtu.be/gE2b68tOESA). The music video of that song (https://youtu.be/Mzybwwf2HoQ) also places a strong emphasis on dance moves that are vaguely based on belly dancing (sans snake), thus using Orientalist vibes to create a sense of feminine sexual submissiveness combined with an implied desire to be dominated.

61   https://youtu.be/rLAam6tke40

62   As Shohat and Alsultany note, "The fluid boundaries between the Orientalist imaginary and Arab popular culture are . . . especially complex, when Arabian/oriental dreams, in a case of commercially motivated 'self-orientalizing,' are marketed and promoted by Middle Easterners themselves" (11).

63   However, the quote reappears in Arabic during the end credits of the clip.

64   For a more recent (and more spectacular) example of the combined appropriation of belly dancing with ancient Egyptian imagery by modern Egyptian culture,

see the video clip for the song "Mish Habki" ("I Won't Cry"), by Lebanese singer-dancer Layali Abboud (https://youtu.be/udyNqWw3-iI). The clip was made to accompany the 2016 Egyptian film *Sattu Muthalath* (*Burglary Triangle*), in which the song is featured. The film, a light silly comedy, actually involves ancient Egyptian tombs, so there is some justification for the imagery, but it's mostly just playful use of well-known images for commercial gain.

65 https://youtu.be/oBTB5qTsqCU
66 https://youtu.be/VyeAiV0HNB0
67 https://youtu.be/aOouS8DEIA8
68 https://youtu.be/gEgJh-Y7lIU
69 https://youtu.be/H6OFrilAlJQ
70 https://youtu.be/c3iSoXGl2Do
71 https://youtu.be/Feg6VWuStPg
72 https://youtu.be/QqspY_D7R78
73 https://youtu.be/y1yv4NwInQw
74 https://youtu.be/TnV5H5MD_74
75 https://youtu.be/X_DeGCloQWg
76 https://youtu.be/yY8HQqcCsU8
77 https://youtu.be/NosVTjkd1rw
78 In 2017, however, al Saber regained custody of her daughter, over the singer's own protests.

Chapter 4

1 In 2011, *Time* magazine named El Général one of the 100 most influential people in the world, acknowledging the importance of his contribution in initiating the Arab Spring uprisings—but also indicating the extent of the coverage he received in Western media.
2 https://youtu.be/JupZw4SOwVQ
3 https://www.youtube.com/watch?v=ay_Wd6IiGOU
4 https://youtu.be/5H0QIM_blZg
5 https://www.youtube.com/watch?v=sCbpiOpLwFg
6 For a succinct summary of the role of rap music in the Arab Spring uprising, within the context of a larger global phenomenon of revolutionary rap, see Fernandes.
7 See, for example, Almeida on Moroccan rap. Also see Salois on recent Moroccan rap as an excellent example of glocalization. Morocco and Algeria have the oldest rap music traditions in the Arab world. The North African hip-hop tradition has evolved along somewhat different lines than the Middle Eastern one, however. Still, the two traditions are certainly interrelated. In addition, Almeida notes that the

evolution of Moroccan rap has centrally relied upon figurations of blackness that link it to African American hip-hop traditions, thus providing another example of the kind of international flows that create conversations among various local manifestations of global hip-hop.

8 https://youtu.be/dFahQz-KPVc
9 https://youtu.be/7Fg6UyDIvs8
10 These lines are delivered mostly in English. The sections in parenthesis are our translations of Qusai's Arabic insertions.
11 Jeff Chang covers this phenomenon well in his history of hip-hop culture, which focuses on the US origins of hip-hop but notes the global nature of the culture as well.
12 See also Khabeer for a discussion of the similar role being played by hip-hop among many young American Muslims.
13 This branching, of course, is not absolute, and some of the most popular rap artists (such as Eminem and Snoop Dogg) have managed effectively to combine these two tendencies.
14 https://youtu.be/Hz97ox1kKfU
15 On this doctrine, see Khabeer (58).
16 On the influence, especially of the Five Percent Nation of Gods and Earths, on American hip-hop, see Miyakawa.
17 For a more positive reading of the work of some less commercial Arab American hip-hop artists, see Maira. Also see Khabeer for a recent extensive study of the ways in which hip-hop culture is providing new definitions of what it means to be a Muslim in America.
18 https://youtu.be/tOwuXkPIl-s
19 There is also another rap song entitled "A.W.A.," this time produced by DJ Outlaw and featuring Qusai and several other performers. Here, Qusai declares himself to be "straight outta the kingdom," in reference to the classic N.W.A. album *Straight Outta Compton* (1988). This song is less vulgar than the one by Lacrim and Montana, but just as politically pointless.
20 "Offendum" is a stage name. The rapper has declined to use his real name in order to avoid endangering his family back in Syria via his political statements and activities.
21 Offendum has stated that his early development as a hip-hop artist was crucially impacted by his study of Arabic poetry, which he describes as "the backbone of the Arabic language" (Davy).
22 See also Grundey for a characterization of Offendum as "Arab hip-hop's poet laureate."
23 Available on YouTube at https://youtu.be/tSLWbIMxd88
24 https://youtu.be/TXjEWrhkb6g

25. There is some uncertainty surrounding these events. In a December 2016 story in *GQ* magazine, James Harkin cited sources in Syria to the effect that this song was actually authored by one Abdul Rahman Farhood and that Qashoush was actually a government informer murdered by the rebels.
26. Maher al-Assad is the brother of Bashar.
27. Offendum here departs from the original lyrics, which identify Maher as an agent of America. Given Offendum's other statements, it is safe to assume that Offendum is not here equating America with Satan (as has sometimes been done in the Arab world), but simply wants to avoid offending Americans, whom he hopes to rally to the cause of the rebels.
28. https://youtu.be/LOpZrd8D-nQ
29. The making of this mixtape is detailed in Alsalman's book *The Diatribes of a Dying Tribe*.
30. https://youtu.be/TtoHCUMpNMY
31. This rather comic and good-spirited take on the treatment of Arabs in American airports is also reflected in a recent ad for the online shopping site Ubuy.com. Here, an obviously affluent Arab couple travels to America just to shop but are grilled in the airport as suspected terrorists. The point of the ad is that Arabs can save themselves the hassle of traveling through Western airports if they simply order online and have their purchases shipped to the Middle East by Ubuy (https://youtu.be/YlCcZhT70aA).
32. https://youtu.be/0ISHZQJdeSw
33. https://youtu.be/21OXQ4m1-Bo
34. https://youtu.be/7LcLqP-GOj0
35. https://youtu.be/iVXFVPGSfc8
36. https://youtu.be/EKGUJXzxNqc
37. https://youtu.be/3y7ah7a6BmQ
38. As Mark LeVine notes, "Tupac Shakur is without a doubt the greatest single influence on Arab, and especially Palestinian, rappers" (101).
39. https://youtu.be/aSDdlmOXzog
40. See Rayya El Zein for a discussion of this film as an emblem of the politics of DAM, which she sees as an attempt to align Palestinians with African Americans and to associate Israelis with white (racist) American culture.
41. https://youtu.be/Z3-v09TQOQE
42. https://youtu.be/6XHZ4OaWbn0
43. https://youtu.be/U0ltbqXmBuQ
44. Available on Facebook at https://www.facebook.com/SamarMediaTv/videos/895045497273380/
45. https://youtu.be/Iidy1qU5bqg
46. https://youtu.be/UjnFbe7D9pY

47 See, for example, Lughod and Mikdashi, who complain that DAM here fails to contextualize honor killings within the larger context of women's political problems in Palestine. We strongly disagree with this criticism, which takes to task a brief video clip for not fully exploring issues that could not be adequately covered in a full-length dissertation. Lughod and Mikdashi also ludicrously complain that the song fails to supply details such as which airport the woman planned to fly out of.
48 https://youtu.be/eJgWkV6alaA
49 One might compare Nafar's statement, included in the documentary *Channels of Rage* that Israelis regard him as a Palestinian Arab, while Arabs regard him as an Israeli.
50 https://youtu.be/T3KpV9hNelk
51 https://youtu.be/4PgxMjmKE0c
52 Available on YouTube at https://youtu.be/hUJrCDjzRQA
53 https://youtu.be/z4OI0GUCI_A
54 Available on YouTube at https://youtu.be/x8_rqO6i4PY
55 Jay-Z's relationship with Obama's successor, Donald Trump, has been less cozy, especially after Trump characterized African countries as "shitholes" in January of 2018. Jay-Z, though, remains a wealthy establishment figure, and Lowkey's basic point remains, especially as Kanye West has expressed a certain sympathy with Trump's policies.
56 https://youtu.be/bB-vYuYhdSE
57 Lowkey has also updated his critique of the American presidency with a strident denunciation of Obama's successor in "McDonald Trump" (2018, https://youtu.be/QTeUmVZrhr0). This mostly English song also includes lines in both Spanish and Arabic, thus showing solidarity with the two groups against whom Trump has directed the most venom.
58 https://youtu.be/kmBnvajSfWU
59 https://youtu.be/iH4wIeF0W4I
60 https://youtu.be/FNqum-_5RhY
61 Though not directly germane to our study, we might note that another recent Lowkey song, "Ghosts of Grenfell" matches the poignancy of "Ahmed" in its response to the tragic Grenfell Tower fire of June 14, 2017 (https://youtu.be/ztUamrChczQ).
62 El Zein also notes rumors (widely circulated in the Western media, though later discredited) that the notorious ISIS commando and executioner "Jihadi John," identified as Mohamed Emwazi, was in fact the British rapper known as "L Jinny."
63 https://youtu.be/42jiILh-Zxo
64 Available on YouTube at https://youtu.be/tTO9vVgsT5U
65 Other recent Lowkey songs have continued his critique of government-supported international arms dealing ("Lords of War") and of the system of late capitalism ("The Death of Neoliberalism").

Chapter 5

1. Established in London in 1991 and now operating from Dubai, Middle East Broadcasting Center (MBC) was the first and is still the largest free-to-air satellite broadcasting company in the Arab world.
2. One Latin American soap, the Brazilian *O Clone* (2001–2) features a transatlantic love affair between a Moroccan Muslim woman and a Brazilian Catholic man, though this one has received considerable criticism for its representation of Moroccan culture. See Shohat and Alsultany.
3. On Syrian television dramas, see Rebecca Joubin.
4. This particular difference is not central to our argument here, though it is not an insignificant one. Much discussion of the American soap opera as a genre has focused on its open-ended form, from Dennis Porter's vision of this form as an aesthetic flaw, to Tania Modleski's vision that this characteristic is a subversive one that is "opposed to classic (male) film narrative" (98).
5. "DAESH" is an acronym for the Arabic version of the name of what is generally referred to in the West as the Islamic State, or ISIS. "DAESH" is considered a derogatory term and is much disliked by DAESH itself.
6. Since the success of *Noor* it has become common practice to dub Turkish soap operas in Syrian for broadcast in the Middle East.
7. Afyon (aka Afyonkarahisar) is a relatively large town with a population of more than 100,000. However, it is located in the center of an agricultural area and is noted for having a somewhat old-fashioned and traditional feel.
8. Both Noor and Muhannad become concerned about rivals for the affection of their mate in the course of the series—most importantly when Muhannad's former fiancée resurfaces (alive, but now confined to a wheel chair), complete with a five-year-old son via her earlier relationship with Muhannad.
9. For an overview of the reaction to *Noor* in the Arab world, see Bucciamanti.
10. Soon afterward, in perhaps the most extreme reaction yet to Arabic soap operas, Saleh Al-Luhaidan (chief justice of the Saudi Arabia's supreme judicial council) responded to a question about the *musalsalat Ramadan* that were broadcast immediately after *Noor* in 2008 by declaring that television channels broadcasting such shows were propagating "depravation and debauchery," posing a threat to the morals of good Muslims everywhere. As a result, he declared that it was lawful from an Islamic point of view to kill the operators of television channels broadcasting such materials ("Okay").
11. This documentary, which describes the impact of Turkish soap operas in the Arab world and the Balkans, can be found online at http://www.aljazeera.com/programmes/witness/2013/11/kismet-how-soap-operas-changed-world-2013 1117152457476872.html. Accessed February 2018.

12 As in all of Sagar's comments in the song, there is a grain of truth here—tourism from the Arab world to Turkey experienced a major spike after the broadcast of the series as devoted viewers traveled north to view the land of Muhannad and Noor.
13 It should be noted, however, that the show has also been broadcast (in appropriately dubbed versions) with some success in Iran and in several Balkan countries. It has not, however, been dubbed into English or any major Western European language.
14 Traditional rural life also receives unsentimental treatment in the relatively lighthearted 2014–15 Turkish soap *Kiraz Mevsimi* (*Cherry Season*, also successfully dubbed in Arabic as *Mawsim al Karaz* and broadcast on MBC 4). Here a group of characters from Istanbul plan an idyllic outing in the countryside only to be beset by comic unpleasantness at every turn.
15 Bakhtin defines the chronotope as "the intrinsic connectedness of temporal and spatial relationships that are artistically expressed in literature" (84). He sees it as a crucial characteristic of individual works, as well as of whole genres.

Chapter 6

1 The only point in the entire season at which Hawsawi performed in Arabic was during his duet with his mentor and team leader, Lebanese singing star Ragheb Alama, during the final episode. Here, Hawsawi briefly broke into Arabic (to great applause from the live audience) in the midst of his otherwise (heavily Bowdlerized) English-language rendition of Justin Timberlake's "Suit and Tie."
2 Originally dominated by state-run channels that offered up little more than pro-regime propaganda, Arab TV expanded into the private sector relatively recently. Muhammad Ayish discusses this phenomenon, expressing skepticism as late as 2011 that Arab television would be able to avoid remaining "captive to patriarchal and authoritarian political traditions" (102). Indeed, even the seemingly cosmopolitan MBC was originally launched by the brother-in-law of Saudi Arabia's King Fahd, causing considerable skepticism in some circles (Sakr, *Satellite Realms*, 42–43). Trends since that time, however, have suggested an increasingly modern and independent direction for Arab television. Some have argued, in fact, that independent television stations such as Al Jazeera Arabic played a key role in the Arab Spring uprisings by evading government control of their broadcast content.
3 As an example of the current Arab mediascape, one of the authors of this volume was recently scanning the channels on satellite TV in Jordan and discovered that the American syndicated medical talk show *The Doctors* was being broadcast (with Arabic subtitles) on MBC 4 at the very same moment a reformulation of the show in Arabic (with an English title, *7 Doctors*) was being broadcast (as part of the same satellite programming package) on Jordan's Roya TV.

4   For a representative performance, see https://youtu.be/NRMDSNXwCm8.
5   Available at https://youtu.be/7DlE_GaWY20
6   For a representative performance, see https://youtu.be/L1MrA3435Ik.
7   The harassment of women is an endemic problem in Egypt, especially in Cairo. The recent film *Cairo 678* (2010) deals with this problem in a way that does have specifically Egyptian intonations. But its feminist message is very much in line with modern Western ideas. Meanwhile, its director, Mohamed Diab, has probably had his greatest success in the film business as the writer of the contemporary crime thrillers *El Gezira* (2007) and *El Gezira 2* (2014), which would be very much at home in American cinemas—and which were big box-office hits in Egypt.
8   Michigan's Mona Haydar, an Arab American, has gotten considerable attention for rapping in her hijab in songs such as "Hijabi" (2017), in the video clip for which (https://youtu.be/XOX9O_kVPeo) she was also visibly pregnant. Meanwhile, in "Dog," her follow-up (2017, https://youtu.be/idMJIEFH_ns), she denounces the hypocrisy of lecherous Muslim men who would declare her rapping in a hijab to be immoral and inappropriate.
9   The success of such music competition shows is a sign of the extensive overlap between the music and television industries in the Middle East, as is the popularity of video clips on Arab television. In addition, singers such as Haifa Wehbe and Myriam Fares have successfully crossed over into acting, while actresses such as Lebanon's Cyrine Abdelnour have ventured into singing.
10 For more on this phenomenon, and on the organization of the Arab media business in general, see Sakr's *Arab Television Today*.
11 Kordahi's later ventures include *Al-Mosameh Karim* ("To Forgive is Generous"), in which he brings together individuals who have had some sort of personal dispute and attempts to help them resolve their differences. The intention is presumably sincere, though it is certainly the case that the show feeds off of a rather lurid interest in the misery of others. It is conducted with considerably more decorum, but it will inevitably remind American viewers of phenomena such as the notorious *Jerry Springer Show*.
12 Letterman had long been considered the likely successor to Carson when Jay Leno was instead tapped to become the new host of *The Tonight Show* upon Carson's retirement in 1992. See Carter for an account of the controversy over this succession.
13 Youssef and his career are the subject of the 2017 documentary film *Tickling Giants*.
14 This phenomenon, in which a singer hosts guests in a relaxed atmosphere, then sings with them, has also been seen in Assala Nasri's *Soula* (which premiered in 2011), in which the host greets guests as if in her own Cairo home. More recently, in 2017, Sherine has begun hosting a bigger-budget version of a similar idea (with more elaborate live performances) in *Sherry Studio*.

15 Wehbe's age has been the subject of considerable tabloid-style controversy, but she seems to have been born some time from 1972 to 1976.
16 The show is successful enough that MBC offered to pick it up for broadcast on one of their channels. Rashed refused the offer, feeling that remaining on YouTube would give him more independence in determining the show's content.
17 https://youtu.be/p9Kxky477FI

Chapter 7

1 Gamal was prominent enough that she had a brief cameo appearance (belly dancing, of course) in the Hollywood film *Valley of the Kings* (1954), even though her appearance there was completely gratuitous and was simply used to provide local color. This film, incidentally, features a search for the tomb of a pharaoh that supposedly contains proof that the Old Testament account of the captivity of the Jews in Egypt is historically accurate.
2 The negative depiction of Islamic fundamentalists, along with the portrayal of homosexuality, caused a number of Muslim clerics in Egypt to demand (unsuccessfully) that the film be banned. Instead, it was submitted as the nation's annual entry for consideration for nomination for the Best Foreign Language Film Oscar.
3 In terms of the film's international status, it might be noted that *Theeb* was shot by the very experienced Austrian cinematographer Wolfgang Thaler, whom Nowar brought to Jordan for the task.
4 Perhaps the most important phenomenon in Jordanian-produced television involves *musalsalat* that feature Bedouins, usually set before the First World War. These productions tend to romanticize Bedouins, featuring beautiful exotic women and fierce, violent men in representations that are themselves stereotypical and even Orientalist. Though supposedly positive in their portrayal of Bedouins, such dramas tend to reproduce Orientalist stereotypes, while at the same time glorifying the past.
5 Among other things, the link to Barnum and Bailey suggests that Lawrence's own famed sympathies with Arab culture might have involved an element of consumerist Orientalism, a phenomenon that was just hitting its stride as Lawrence was participating in the Arab Revolt.
6 This roadshow itself was part of the general fascination with Orientalist motifs that, as we note in Chapter 1, played a prominent role in the American culture of the time.
7 Interestingly, *Lawrence* does not appear on the British Film Institute's (BFI) list of the fifty greatest films of all time, published in the September 2012 issue of *Sight & Sound* magazine. The list of greatest British films of the twentieth century compiled by the BFI did rank *Lawrence* third, however.

8   Critics such as Caton and Stollery have detailed the Orientalism inherent in *Lawrence*'s depiction of Arabs.

9   In the film, however, Lawrence is unaware of the secret Sykes-Picot Treaty, by which the British and French arranged to divvy up the Middle East after the war. In reality, he was well aware of the treaty, though deeply troubled by it. It was, according to Jackson, "one of his deepest sources of torment" (21).

10 See Raw for a comparison of *Lawrence of Arabia* with the 1952 Turkish film *Ingiliz Kemal Lavrens'e Karsi* ("Ingiliz Kemal Against Lawrence"), which depicts the Turks as heroic crusaders against the efforts of Lawrence and the British to colonize the Middle East. Raw notes that Western critics have largely ignored the Orientalism of *Lawrence* in its depiction of the Turks as "inefficient, ruthless, or perverted" (252).

11 Shohat and Stam have argued that the film shows an *anti-*Arab bias, consistently associating the British with "productive, creative pioneering" and the Arabs with "underdevelopment" (148).

12 Lawrence, however disgusted he might have been by the British and French efforts to carve up the Middle East after the First World War, would also play a key role in the postwar negotiations that laid out the political future of the region. As Anderson notes, Lawrence was particularly central to the construction of what would become the nation of Jordan.

13 The same might be said about the representation of desert tribesmen in other Western attempts at the desert epic, such as *The Wind and the Lion* (1975), which features Sean Connery as the historical Moroccan Berber anticolonial leader Mulai Ahmed er Raisuli. Connery plays the role in full Scottish accent, which is no problem at all, given that the entire film fails to take itself seriously and plays its important historical subject matter largely for jokes. Even beheadings are used as opportunities for humor in this truly strange film, which largely romanticizes Raisuli and his desert followers as a jolly band of misfits. And the portrayal of the court of the sultan of Morocco in *The Wind and the Lion* is one of the most extreme depictions of Oriental decadence to appear anywhere in Hollywood film.

14 Given that Istanbul was already linked to Damascus by rail, this railway was intended to provide a direct link from the Ottoman capital all the way to Mecca.

15 The Stranger's namelessness (along with his generally laconic nature and his moral ambiguity) clearly echoes that of the "Man with No Name" character played by Clint Eastwood in Sergio Leone's The Dollars Trilogy of Spaghetti Westerns: *A Fistful of Dollars* (1964), *For a Few Dollars More* (1965), and *The Good, the Bad, and the Ugly* (1966). Eastwood also plays a similar nameless character in the American Western *High Plains Drifter* (1973), in which the character is also listed in the credits as "The Stranger"—as is the incongruous cowboy figure who appears in the Coen Brothers' *The Big Lebowski* (1998).

16 Nowar told the authors of this volume in a private communication (August 12, 2018) that the railway motif in *Theeb* derives partly from the fact that, to this day, the Bedouins tell stories about the impact of this railway on their culture, suggesting that the magnitude of this impact was great.
17 See Caton for a further discussion of this notion. In particular, Caton argues that Lean used the Western "as a frame of reference for understanding his epic" (189).
18 Though there is little convincing evidence concerning the real Lawrence's sexuality, the consensus is that he was either asexual or homosexual. However, the only mention of Lawrence's sexuality in the film (in an episode based on Lawrence's account in *Seven Pillars*) occurs when he is captured at Deraa and propositioned by the Turkish Bey, a proposition that he strongly rebuffs, leading to a vicious reprisal.
19 Much of the action in two other Scott films, *Kingdom of Heaven* (2005) and *Body of Lies* (2008) takes place in what is now Jordan (though not in Wadi Rum), though the Jordan scenes in both of these films were shot in Morocco.
20 Many of the Hollywood films shot in Wadi Rum employed locals on their crews, which meant that, for the making of *Theeb*, there were already a number of experienced crew members in place in the area. According to Al Jazeera ("Jordan Shoots") Bassel Ghandour, who cowrote and coproduced *Theeb*, has argued that the filming of Hollywood movies in Jordan "paved the way" for this new generation of Jordanian filmmakers. "These films," Ghandour said, "came to Jordan and we crewed up on them. That's how we learned the craft, that's how we learned what a set looks like, and that's how we became really world class." Similarly, *Theeb* coproducer Laith Majali has said that the making of the film was greatly facilitated by the availability of a local crew with extensive professional experience: "There is no way we could have made *Theeb* in the quality we did if it weren't for our Jordanian crews having worked with some of [Hollywood's] best directors, such as Ridley Scott and Kathryn Bigelow" ("Jordan Shoots").
21 At least one Western, *Hawmps!* (1976), deals (though in a largely comic mode) with an actual program in the mid-nineteenth century in which the US Cavalry experimented with using camels to ease travel across the arid expanses of the American Southwest.
22 Arab film even has its own (comedy-infused) Zapata Western in the form of Hassan Hafez's *Viva Zalata* (1976), which includes Western legend Billy the Kid as a central character.
23 For one of the better interviews in which Nowar discusses the influence of Western films on his cinematic vision, see Talu. Nowar told the authors of this volume (August 12, 2018) that he was influenced by so many films it would be hard to name them all, though he did single out John Ford's *The Searchers* (1956), Sam Peckinpah's *Straw Dogs* (1971), Mel Gibson's *Apocalypto* (2006), and Akira Kurosawa's *Sanshiro Sugata* (1943) and *Sanjuro* (1962). Interestingly,

Nowar suggested to us that classic animated Disney films such as *Pinocchio* (1940), *Bambi* (1942), and *The Jungle Book* (1967) should also be credited as influences.

24 The Arab Revolt, commonly designated in Jordan as the "Great Arab Revolt," is regarded as a key event in the founding of the nation of Jordan, though it is looked upon negatively in much of the Arab world due to the French-British colonial collusion after the war. After all, Jordan's King Abdullah II is a direct descendent of Sharif Hussein bin Ali, the key figure in the revolt and a figure who is still regarded as a national hero in Jordan—which is also the only one of the monarchies growing out of the Arab Revolt that still survives. The centennial of the Arab Revolt was celebrated in Jordan in 2016 with much aplomb. See "Jordan Marks."

Conclusion

1 See the collection edited by Alsultany and Shohat for a number of perspectives on the influence of Arab culture in both the United States and Latin America. And see Robbert Woltering's study of Occidentalist discourse in the Egyptian media, which concludes that the uneven distribution of power makes Occidentalism in the East (driven by both a real and a perceived inferiority) function far differently than Orientalism in the West (driven by an advantage in both real material power and media-driven discursive power).

2 For a much more extensive, Sartre-inflected reading of this aspect of *Jude the Obscure*, see Daraiseh.

3 Bollywood films, of course, have become increasingly popular in a variety of global contexts in recent years. See, for example, Larkin's discussion of the popularity of Bollywood products in the Muslim Hausa community of Nigeria. For Larkin, this popularity in such areas results partly because watching Bollywood films is seen "as a means of establishing distance from the ideologically loaded presence of American film" (173). Then again, Bollywood films are often heavily influenced by Hollywood, adding its own local touches to Hollywood models. See Rao on glocalization in Bollywood films.

4 See M. Keith Booker's *Postmodern Hollywood* for a similar argument that, even if postmodern directors lack individual styles as Jameson claims, they can still borrow from the styles of others in new and creative ways, especially through combining different styles in a single work (187–89).

Works Cited

"13-year-old Hala Turk Pictured with Her Ass Up against a Male Singer's Private Parts!" *Albawaba* (June 30, 2015). https://www.albawaba.com/entertainment/13-year-old-hala-turk-pictured-her-ass-against-male-singers-private-parts-713890. Web. Accessed April 2019.

Abou-Bakr, Omaima. "Satellite Piety: Contemporary TV Islamic Programs in Egypt." *Popular Culture in the Middle East and North Africa: A Postcolonial Outlook.* Eds. Walid El Hamamsy and Mounira Soliman. London: Routledge, 2013. 113–29.

Achebe, Chinua. *Things Fall Apart.* 1958. New York: Anchor-Random House, 1994.

Agamben, Giorgio. *What Is an Apparatus?* Trans. David Kishik and Stefan Pedatella. Palo Alto, CA: Stanford University Press, 2009.

Ahmad, Aijaz. *In Theory: Classes, Nations, Literatures.* London: Verso, 1992.

Ahmad, Jalal Al-i. *Occidentosis: A Plague from the West.* 1978. Trans. R. Campbell. Berkeley, CA: Mizan Press, 1984.

Aidi, Hisham. *Rebel Music: Race, Empire, and the New Muslim Youth Culture.* New York: Pantheon, 2014.

Al-Atiq, Fahd. *Life on Hold.* 2004. Trans. Jonathan Wright. Cairo: American University in Cairo Press, 2012.

Al-Barghouti, Tamim. "Caliphs and Clips." *Music and Media in the Arab World.* Ed. Michael Frishkopf. New York: The American University in Cairo Press, 2010. 225–30.

Ali, Tariq. "Literature and Market Realism." *New Left Review* 199 (May–June 1993): 140–45.

Almeida, Cristina Moreno. "'Race' and 'Blackness' in Moroccan Rap: Voicing Local Experiences of Marginality." *American Studies Encounters the Middle East.* Eds. Alex Lubin and Marwan M. Kraidy. Chapel Hill: University of North Carolina Press, 2016. 81–105.

Alsalman, Yassin. *Diatribes of a Dying Tribe.* Montreal: Write or Wrong Publishing, 2010.

Alsanea, Rajaa. *Girls of Riyadh.* 2005. Trans. Rajaa Alsanea and Marilyn Booth. London: Penguin, 2007.

Alsultany, Evelyn. *Arabs and Muslims in the Media: Race and Representation after 9/11.* New York: New York University Press, 2012.

Alsultany, Evelyn, and Ella Shohat, ed. *Between the Middle East and the Americas: The Cultural Politics of Diaspora.* Ann Arbor: University of Michigan Press, 2013.

Ambah, Faiza Saleh. "A Subversive Soap Roils Saudi Arabia." *The Washington Post.* August 3, 2008. http://www.washingtonpost.com/wp-dyn/content/article/2008/08/02/AR2008080201547.html. Web. Accessed April 2019.

Anderson, Scott. *Lawrence in Arabia: War, Deceit, Imperial Folly and the Making of the Modern Middle East*. Garden City, NY: Anchor Books, 2014.

Appadurai, Arjun. *Modernity at Large*. Minneapolis: University of Minnesota Press, 1996.

Armbrust, Walter. "What Would Sayyid Qutb Say?: Some Reflections on Video Clips." *Music and Media in the Arab World*. Ed. Michael Frishkopf. New York: The American University in Cairo Press, 2010. 231–54.

Ashcroft, Bill. *Post-Colonial Transformation*. London: Routledge, 2001.

Ayish, Muhammad. "Television Broadcasting in the Arab World." *Arab Media: Globalization and Emerging Media Industries*. Eds. Noha Mellor, Muhammad Ayish, Nabil Dajani, and Khalil Rinnawi. Cambridge: Polity Press, 2011. 85–102.

Azaiez, Tamara Wong. "Beyoncé Appropriates Oum Kalthoum Song on Tour." *Arab America* (June 30, 2016). https://www.arabamerica.com/beyonce-appropriates-oum-kalthoum-song-tour/. Web. Accessed April 2019.

Aziz, Moataz Abdel. "Arab Music Videos and Their Implications for Arab Music and Media. *Music and Media in the Arab World*. Ed. Michael Frishkopf. New York: The American University in Cairo Press, 2010. 77–90.

Bakhtin, M. M. *The Dialogic Imagination*. Ed. Michael Holquist. Trans. Caryl Emerson and Michael Holquist. Austin: University of Texas Press, 1981.

Berman, Jacob Rama. *American Arabesque: Islam, Arabs and the Nineteenth-Century Imaginary*. New York: New York University Press, 2012.

Bernal, Martin. *Black Athena: The Afroasiatic Roots of Classical Civilization*. New Brunswick, NJ: Rutgers University Press, 1987.

Bhabha, Homi. *The Location of Culture*. London: Routledge, 1994.

Bhaduri, Aditi. "Interview: Dr. Nawal El Saadawi." *Newsline* (July 2006). https://newslinemagazine.com/magazine/interview-dr-nawal-el-saadawi/. Web. Accessed April 2019.

Bloch, Ernst. *The Principle of Hope*. 3 vols. Trans. Neville Plaice, Stephen Plaice, and Paul Knight. Cambridge, MA: MIT Press, 1995. (Original German version published in 1959.)

Booker, M. Keith. *Colonial Power, Colonial Texts: India in the Modern British Novel*. Ann Arbor: University of Michigan Press, 1997.

Booker, M. Keith. *Disney, Pixar, and the Hidden Messages in Children's Film*. Santa Barbara, CA: Praeger, 2009.

Booker, M. Keith. *Postmodern Hollywood: What's New in Film and Why It Makes US Feel So Strange*. Westport, CT: Praeger, 2007.

Booker, M. Keith, and Dubravka Juraga. "The Reds and the Blacks: The Historical Novel in the Soviet Union and Postcolonial Africa." *Socialist Cultures East and West: A Post–Cold War Reassessment*. Ed. Dubravka Juraga and M. Keith Booker. New York: Praeger, 2002. 11–30.

Boone, Joseph Allen. *The Homoerotics of Orientalism*. New York: Columbia University Press, 2014.

Bradbury, Ray. *Fahrenheit 451*. 1953. New York: Ballantine Books, 1979.

Brandt, Allan. *The Cigarette Century: The Rise, Fall, and Deadly Persistence of the Product that Defined America*. New York: Basic Books, 2009.

Bucciamanti, Alexandra. "Turkish Soap Operas in the Arab World: Social Liberation or Cultural Alienation?" *Arab Media & Society* 10 (Spring 2010). https://www.arabmediasociety.com/turkish-soap-operas-in-the-arab-world-social-liberation-or-cultural-alienation/. Web. Accessed April 2019.

Bulos, Nabih. "The *Theeb* Director Describes the Film's Arduous Journey to a Foreign Language Film Oscar Nomination." *The Los Angeles Times* (February 19, 2016). https://www.latimes.com/entertainment/movies/la-et-mn-oscars-theeb-jordan-naji-abu-nowar-20160218-story.html. Web. Accessed April 22, 2019.

Buruma, Ian, and Avishai Margalit. *Occidentalism: The West in the Eyes of Its Enemies*. New York: Penguin, 2004.

Carter, Bill. *The Late Shift: Letterman, Leno, and the Network Battle for the Night*. New York: Hachette, 1995.

Castillo, Edward D. "*Dances with Wolves*." *Multiculturalism, Postcoloniality, and Transnational Media*. Ed. Ella Shohat and Robert Stam. New Brunswick, NJ: Rutgers University Press, 2003. 63–76.

Caton, Steven C. Lawrence of Arabia: *A Film's Anthropology*. Berkeley: University of California Press, 1999.

Çelik, Zeynep. "Speaking Back to Orientalist Discourse at the World's Columbian Exposition." *Noble Dreams, Wicked Pleasures: Orientalism in America, 1870-1930*. Ed. Holly Edwards. Princeton, NJ: Princeton University Press, 2000. 77–97.

Cestor, Elisabeth. "Music and Television in Lebanon." *Music and Media in the Arab World*. Ed. Michael Frishkopf. New York: The American University in Cairo Press, 2010. 97–110.

Chang, Jeff. *Can't Stop Won't Stop: A History of the Hip-Hop Generation*. London: Picador, 2005.

Christie, Ian. "The 50 Greatest Films of All Time." *British Film Institute Sight & Sound Poll* (Updated December 2015). https://www.bfi.org.uk/news/50-greatest-films-all-time. Web. Accessed April 2019.

Cockburn, Patrick. *The Age of Jihad: Islamic State and the Great War for the Middle East*. London: Verso, 2016.

Crary, Robert. *24/7: Late Capitalism and the Ends of Sleep*. London: Verso, 2013.

Curtis, Carl C. III. "David Lean's Lawrence: 'Only Flesh and Blood.'" *Literature Film Quarterly* 40.4 (2012): 274–87.

Daraiseh, Isra. "The Literary Unconscious: Ideology and Utopia in the Nineteenth-Century Realist Novel in England and Russia." Diss. University of Arkansas, 2015.

Darwish, Hany. "Images of Women in Advertising and Video Clips: A Case Study of Sherif Sabri." *Music and Media in the Arab World*. Ed. Michael Frishkopf. New York: The American University in Cairo Press, 2010. 255–64.

Davis, Janet M. *The Circus Age: Culture and Society under the American Big Top*. Chapel Hill: University of North Carolina Press, 2002.

Davy, Steven. "For Hip-Hop Artist Omar Offendum, Apathy toward Syria Is Not an Option." *PRI's The World* (May 4, 2014). https://www.pri.org/stories/2015-05-04/hip-hop-artist-omar-offendum-apathy-toward-syria-not-option. Web. Accessed April 2019.

DeGhett, Torie Rose. "Hip-Hop-Academia: Omar Offendum and Arab Diaspora Rap." *Los Angeles Review of Books* (September 16, 2012). https://lareviewofbooks.org/article/hip-hop-academia-omar-offendum-and-arab-diaspora-rap/. Web. Accessed April 2019.

DeGhett, Torie Rose. "'Record! I Am an Arab!': Paranoid Arab Boys, Global Ciphers, and Hip Hop Nationalism." *The Hip Hop and Obama Reader*. Ed. Travis L. Ghosa and Erik Nielson. New York: Oxford University Press, 2015. 94–106.

Derr, Holly L. "We Need to Talk about Katy Perry: Why Orientalism in Pop Culture Matters?" *HowlRound* (December 6, 2013). https://howlround.com/we-need-talk-about-katy-perry. Web. Accessed April 2019.

D'Haen, Theo. "Postmodernism in American Fiction and Art." *Approaching Postmodernism*. Ed. Douwe Fokkema and Hans Bertens. Amsterdam: John Benjamins, 1986. 211–31.

Ditmars, Hadani. "Jordan Film Receives Oscar Nomination." *Middle East Institute* (January 13, 2016). https://www.mei.edu/publications/jordanian-film-receives-oscar-nomination. Web. Accessed April 2019.

Dos Passos, John. *John Dos Passos: U.S.A.* New York: Library of America, 1996 (1930–36).

Dos Passos, John. *Manhattan Transfer*. Boston, MA: Mariner Books, 2003 (1925).

Dos Passos, John. *Orient Express: A Travel Memoir*. La Vergne, TN: Open Road Distribution, 2015 (1927).

Dyer, Richard. "Entertainment and Utopia." *Only Entertainment*. 2nd ed. London: Routledge, 2002. 19–35.

Eagleton, Terry. *The Ideology of the Aesthetic*. London: Basil Blackwell, 1990.

Eagleton, Terry. *The Illusions of Postmodernism*: Oxford: Blackwell, 1996.

Eagleton, Terry. "Thomas Hardy and *Jude the Obscure*." *The Eagleton Reader*. Ed. Stephen Regan. Oxford: Blackwell, 1998. 36–48.

Edwards, Brian T. *After the American Century: The Ends of U.S. Culture in the Middle East*. New York: Columbia University Press, 2016.

Edwards, Holly, "A Million and One Nights: Orientalism in American 1870-1930." *Noble Dreams, Wicked Pleasures: Orientalism in America, 1870-1930*. Ed. Holly Edwards. Princeton, NJ: Princeton University Press, 2000. 11–57.

Elouardaoui, Ouidyane. "Contemporary Arab Music Video Clips: Between Simulating MTV's Gender Stereotypes and Fostering New Ones." *Imaginations: Journal of Cross-Cultural Image Studies* 4.1 (August 22, 2013). http://imaginations.glendon.yorku.ca/?p=4358. Web. Accessed April 2019.

Fanon, Frantz. *The Wretched of the Earth*. Trans. Constance Farrington. New York: Grove Press, 1963.

Fernandes, Sujatha. "'Obama Nation': Hip Hop and Global Protest." *The Hip Hop and Obama Reader*. Ed. Travis L. Ghosa and Erik Nielson. New York: Oxford University Press, 2015. 88–93.

Fisher, Mark. *Capitalist Realism: Is There No Alternative?* London: Zero Books, 2009.

Freij, Muath. "*Theeb* Cast, Crew Hailed for "Landmark" Oscar Nomination." *Jordan Times* (February 29, 2016). http://www.jordantimes.com/news/local/theeb-cast-c rew-hailed-landmark-oscar-nomination. Web. Accessed April 2019.

Geraghty, Christine. *Women and Soap Operas: A Study of Prime Time Soaps*. Cambridge: Polity Press, 1991.

Gibb, H. A. R. "Literature." *The Legacy of Islam*. Ed. Sir Thomas Arnold and Alfred Guillaume. 1931. Oxford: Oxford University Press, 1965. 180–209.

Greene, Naomi. *From Fu Manchu to Kung Fu Panda: Images of China in American Film*. Honolulu: University of Hawaii Press, 2014.

Gross, Joan, David McMurray, and Ted Swedenburg. "Rai, Rap, and Ramadan Nights: Franco-Maghribi Cultural Identities." *Middle East Report* 178 (1992): 11–24.

Grundey, Adam. "Meet Arab Hip-Hop's Poet Laureate, Omar Offendum." *Redbull.com* (January 24, 2017). https://www.redbull.com/mea-en/meet-arab-hip-hops-poet-laureate-omar-offendum. Web. Accessed April 2019.

Hall, Stuart, and Paddy Whannel. *The Popular Arts: A Critical Guide to the Mass Media*. New York: Pantheon Books, 1965.

Hassan, Waïl S. *Tayeb Salih: Ideology and the Craft of Fiction*. Syracuse, NY: Syracuse University Press, 2003.

Hayden, Patrick. "Globalization, Reflexive Utopianism, and the Cosmopolitan Social Imaginary." *Globalization and Utopia*. Eds. Patrick Hayden and Chamsy el-Ojeili. New York: Palgrave Macmillan, 2009. 51–68.

Hayden, Patrick and Chamsy el-Ojeili, eds. *Globalization and Utopia*. New York: Palgrave Macmillan, 2009.

Hazbun, Waleed. "The Uses of Modernization Theory: American Foreign Policy and Mythmaking in the Arab World." *American Studies Encounters the Middle East*. Eds. Alex Lubin and Marwan M. Kraidy. Chapel Hill: University of North Carolina Press, 2016. 175–206.

Hebdige, Dick. *Subculture: The Meaning of Style*. Rev. ed. London: Routledge, 1979.

Hobsbawm, Eric. *The Age of Revolution, 1789–1848*. New York: Vintage-Random House, 1996.

Hobson, Dorothy. *Soap Opera*. London: Polity, 2003.

hooks, bell. "Moving Beyond Pain." *bell hooks Institute* (May 9, 2016). Accessed April 2019.

"ISIS Threatens Producers, Cast of 'Black Crows' TV Show." *ANSAmed* (May 31, 2017). http://www.ansamed.info/ansamed/en/news/sections/politics/2017/05/31/isis-threat ens-producers-cast-of-black-crows-tv-show_95aec5ff-ad3f-4f7f-86d1-59e513ac3 8b0.html. Web. Accessed April 2019.

Iskandar, Adel. "'Whenever, Wherever!': The Discourse of Orientalist Transnationalism in the Construction of Shakira." *The Ambassadors* 6.2 (July 2003). https://ambassadors.net/archives/issue14/selected_studies4.htm. Web. Accessed April 2019.

Jackson, Kevin. *Lawrence of Arabia*. London: British Film Institute, 2007.

Jarmakani, Amira. "They Hate Our Freedom, But We Love Their Belly Dance." *Between the Middle East and the Americas: The Cultural Politics of Diaspora*. Eds. Evelyn Alsultany and Ella Shohat. Ann Arbor: University of Michigan Press, 2013. 130–52.

Jameson, Fredric. *Archaeologies of the Future: The Desire Called Utopia and Other Science Fictions*. London: Verso, 2005.

Jameson, Fredric. *The Political Unconscious: Narrative as a Socially Symbolic Act*. Ithaca, NY: Cornell University Press, 1981.

Jameson, Fredric. *Postmodernism, or, The Cultural Logic of Late Capitalism*. Durham, NC: Duke University Press, 1991.

Jameson, Fredric. *Signatures of the Visible*. New York: Routledge, 1992.

Jameson, Fredric. "Third-World Literature in the Era of Multinational Capitalism." *Pretexts* 3.1–2 (1991): 82–104.

JanMohamed, Abdul R. "The Economy of Manichean Allegory: The Function of Racial Difference in Colonialist Literature." *Critical Inquiry* 12.1 (1985): 59–87.

"Jordan Marks Great Arab Revolt Centennial with Parade." *Business Insider* (June 3, 2016). https://www.businessinsider.com/ap-jordan-marks-great-arab-revolt-centennial-with-parade-2016-6. Web. Accessed April 2019.

Joubin, Rebecca. *The Politics of Love: Sexuality, Gender, and Marriage in Syrian Television Drama*. Lanham, MD: Lexington Books, 2013.

Kaplan, E. Anne. *Rocking around the Clock: Music Television, Postmodernism, and Consumer Culture*. London: Methuen, 1987.

Khabeer, Su'ad Abdul. *Muslim Cool: Race, Religion and Hip Hop in the United States*. New York: NYU Press, 2016.

Khalaf, Hala. "The Judges of *The Voice Ahla Sawt* Feel the Show Is the Perfect Platform to Dispel Misconceptions about Arabs." *The National* (December 22, 2015). https://www.thenational.ae/arts-culture/television/the-judges-of-the-voice-ahla-sawt-feel-the-show-is-the-perfect-platform-to-dispel-misconceptions-about-arabs-1.101454. Web. Accessed April 2019.

Khalaf, Hala. "Nedaa Shrara Wins *The Voice Ahla Sawt*: 'I Came with One Goal: To Win.'" *The National* (December 27, 2015). https://www.thenational.ae/arts-culture/television/nedaa-shrara-wins-the-voice-ahla-sawt-i-came-with-one-goal-to-win-1.1108368. Web. Accessed April 2019.

Kraidy, Marwan, and Joe Khalil. *Arab Television Industries*. London: Palgrave Macmillan, 2009.

Kramer, Martin. *Ivory Towers on Sand: The Failure of Middle Eastern Studies in America*. Washington, DC: Washington Institute for Near East Policy, 2001.

Kristeva, Julia. *Powers of Horror: An Essay on Abjection*. Trans. Leon S. Roudiez. New York: Columbia University Press, 1982.

Kubala, Patricia. "The Controversy over Satellite Music Television in Contemporary Egypt." *Music and Media in the Arab World*. Ed. Michael Frishkopf. New York: The American University in Cairo Press, 2010. 173–224.

Larkin, Brian. "Itineraries of Indian Cinema: African Videos, Bollywood, and Global Media." *Multiculturalism, Postcoloniality, and Transnational Media*. Ed. Ella Shohat and Robert Stam. New Brunswick, NJ: Rutgers University Press, 2003. 170–92.

Lawrence, T. E. *Seven Pillars of Wisdom: A Triumph*. The Complete 1922 Text. Radford, VA: Wilder Publications, 2011.

Leach, William. *Country of Exiles: The Destruction of Place in American Life*. New York: Pantheon Books, 1999.

Leach, William. *Land of Desire: Merchants, Power, and the Rise of a New American Culture*. New York: Vintage-Random House, 1993.

Lefkowitz, Mary R., and Guy MacLean Rogers, eds. *Black Athena Revisited*. 2nd ed. Chapel Hill: University of North Carolina Press, 1996.

LeVine, Mark. *Heavy Metal Islam: Rock, Resistance, and the Struggle for the Soul of Islam*. New York: Broadway Books, 2008.

Lewis, Bernard. *What Went Wrong?: The Clash between Islam and Modernity in the Middle East*. New York: Oxford University Press, 2002.

Lorde, Audre. "The Master's Tools Will Never Dismantle the Master's House." *Sister Outsider: Essays and Speeches*. New York: Crossing Press, 2007. 110–13.

Louis, J. C., and Harvey J. Yazijian. *The Cola Wars: The Story of the Global Battle between the Coca-Cola Company and Pepsico, Inc*. New York: Everest House, 1980.

Lughod, Lila Abu, and Maya Mikdashi. "Tradition and the Anti-Politics Machine: DAM Seduced by the 'Honor Crime.'" *Jadaliyya* (November 23, 2012). Web. Accessed April 2019.

Lukács, Georg. *The Historical Novel*. Trans. Hannah and Stanley Mitchell. Lincoln: University of Nebraska Press, 1983.

Mahfouz, Naguib. *The Cairo Trilogy: Palace Walk, Palace of Desire, Sugar Street*. 1956–1957. Trans. William Maynard Hutchins, Olive E. Kinny, Lorne M. Kenny, and Angela Boutros Samaan. New York: Everyman's Library, 2001.

Maira, Sunaina. "'A Strip, A Land, A Blaze': Arab American Hip-Hop and Transnational Politics." *Between the Middle East and the Americas: The Cultural Politics of Diaspora*. Eds. Evelyn Alsultany and Ella Shohat. Ann Arbor: University of Michigan Press, 2013. 195–213.

Mandel, Ernest. *Late Capitalism*. Trans. Joris De Bres. London: NLB, 1975.

Marx, Karl, and Friedrich Engels. *The Communist Manifesto*. 1848. Ed. David McClellan. New York: Oxford University Press, 1992.

May, Lary. *Screening Out the Past: The Birth of Mass Culture and the Motion Picture Industry*. Chicago, IL: University of Chicago Press, 1983.

"MBC's CEO on Running One of the Largest TV Stations in the Middle East." *Albawaba Business* (January 16, 2014). https://www.albawaba.com/business/sam-barnett-interview-547715. Web. Accessed April 2019.

McAlister, Melani. *Epic Encounters: Culture, Media, & U.S. Interests in the Middle East since 1945*. Berkeley: University of California Press, 2005.

Mead, Margaret. *Culture and Commitment: The New Relationships between the Generations in the 1970s*. Rev. and updated edition. Garden City, NY: Anchor Books, 1978.

Mellor, Noha. "Arab Media: An Overview of Recent Trends." *Arab Media: Globalization and Emerging Media Industries*. Ed. Noha Mellor, Muhammad Ayish, Nabil Dajani, and Khalil Rinnawi. Cambridge: Polity Press, 2011. 12–28.

Meyer, Stefan G. *The Experimental Arabic Novel: Postcolonial Literary Modernism in the Levant*. Albany: State University of New York Press, 2000.

"Middle East Content Creators 'Need Shows with International Appeal.'" *Digital TV Europe.com* (October 16, 2017). https://www.digitaltveurope.com/2017/10/16/middle-east-content-creators-need-shows-with-international-appeal/. Web. Accessed April 10, 2019.

Mitchell, Timothy. "McJihad: Islam in the US Global Order." *Social Text* 20.4 (2002): 1–18.

Miyakawa, Felicia. *Five Percenter Rap*. Bloomington: Indiana University Press, 2005.

Modleski, Tania. *Loving with a Vengeance: Mass-Produced Fantasies for Women*. London: Routledge, 1990.

Mokhtar, Hosna'a. "Kingdom's Grand Mufti Condemns 'Malicious' Turkish Soap Operas." *Arab News*. July 28, 2008. http://www.arabnews.com/node/314149. Web. Accessed April 2019.

Mordden, Ethan. *Broadway Babies: The People Who Made the American Musical*. New York: Oxford University Press, 1988.

Munif, Abdelrahman. *Cities of Salt*. Trans. Peter Theroux. New York: Random House, 1987.

Naficy, Hamid. *An Accented Cinema: Exilic and Diasporic Filmmaking*. Princeton, NJ: Princeton University Press, 2001.

"Okay to Kill Owners Immoral TV Stations—Cleric." *Arabian Business.com*. September 13, 2008. https://www.arabianbusiness.com/okay-kill-owners-immoral-tv-stations-cleric-43460.html. Web. Accessed April 2019.

Ortiz, Fernando. *Cuban Counterpoint: Tobacco and Sugar*. Trans. Harriet de Onís. Durham, NC: Duke University Press, 1995.

Pennycook, Alastair, and Tony Mitchell. "Hip Hop as Dusty Foot Philosophy: Engaging Locality." *Global Linguistic Flows: Hip Hop Cultures, Youth Identities, and the Politics of Language*. Eds. H. Samy Alim, Awad Ibrahim, and Alastair Pennycook. London: Routledge, 2008. 25–42.

Pieterse, Jan Nederveen. *Globalization and Culture: Global Mélange*. 3rd ed. Lanham, MD: Rowman and Littlefield, 2015.

Pietz, William. "The 'Post-Colonialism' of Cold War Discourse." *Social Text* 19–20 (Fall 1988): 55–75.

Prakash, Gyan. "*Orientalism* Now." *History and Theory* 34 (1995): 199–212.

Radway, Janice. *Reading the Romance: Women, Patriarchy, and Popular Literature*. Chapel Hill: University of North Carolina Press, 1991.

Rao, Shakuntala. "'I Need an Indian Touch': Glocalization and Bollywood Films." *Journal of International and Intercultural Communication* 3.1 (2010): 1–19.

Raw, Laurence. "T. E. Lawrence, the Turks, and the Arab Revolt in the Cinema: Anglo-American and Turkish Representations." *Literature/Film Quarterly* 33.4 (2005): 252–61.

Rinnawi, Khalil. "When Global Meets Local." *Arab Media: Globalization and Emerging Media Industries*. Ed. Noha Mellor, Muhammad Ayish, Nabil Dajani, and Khalil Rinnawi. Cambridge: Polity Press, 2011. 149–69.

Ritzer, George. *The McDonaldization of Society*. 8th ed. New York: Sage Publications, 2014.

Robertson, Roland. "Glocalization: Time-Space and Homogeneity-Heterogeneity." *Global Modernities*. Eds. Mike Featherstone, Scott Lash, and Roland Robertson. Thousand Oaks, CA: Sage Publications, 1996. 25–44.

Robinson, Kim Stanley. *New York 2140*. New York: Orbit, 2017.

Rothman, Lily. "There's a Very Good Reason Why Katy Perry's 'Dark Horse' Video Is Set in Ancient Egypt." *Time* (February 21, 2014). http://time.com/9233/katy-perry-dark-horse-egypt/. Web. Accessed April 2019.

Rowe, John Carlos. "Arabia Fantasia: U.S. Literary Culture and the Middle East." *Alif: Journal of Comparative Poetics* 32 (2012): 55–77.

Saadawi, Nawal El. "Men Are Not My Enemies." Interview. *BBC*. https://www.bbc.co.uk/programmes/p0369vkx. Web. Accessed April 2019 .

Said, Edward W. *Culture and Imperialism*. New York: Alfred A. Knopf, 1993.

Said, Edward W. *Orientalism*. New York: Vintage-Random House, 1978.

Sakr, Naomi. *Arab Television Today*. London: I. B. Tauris, 2007.

Sakr, Naomi. *Satellite Realms: Transnational Television, Globalization, and the Middle East*. London: I. B. Tauris, 2001.

Salois, Kendra. "Fleas in the Sheepskin: Glocalization and Cosmopolitanisn in Moroccan Hip-Hop." *Islam and Popular Culture*. Eds. Karin van Nieuwkerk, Mark LeVine, and Martin Stokes. Austin: University of Texas Press, 2016.

Sarsar, Saliba, and Manal Stephan. "Overcoming the Divide: Arab Women between Traditional Life and a Globalizing Culture." *Globalizing Cultures: Theories, Paradigms, Actions*. Ed. Vincenzo Mele and Marina Vujnovic. Chicago, IL: Haymarket Books, 2015. 331–52.

Schueller, Malini Johar. *U.S. Orientalisms: Race, Nation, and Literature, 1790–1890*. Ann Arbor: University of Michigan Press, 2001.

Semmerling, Tim Jon. *Evil Arabs in American Popular Film: Orientalist Fear*. Austin: University of Texas Press, 2006.

Shaheen, Jack G. *Reel Bad Arabs: How Hollywood Vilifies a People*. Northampton, MA: Olive Branch Press, 2009.

Shaheen, Jack G. *The TV Arab*. Bowling Green, OH: Bowling Green State University Popular Press, 1984.

Shay, Anthony. *Dancing across Borders: The American Fascination with Exotic Dance Forms*. Jefferson, NC: McFarland, 2008.

Shechter, Relli. *Smoking, Culture, and Economy in the Middle East: The Egyptian Tobacco Market 1850–2000*. London: I. B. Tauris, 2006.

Shohat, Ella, and Evelyn Alsultany. "The Cultural Politics of 'the Middle East' in the Americas: An Introduction." *Between the Middle East and the Americas: The Cultural Politics of Diaspora*. Eds. Evelyn Alsultany and Ella Shohat.Ann Arbor: University of Michigan Press, 2013. 1–41.

Shohat, Ella, and Robert Stam. *Unthinking Eurocentrism: Multiculturalism and the Media*. 2nd ed. London: Routledge, 2014.

Shoup, John A. "Rai: North Africa's Music of the Working Class." *Popular Culture in the Middle East and North Africa: A Postcolonial Outlook*. Eds. Walid El Hamamsy and Mounira Soliman. London: Routledge, 2013. 46–62.

Slotkin, Richard. *Gunfighter Nation: The Myth of the Frontier in Twentieth-Century America*. 1992. Norman: University of Oklahoma Press, 1998.

Stiffler, Matthew Jaber. "Consuming Orientalism: Public Foodways of Arab American Christians." *Mashriq & Mahjar* 2.2 (2014): 111–38.

Stollery, Martin. *Lawrence of Arabia*. London: York, 2000.

Swedenburg, Ted. "Palestinian Rap: Against the Struggle Paradigm." *Popular Culture in the Middle East and North Africa: A Postcolonial Outlook*. Eds. Walid El Hamamsy and Mounira Soliman. London: Routledge, 2013. 17–32.

Tagharobi, Kaveh, and Ali Zarei. "Modernism in the Middle East and Arab World." *Routledge Encyclopedia of Modernism*. September 5, 2016. https://www.rem.rout ledge.com/articles/overview/accommodating-an-unexpected-guest. Web. Accessed April 2019.

Tally, Robert T., Jr. *Utopia in The Age of Globalization*. New York: Palgrave Macmillan. 2013.

Talu, Yonca. "Interview: Naji Abu Nowar." *Filmcomment* (April 24, 2015). https://ww w.filmcomment.com/blog/interview-naji-abu-nowar-theeb/. Web. Accessed April 2019.

Taylor, Stephanie d'Arc. "Jordan Shoots for a Victory at the Oscars." *AlJazeera* (February 29, 2016). https://www.aljazeera.com/news/2016/02/jordan-shoots-victory-osca rs-160221091726699.html Web. Accessed April 2019.

Towfik, Ahmed Khaled. *Utopia*. Trans. Chip Rosetti. Doha: Bloomsbury Qatar Foundation, 2011.

"Turkish Soap Star Sparks Divorces in Arab World." *Ummah.com*. July 22, 2008. https:// www.ummah.com/forum/forum/family-lifestyle-community-culture/marriage/18 2805-turkish-soap-star-sparks-divorces-in-arab-world. Web. Accessed April 2019.

Varisco, Daniel Martin. *Reading Orientalism: Said and the Unsaid*. Seattle: University of Washington Press, 2007.
Warraq, Ibn. *Defending the West: A Critique of Edward Said's* Orientalism. Amherst, NY: Prometheus Books, 2007.
Webb, Sam. "ISIS Tells Muslims to Destroy Their Satellite TV Sets So They Don't 'Pollute Their Ethics.'" *The Mirror* (June 1, 2016). https://www.mirror.co.uk/news/world-news/isis-tells-muslims-destroy-satellite-8092190 Web. Accessed April 2019.
Weber, Max. *The Protestant Ethic and the Spirit of Capitalism*. 1904–1905. Trans. Talcott Parsons. 1930. London: Routledge, 1995.
Wilson, G. Willow. *Alif the Unseen*. New York: Grove Press, 2012.
Wilson, G. Willow. *The Butterfly Mosque: A Young American Woman's Journey to Love and Islam*. New York: Grove Press, 2010.
Woltering, Robbert. *Occidentalisms in the Arab World: Ideology and Images of the West in the Egyptian Media*. London: I. B. Tauris, 2011.
Worth, Robert F. "Arab TV Tests Societies' Limits with Depictions of Sex and Equality." *The New York Times*. September 26, 2008. https://www.nytimes.com/2008/09/27/world/middleeast/27beirut.html. Web. Accessed April 2019.
Zein, Rayya El. "From 'Hip Hop Revolutionaries' to 'Terrorist-Thugs': 'Blackwashing' between the Arab Spring and the War on Terror." *Lateral: Journal of the Cultural Studies Association* 5.1 (Spring 2016). http://csalateral.org/issue/5-1/hip-hop-blackwashing-el-zein/. Web. Accessed April 2019.
Žižek, Slavoj. "*Junction 48:* Sexual Is Political." *The Huffington Post* (April 26, 2016). https://www.huffpost.com/entry/junction-48-sexual-is-pol_b_9777038. Web. Accessed April 2019.

Films cited

8 Mile. Dir. Curtis Hanson, 2002.
Aladdin. Dir. Ron Clements and John Musker. Disney, 1992.
Alien. Dir. Ridley Scott, 1979.
Apocalypto, Dir. Mel Gibson, 2006.
Argo. Dir. Ben Affleck, 2012.
Bab el hadid (*Cairo Station*). Dir. Youssef Chahine. 1958.
The Ballad of Cable Hogue. Dir. Sam Peckinpah, 1970.
Bambi. Dir. David Hand et al., 1942.
Ben-Hur. Dir. William Wyler, 1959.
The Big Lebowski. Dir. Joel and Ethan Coen, 1998.
The Big Sleep. Dir. Howard Hawks, 1946.
Black Sunday. Dir. John Frankenheimer, 1977.
Body of Lies. Dir. Ridley Scott, 2008.
The Bodyguard. Dir. Mick Jackson, 1992.

Buffalo Bill and the Indians, or Sitting Bull's History Lesson. Dir. Robert Altman, 1976.
A Bullet for the General. Dir. Damiano Damiani, 1967.
Butch Cassidy and the Sundance Kid. Dir. George Roy Hill, 1969.
Cairo 678. Dir. Mohamed Diab, 2010.
Captain Abu Raed. Dir. Amin Matalqa, 2008.
Channels of Rage. Dir. Anat Halachmi, 2003.
Chinatown. Dir. Roman Polanski, 1973.
Citizen Kane. Dir. Orson Welles, 1941.
Cleopatra. Dir. Joseph L. Mankiewicz, 1963.
Compañeros. Dir. Sergio Corbucci, 1970.
Dances with Wolves. Dir. Kevin Costner, 1990.
Dracula. Dir. Tod Browning, 1931.
Duck, You Sucker! Dir. Sergio Leone, 1971.
El Feel el Azraq (The Blue Elephant). Dir. Marwan Hamed, 2014.
The Exorcist. Dir. William Friedkin, 1973.
A Fistful of Dollars. Dir. Sergio Leone, 1964
Footloose. Dir. Herbert Ross, 1984.
For a Few Dollars More. Dir. Sergio Leone, 1965.
Frankenstein. Dir. James Whale, 1931.
Frozen. Dir. Chris Buck and Jennifer Lee, 2013.
The Garden of Allah. Dir. Richard Boleslawski, 1936.
Garden of the Moon. Dir. Busby Berkeley, 1938.
The Good, the Bad, and the Ugly. Dir. Sergio Leone, 1966.
Harum Scarum. Dir. Gene Nelson, 1965.
Hawmps! Dir. Joe Camp, 1976.
High Plains Drifter. Dir. Clint Eastwood, 1973.
The Hurt Locker. Dir. Kathryn Bigelow, 2008.
Jarhead. Dir. Sam Mendes, 2005.
Junction 48. Dir. Udi Aloni, 2016.
The Jungle Book. Dir. Wolfgag Reitherman, 1967.
King of Kings. Dir. Nicholas Ray, 1961.
The Kingdom. Dir. Peter Berg, 2007.
Kingdom of Heaven. Dir. Ridley Scott, 2005.
Kismet: How Turkish Soap Operas Change the World. Dir. Nina Maria Pashalidou, 2014.
The Lady from Shanghai. Dir. Orson Welles, 1947.
Lawrence of Arabia. Dir. David Lean, 1962.
Lion of the Desert. Dir. Moustapha Akkad, 1980.
The Martian. Dir. Ridley Scott, 2015.
The Mask of Fu Manchu. Dir. Charles Brabin, 1932.
The Message. Dir. Moustapha Akkad, 1976.
Morocco. Dir. Josef von Sternberg, 1930.
The Mummy. Dir. Karl Freud, 1932.

Nanook of the North. Dir. Robert J. Flaherty, 1922.
The Old Dark House. Dir. James Whale, 1932.
Once Upon a Time in the West. Dir. Sergio Leone, 1968.
The Outlaw Josey Wales. Dir. Clint Eastwood, 1976.
Pinocchio. Dir. Ben Sharpsteen et al., 1940.
The Professionals. Dir. Richard Brooks, 1966.
Prometheus. Dr. Ridley Scott, 2012.
Raiders of the Lost Ark. Dir. Steven Spielberg, 1981.
Rango. Dir. Gore Verbinski, 2011.
Red Planet. Dir. Antony Hoffman, 2000.
Rogue One: A Star Wars Story, 2016.
Rooster Cogburn. Dir. Stuart Miller, 1975.
Sanjuro. Dir. Akira Kurosawa, 1962.
Sanshiro Sugata. Dir. Akira Kurosawa, 1943.
The Searchers. Dir. John Ford, 1956.
Shane. Dir. George Stevens, 1953.
Shanghai Express. Dir. Josef von Sternberg, 1932.
The Shanghai Gesture. Dir. Josef von Sternberg, 1941.
The Sheik. Dir. George Melford, 1921.
Shrek 2. Dir. Andrew Adamson, Kelly Asbury, and Conrad Vernon, 2004.
The Siege. Dir. Edward Zwick, 1998.
Slingshot Hip Hop. Dir. Jackie Salloum, 2008.
The Son of the Sheik. Dir. George Fitzmaurice, 1926.
Stagecoach. Dir. John Ford, 1939.
Star Trek Beyond. Dir. Justin Lin, 2016.
Straw Dogs. Dir. Sam Peckinpah, 1971.
Syriana. Dir. Stephen Gaghan, 2005.
The Ten Commandments. Dir. Cecil B. DeMille, 1956.
Theeb. Dir. Naji Abu Nowar, 2014.
The Thief of Bagdad. Dir. Raoul Walsh, 1924.
Tickling Giants. Dir. Sara Taksler, 2017.
Tin Pan Alley. Dir. Walter Lang, 1940.
The Treasure of the Sierra Madre. Dir. John Huston, 1948.
True Lies. Dir. James Cameron, 1994.
United 93. Dir. Paul Greenglass, 2006.
Viva Zalata. Dir. Hassan Hafez, 1976.
Viva Zapata! Dir. Elia Kazan, 1952.
Valley of the Kings. Dir. Robert Pirosh, 1954.
The Wild Bunch. Dir. Sam Peckinpah, 1969.
The Wind and the Lion. Dir. John Milius, 1975.
World Trade Center, Dir. Oliver Stone, 2006.
Zero Dark Thirty. Dir. Kathryn Bigelow, 2012.

Index

abjection   11
Abou-Bakr, Omaima   224 n.12
Achebe, Chinua   186, 206
Agamben, Giorgio   224 n.14
Aguilera, Christina   73–4, 100, 110
Ahlam   89, 106, 170
Ahmad, Aijaz   209, 216–17, 223 n.3
Ahmad, Jalal Al-i   224 n.10
Aidi, Hisham   115, 132
Ajram, Nancy   86–7, 89–93, 98–9, 101, 171, 173, 230 n.3, 232 n.35
Akkad, Moustapha   208–9
Akon   76, 78, 103
Aladdin (1992)   53, 54
Al-Atiq, Fahd
   Life on Hold (2004)   7
Ali, Tariq   221
"Ali-Baba Bound"   51–2
Alien (1979)   169
Almeida, Cristina Moreno   234 n.7
Alsalman, Yassin, *see* Narcy
Alsanea, Rajaa
   Girls of Riyadh   28
Alsultany, Evelyn   227 n.30, 233 n.62, 238 n.2, 244 n.1
Ambah, Faiza Saleh   137
Anderson, Scott   187, 242 n.12
Apocalypto (2006)   243 n.23
Appadurai, Arjun   215–16
Arab competition shows
   Arab Idol   90, 104, 111, 126–7
   Arabs Got Talent   110–11, 114, 164–5
   Star Sghar   110
   Superstar   90
   The Voice   164
   X Factor Arabia   161–3
Arab talk shows   168
   Ana wel Assal ("The Honey and I")   171
   Al-Bernameg ("The Show")   169
      (*see also* Youssef, Bassem)

   Bidoon Rakabah ("Uncensored")   170–1
   Ghanili Ta Ghanilak ("Sing to Me and I'll Sing to You")   172
   Hayda Haki ("Now You're Talking")   173–4
   Kalam Nawaem ("Soft Talk")   168
   Al Mataha ("The Maze")   169–70
   Siwar Shuaib ("Corralled by Shuaib")   174–5
   Talk of the Town   169
Argo (2012)   58
Armbrust, Walter   85–6
Ashcroft, Bill   20
Assaf, Mohammed   89, 104, 126–7, 233 n.57
Avishai Margalit
   Occidentalism (2004)   16–17, 25
Ayish, Muhammad   239 n.2
Azaiez, Tamara Wong   63
Aziz, Moataz Abdel   230 n.4

Bab Al-Hara (TV)   138
Bab el hadid (*Cairo Station*) (1958)   181–2
Bakhtin, M. M.   155, 239 n.15
The Ballad of Cable Hogue (1970)   193
Bambi (1942)   244 n.23
The Bangles   67–9
The Beatles   51
Belly dancing   228 n.22
   American music videos   67, 73–7, 79, 229 n.25, 233 n.60
   Arab video clips   94–5, 105–8, 233 n.64
   Orientalism   12, 29, 57, 227 n.7, 229 n.25
   World's Columbian Exposition   35–6, 57
Ben-Hur (1959)   54
Berman, Jacob Rama   225 n.2

Bernal, Martin   73, 228 n.19
Beyoncé   63–5, 227 n.2
Bhabha, Homi   214–15
Bieber, Justin   111, 163
Black Sunday (1977)   58
Bloch, Ernst   166–7, 218
The Bodyguard (1992)   163
Body of Lies (2008)   243 n.19
Bollywood   8, 102, 103, 106, 220, 244 n.3
Booker, M. Keith   52–3, 88, 229 n.37, 244 n.4
Boone, Joseph Allen   69, 228 n.12
Bradbury, Ray
   Fahrenheit 451   168
Brandt, Allan   42, 225 n.8
Bucciamanti, Alexandra   238 n.9
Buffalo Bill and the Indians, or Sitting Bull's History Lesson (1976)   188
A Bullet for the General (1967)   203
Bulos, Nabih   207
Buruma, Ian
   Occidentalism (2004)   16–17, 25
Butch Cassidy and the Sundance Kid (1969)   204

Cairo 678   240 n.7
Cairo Trilogy, see Mahfouz, Naguib
Captain Abu Raed (2008)   184, 208
Cardi B   83, 97–8
Carson, Johnny   167–8, 172, 240 n.12
Carter, Bill   240 n.12
Carter, Howard   46
Castillo, Edward D.   186
Caton, Steven C.   242 n.8, 243 n.17
Çelik, Zeynep   225 n.3
Cestor, Elisabeth   91, 94, 98
Chang, Jeff   235 n.11
Channels of Rage (2003)   237 n.49
Chopra, Priyanka   102
Citizen Kane (1941)   183, 188
Cleopatra   55, 57, 69–71, 74, 226 n.12
Cleopatra (1963)   55, 57
Cockburn, Patrick   223 n.5
Cody, Buffalo Bill   45
Coldplay   64–5
Cold War   3, 68, 81, 151, 219, 229 n.37
Compañeros (1970)   203
Crary, Robert   22–3, 224 n.14
Curtis, Carl C. III   191

DAM (rap group), see Nafar, Tamer
Dances with Wolves (1990)   186, 196, 202
Daraiseh, Isra   244 n.2
Darwish, Hany   108
Darwish, Mahmoud   128
Davis, Janet M.   44
Davy, Steven   119, 235 n.21
DeGhett, Torie Rose   114, 119, 133
Derr, Holly L.   228 n.16
Derulo, Jason   76–7, 101, 232 n.51
D'Haen, Theo   230 n.35
Diab, Maya   77, 101
Diddy   78, 117
Ditmars, Hadani   186
Dos Passos, John   38
Dracula (1931)   48
Duck, You Sucker! (1971)   195, 203
Dyer, Richard   141–4, 152

Eagleton, Terry
   the aesthetic   141–2
   Jude the Obscure   218
   postmodernism   221
Edwards, Brian T.   8, 20, 224 n.20
Edwards, Holly   34–6, 44, 226 n.11
8 Mile (2002)   125
Elissa   86, 89, 99–101, 171, 173, 178, 230 n.3
Elmessiri, Abdel-Wahab   108
Elouardaoui, Ouidyane   19
Eminem   125, 163, 235 n.13
Engels, Friedrich   16–17, 216
ET bil Arabi (TV)   111, 177–8
The Exorcist (1973)   226 n.15

Fairuz   85, 94
Fanon, Frantz   5, 131, 223 n.4
Fares, Myriam   86, 93–4, 98–101, 109, 170–1, 232 n.29, 240 n.9
El Feel el Azraq ("The Blue Elephant") (2014)   183
Feghali, Bassem   98, 170, 232 n.29
Fernandes, Sujatha   234 n.6
Fisher, Mark
   capitalist realism   221
A Fistful of Dollars (1964)   242 n.15
Footloose (1984)   163
For a Few Dollars More (1965)   242 n.15
Foucault, Michel   5, 14, 15, 223 n.4

Frankenstein (1931)   183
Freij, Muath   207
Frozen (2013)   2

Galsworthy, John
   The Forsyte Saga   27
Gamal, Samia   182, 241 n.1
The Garden of Allah (1904 novel)   34, 40
The Garden of Allah (1936 film)   40, 47
Garden of the Moon (1938)   52
El Général   113, 115, 132, 234 n.1
Geraghty, Christine   142, 145–7
Gharabeeb Soud (TV, "Black
   Crows")   138–9
Gibb, H. A. R.   10, 150
The Good, the Bad, and the Ugly
   (1966)   202, 242 n.15
Grande, Ariana   111
Grauman's Egyptian Theater   46–7
Great Arab Revolt   31, 244 n.24
Greene, Naomi   226 n.16
Grundey, Adam   235 n.22

Hall, Stuart   19
Harum Scarum (1965)   227 n.5
Hassan, Ihab   221
Hassan, Waïl S.   224 n.16
Hawmps! (1976)   243 n.21
Hawsawi, Hamza (AyZee)   162–3,
   239 n.1
Al Hayba (TV)   139–40, 178
   Narcos (TV)   139
Haydar, Mona   240 n.8
Hayden, Patrick   114, 223 n.9
Hazbun, Waleed   224 n.13
Hebdige, Dick   117
High Plains Drifter (1973)   242 n.15
Hobsbawm, Eric   7
Hobson, Dorothy   153
hooks, bell   227 n.3
Hosny, Tamer   89, 103, 115
The Hurt Locker (2008)   58, 201

I Dream of Jeannie (TV)   74
Iskandar, Adel   229 n.34
Islamic State of Iraq and the Levant (aka
   DAESH, ISIL, and ISIS)   3, 13, 139
   opposition to satellite television   18,
      166–7, 210, 237 n.62, 238 n.5

Jackson, Kevin   242 n.9
Jackson, Michael   70–2, 90, 100, 131, 161
Jarmakani, Amira   228 n.22
Jameson, Fredric   218
   Archaeologies of the Future (2005)   14
   The Political Unconscious (1981)   40–1
   Postmodernism (1991)   8–9, 21–3,
      72–3, 81, 83–4, 87–8, 91, 106,
      116–17, 215, 221–2, 230 n.41,
      244 n.4
   Signatures of the Visible (1992)
      116–17
   "Third-World Literature in the Era
      of Multinational Capitalism"
      (1986)   149–53, 209–10
JanMohamed, Abdul R.   215
Jarhead (2005)   58
Jay-Z   117, 129, 237 n.55
Joubin, Rebecca   238 n.3
Junction 48 (2015)   125–6
The Jungle Book (1967)   52–3, 243 n.23

Kaplan, E. Anne   87
Kelly, R.   74–5, 97–8
Khabeer, Su'ad Abdul   235 nn.12, 15, 17
Khalaf, Hala   164
Khalas (Israeli heavy metal band)   64
Khalifa, Wiz   77, 233 n.55
Khawatir (TV)   175–7
El Kilani, Wafaa   169–70
The Kingdom (2007)   58
King of Kings (1961)   54–6
*Kismet: How Turkish Soap Operas Change
   the World* (2014)   148
Kraidy, Marwan   230 n.2
Kramer, Martin   223 n.2
Kristeva, Julia   11
Kubala, Patricia   85

Labaki, Nadine   87
The Lady from Shanghai (1947)   50
Lamjarred, Saad   89–90, 104
Larkin, Brian   244 n.3
late capitalism   8, 9, 11, 12, 21–4, 35,
   72–3, 80–2, 84, 88, 98, 106, 109,
   116–17, 140, 168, 172, 215, 220–1,
   230 n.41, 237 n.65
Lawrence, T. E.   187–8, *see also* Lawrence
   of Arabia

Lawrence of Arabia (1962)
   heroism   188, 190–3
   historical background   185, 187
   Orientalism   186, 189–90, 192
   Westerns   31
Leach, William   33–4, 36–7, 41–2, 216
Letterman, David   167–8, 173, 240 n.12
LeVine, Mark   230 n.5, 236 n.38
Lewis, Bernard   8, 10
Lion of the Desert (1980)   208
Lorde, Audre   206
Lowkey (Kareem Dennis)   3, 123, 127–34
   American imperialism   123, 129–30
   capitalism   133–4, 237 n.65
   Iraq   128
   Palestine   116, 128
   refugee crisis   130–1
   Trump, Donald   237 n.57
Lukács, Georg   218, 228 n.9
Lyotard, Jean-François   221

McAlister, Melani   20
McDonaldization   8, 213, 223 n.6
Madonna   70, 226 n.25
Mahfouz, Naguib   26
   Cairo Trilogy   26–7, 103
Maira, Sunaina   235 n.17
Mandel, Ernest   8, *see also* late capitalism
Mansour, Shadia   30, 116, 119, 122–4, 126–8, 131, 133
The Martian (2015)   201
Marx, Karl   16–17, 150, 222
   India   216–17
The Mask of Fu Manchu (1932)   48–9
Massari   78–9, 82, 104, 118, 235 n.19
May, Lary   226 n.13
Mead, Margaret   22, 215
Mellor, Noha   19
The Message (1976)   209
Meyer, Stefan G.   224 n.19
Middle East Broadcasting Center (MBC)   89, 95, 100, 102, 106, 111, 137–9, 162, 164, 166, 168, 175, 177–8, 238 n.1, 239 nn.2–3, 14, 241 n.16
Mitchell, Timothy   8, 115
Miyakawa, Felicia   235 n.16
Modleski, Tania   146, 238 n.4
Montana, French   79, 82, 118, 235 n.19

Mordden, Ethan   225 n.6
Morocco (1930)   47
The Mummy (1932)   48
Munif, Abdelrahman
   Cities of Salt   27

Nafar, Tamer   116, 124–7, 131–2, 237 n.49
Naficy, Hamid   122
Nanook of the North (1922)   187
The Narcicyst, *see* Narcy
Narcos (TV)   139–40
Narcy   30, 78, 113, 121–2, 128, 131
Nasri, Assala   230 n.3, 240 n.14
Noor (TV)   30, 135–59, 238 nn.6–10, 239 n.12
Nowar, Naji Abu   181, 185, 186, 200, 207–8, 241 n.3, 243 nn.16, 23

Offendum, Omar   30, 113, 115, 118–23, 131, 133, 235 nn.20–2, 236 n.27
The Old Dark House (1932)   48
Omran, Aseel   102, 232 n.51
Once Upon a Time in the West (1968)   204
Ortiz, Fernando   21
The Outlaw Josey Wales (1976)   202

Paar, Jack   167
Peckinpah, Sam   193, 204, 208–9, 243 n.23
Perry, Katy   69–71, 228 n.14
Pieterse, Jan Nederveen   8, 20, 23
Pietz, William   229 n.37
Pinocchio (1940)   243 n.23
Pitbull   102–3
postmodernism
   Arabic literature   27–8
   commodification of culture   87–8, 116–17
   fragmentation   87, 91, 230 nn.39, 41
   global capitalism   8, 82, 88, 106, 221
   modernization   9, 21–4, 116, 215, 222
   nostalgia   71
   pastiche   63, 64, 69, 72–3, 79–82, 88, 90, 92, 105–7, 215, 244 n.4
Prakash, Gyan   223 n.2
Presley, Elvis   65, 227 n.5

The Professionals (1966)   202
Prometheus (2012)   201
Public Enemy   117, 121

Qabbani, Nizar   119, 224 n.18
Qusai   114–15, 131, 235 n.19

Radway, Janice   145–6, 149
Raiders of the Lost Ark (1981)   58–9
Raï music   101, 232 n.46, 232 n.47
Rango (2011)   193
Rao, Shakuntala   244 n.3
Raw, Laurence   242 n.10
RedOne   102
Red Planet (2000)   201
Rhymes, Busta   78, 122, 229 n.33
Rinnawi, Khalil   224 n.12
Ritzer, George   223 n.6
Robertson, Roland   223 n.8
Robinson, Kim Stanley
  New York 2140   1
Rogue One: A Star Wars Story (2016)   201
Rooster Cogburn (1975)   195
Rotana   89, 91, 97, 162, 230 n.5
Rothman, Lily   228 n.14, 18
Rowe, John Carlos   35, 67
Ruby   86, 105–9

El Saadawi, Nawal   14, 169
Sabah   85
Said, Edward W.   128, 131
  Culture and Imperialism (1993)   1, 214, 218, 223 n.4, 228 n.21
  Orientalism (1978)   4–7, 9–12, 14–15, 20, 25, 33, 35, 40, 51, 59, 72, 150, 177, 182, 213–14, 216, 223 n.3, 228 n.9
Sakr, Naomi   224 n.12, 239 n.2, 240 n.10
Salois, Kendra   234 n.7
Sanjuro (1962)   243 n.23
Sanshiro Sugata (1943)   243 n.23
Sarsar, Saliba   136
Schueller, Malini Johar   35
The Searchers (1956)   202
Semmerling, Tim Jon   226 n.15
Shaggy   103, 115, 229 n.30
Shaheen, Jack G.   227 n.30
Shakur, Tupac   117, 124
Shane (1953)   194, 198
Shanghai Express (1932)   47–8

The Shanghai Gesture (1941)   49–50
Sharara, Nedaa   164
Shawq (TV)   138, 140
Shay, Anthony   227 n.7
Shechter, Relli   225 n.9
The Sheik (1921)   46, 51, 227 n.5
Sherine   86, 89, 101, 164, 171, 240 n.14
Sheyaab   164–5
Shohat, Ella   75, 233 n.62, 238 n.2, 242 n.11, 244 n.1
Shoup, John A.   101, 232 n.47
Shrek 2 (2004)   163
Al Shugairi, Ahmad   175–7
The Siege (1998)   58
Slingshot Hip Hop (2008)   124–5
Slotkin, Richard   44, 51, 198–200
Snoop Dogg   103, 115, 235 n.13
Soap operas   137–8, 141–3, 145, 147, 149, 152
The Son of the Sheik (1926)   46
Spears, Britney   99, 110, 233 n.60
Stagecoach (1939)   201
Star Trek (TV)   56–8, 74
Star Trek Beyond (2016)   224 n.15
Stephan, Manal   136
Stevens, Ray   65–6
St. Louis World's Fair (1904)   46
Stiffler, Matthew Jaber   223 n.1
Stollery, Martin   242 n.8
Straw Dogs (1971)   243 n.23
Swedenburg, Ted   116, 125, 232 n.46
Swift, Taylor   87
Syriana (2005)   58

Tally, Robert T., Jr.   14
Taylor, Elizabeth   55, 57
telenovelas   137–8, 140
The Ten Commandments (1956)   54, 56
Theeb (2014)   31, 181–211, 241 n.3, 243 nn.16, 20
The Thief of Bagdad (1924)   46–7
Tickling Giants (2017)   240 n.13
Tin Pan Alley (1940)   51
Towfik, Ahmed Khaled
  Utopia   28
transnational flow   1, 27–30, 64, 80, 87, 89, 102, 115, 134, 139, 165, 213
True Lies (1994)   58
Al Turk, Hala   89, 109–11

Turner, Frederick Jackson
    frontier hypothesis   35
Twain, Shania   65, 87

Umm Kulthum   63–4, 85, 164, 230 n.1
United 93 (2006)   58

Varisco, Daniel Martin   223 n.3
Viva Zalata (1976)   243 n.22
Viva Zapata! (1952)   203

Warraq, Ibn   223 n.3
Weber, Max   36–7
Wehbe, Haifa   86, 89, 94–8, 101, 106,
    109, 111–12, 171, 173–4, 229 n.30,
    232 n.35, 233 n.56, 240 n.9, 241 n.15

The Wild Bunch (1969)   204
Wilson, G. Willow   17–18
The Wind and the Lion (1975)
    242 n.13
Woltering, Robbert   244 n.1
World's Columbian Exposition
    (1893)   35, 57
World Trade Center (2006)   58
Worth, Robert F.   147

Youssef, Bassem   169–70, 240 n.13

El Zein, Rayya   132, 133, 236 n.40,
    237 n.62
Zero Dark Thirty (2012)   58
Žižek, Slavoj   125